Wiebke Gronemeyer
The Curatorial Complex:
Social Dimensions of Knowledge Production

D1663434

Wiebke Gronemeyer

The Curatorial Complex

Social Dimensions of Knowledge Production

Wilhelm Fink

Printed with kind support of
Gerda Henkel Stiftung, Düsseldorf.

Cover illustration:
Robert Morris, *Bodymotionspacesthings*, 1971.
Interactive installation at Turbine Hall, Tate Modern, London, 2009.
Copyright VG Bild-Kunst, Bonn 2017.
Photo: Wiebke Gronemeyer

Bibliographic information published by the Deutsche Nationalbibliothek

The Deutsche Nationalbibliothek lists this publication
in the Deutsche Nationalbibliografie; detailed bibliographic data
available online: http://dnb.d-nb.de

© 2018 Wilhelm Fink Verlag, ein Imprint der Brill-Gruppe
(Koninklijke Brill NV, Leiden, Niederlande; Brill USA Inc., Boston MA, USA;
Brill Asia Pte Ltd, Singapore; Brill Deutschland GmbH, Paderborn, Deutschland)

Internet: www.fink.de

Cover design: Evelyn Ziegler, München
Production: Brill Deutschland GmbH, Paderborn

ISBN 978-3-7705-6312-8

Table of Contents

List of Illustrations

Acknowledgements

For her invaluable advice, motivation, enthusiasm, and critique during the conceptualization of this research and the writing process, I am indebted to Andrea Phillips. For his guidance, insightful comments, and challenging questions, I wish to thank Boris Groys. For his hospitality and advice, I am grateful to Tony Bennett and his colleagues at the Institute for Culture and Society, University of Western Sydney, Australia. I am forever grateful to Professor Isabel Wünsche for encouraging me to bring this publication forward. For their advice, suggestions, and valuable critique, I wish to thank Ute Meta Bauer, John Chilver, Maria Hlavajova, Lisa Le Feuvre, Maria Lind, Birgit Mersmann, Kirsty Ogg, Helena Reckitt, Andrew Renton, Irit Rogoff, Edgar Schmitz, and Gilda Williams. I would especially like to thank Beatrice von Bismarck, Erika Fischer-Lichte, Sokratis Georgiadis, Verena Krieger, Vera Mey, Caterina Riva, and Ulf Wuggenig for their hospitality, and for giving me the opportunity to present parts of this research at various stages of its completion. I wish to thank Joel Furness at Chisenhale Gallery, London, Anne Maier at Haus der Kulturen der Welt, Berlin, Anton Vidokle, Magdalena Magiera and Amal Issa at e-flux, Michel Müller, and Arjan van Meeuwen at Basis voor actuele Kunst, Utrecht, for supplying me with materials relating to the projects discussed in this thesis. Most significantly, I wish to thank the artists and curators involved in the projects for their work, which inspired this research in the first place. For their editorial support, I am grateful to the Wilhelm Fink Verlag, especially Henning Siekmann and Anna Kaiser. Carrying out this research would have not been possible without a PhD scholarship from the Gerda Henkel Foundation, Düsseldorf, and further financial support of Goldsmiths, University of London. This book has been published with the support of the Gerda Henkel Foundation, Düsseldorf. Finally, I would like to thank my family, especially my parents, my partner, and daughters for their unconditional support and endless encouragement.

Introduction

This book questions whether curatorial practices assume a social function, and if so, what form this function takes. Pursuing this question presumes a relation between what curators do and how what they do is experienced in the world, which approaches and positions curatorial practice as a dialogical activity. By analyzing how artistic and curatorial practices can activate processes and generate structures that facilitate dialogical spaces of negotiation between curators, artists, and their publics, this book addresses the social dimensions of knowledge production for the ways people and art come together in the curated encounter. More specifically, I argue for an intrinsic social dimension to the "curatorial complex"—an articulation I develop for the curatorial as a field of research and practice constituted by concurrent processes of production and reflection. These processes engage in not only discursive, but also, and particularly, material forms of enquiry into knowledge production in the domain of art.

A number of exhibitions and discursive projects are discussed here that seek to provide art with a more political context in which to begin an enquiry into rethinking the category of art production and the modalities of spectatorship it produces, as distinct from the narrative and methodical perspectives of academic or established disciplinary thinking. This discussion is set against the backdrop of recent discourse engaged in developing concepts of the "curatorial" as a research-based practice of forms of knowledge production that connects the aesthetic and the cognitive.

Rather than furthering the construction of an opposition between the "curatorial" and curating as exhibition-making, I intend to elaborate on the differences of exhibitionary, discursive, and performative forms of engagement in the context of a diversification of the exhibition as a medium of practice, not its dismissal. A central claim of this book is to perceive the exhibition as an embodied form of knowledge production that generates forms of sociality whose material quality is as important as its discursive capacity for emergence and enquiry.

Research Questions

As well as examining how the social, political, and cultural factors that condition curatorial practices are addressed, negotiated, and reflected in the curated encounter, this book enquires into their constituent modalities and strategies of production.

Attempting to answer a question of such broad scope entails the risk of becoming entangled in a web of generalizations, unsustainable assumptions, and superficial arguments. It has therefore been necessary to develop a set of more specific research questions that map a field of knowledge in order to reflect upon it and contribute to it. The idea is to further develop the prolific interest of curatorial practices in order to explore and argue for their own epistemic quality as active forms of knowledge production.

The projects that this book analyzes and explores are: (1) Michael Fullerton's solo exhibition *Columbia* (2010), Chisenhale Gallery, London; (2) *The Potosí Principle* (2010), curated by artists Alice Creischer, Andreas Siekmann, and writer and curator Max Jorge Hinderer, at Haus der Kulturen der Welt, Berlin, Museo Nacional Centro de Arte Reina Sofía, Madrid, and Museo Nacional de Arte and Museo Nacional de Etnografía y Folklore, La Paz; (3) unitednationsplaza (2006), a discursive art project organized by Anton Vidokle with a number of collaborators and based in Berlin; and (4) *Former West* (2008–2016), an international long-term research, exhibition, publishing and education project, coordinated by BAK, Utrecht.

These projects lend themselves to an analysis of the terms of knowledge production in the space of a contention with art. Questions around what knowledge is and how it can be produced are paired with a critical interest in the proliferation of knowledge production in the field of art as part of the "intellectualization of the art field" (Hlavajova et al., *On Knowledge Production* 7). The research question pertaining to the function that knowledge production assumes in the context of curatorial practices, and vice versa, is located in the context of how the term "knowledge production" is often used very broadly to indicate everything ranging from immaterial realms of production in curatorial practice to resurrected forms of pedagogy in art education. The approach this research takes towards this large field of discourse is also critically directed at the endless use and appropriation of the term knowledge production in the information society, a phenomenon that generally parallels how cultural production operates in accordance with free-market thinking. The research question "What is knowledge production?" can therefore be recast as: "What is knowledge if it is in production?" Such question enquires not only what it means when knowledge is being produced, but also what knowledge is produced from within the context of curatorial practices. Thereby this research enquires into the process of knowledge production as a generation and transformation of information, interpretation, and meaning. Furthermore, such question attempts to contrast the result-oriented language of capitalist society. This research challenges both the epistemic context in which the term "knowledge" has been situated throughout the history of the development of modern academic disciplines, and affirms the potential of artistic and curatorial practices producing knowledge as thinking processes fostering dialogical forms of engagement.

By engaging in a debate around the diversification of the exhibition form, this research examines curatorial practices in the discursive sphere in relation to the idea of dematerializing processes of knowledge production. It also critically addresses the ramifications processes of knowledge production can suffer as situated within the cognitive cultural economy of post-Fordist society.

It is not the intention of this book to promote curatorial practices as unequivocally preeminent and/or dominant realms of knowledge production. Rather, it attempts to locate the observations it makes and analyzes with regard to processes of knowledge production in the discourse on knowledge production provoking a debate on the dissemination, obtainability, and exploitation of knowledge.

Referring to different positionalities in the field with regard to the distinction between "curating" and "curatorial," this research avoids arguing for a consolidation of these terminologies or prescribing limitations to the practice of curating or determining with which bodies of knowledge the curatorial should associate or identify. Such an undertaking would rest on commonplaces and presuppositions about notions of practice and discourse and run the risk of not producing more than a repetition and replication of the self-referentiality of established jargons around curatorial practices in contemporary art. Distinctions between curating and curatorial, or between artist and curator are, to a certain extent, obliterated by assuming a perspective that—rather than scrutinizing positionalities in the field of art and questioning what something is or who somebody is—examines the kind of activities that take place, and enquires into how something or somebody comes into being and is manifested. In this sense, curatorial practices are discussed as an activity encompassing as much thinking as doing, oscillating between reflection and production, determination and disruption, and representation and presentation.

Elaborating on the meaning of the term "practice" as a concept of action and reflection, while setting it in relation to artistic and curatorial practices, is intrinsically linked to conceptions of agency. What forms of agency does the curatorial entail and enable, and in what ways are these forms of agency conditioned socially, culturally, and politically? The common thread that runs through the book is not the presentation of curatorial practice as a form of exhibiting and collecting the views and values belonging to a particular society, but an argument for a model of practice first and foremost as an activity of observing, communicating, mediating—thereby negotiating expectations, attitudes, and sensitivities affecting how sociality comes into being.

The argument that this book develops on an intrinsic social dimension to the curatorial complex rests on research questions pertaining to how cultural practitioners in the curatorial complex allocate a social and political relevance to their practices, and how they articulate it. With regard to the examples discussed, particularly those operating in the discursive sphere, I enquire into the nature of the relations established in the curated encounter and proposes a notion of curatorial practices that provide a speculative realm of thinking and doing, where the social, political, and cultural realities in which the practices are situated can be imagined differently and alternatively. This enquiry starts by challenging epistemic schemata within the field of cultural production, such as forms of passive spectatorship, the culture of spectacle, practices of representation and narrative production of the past, which together have, to a large extent, characterized the production and reception of art. Emphasis is instead placed on the creation of dialogical spaces of communication between curators, artists, and their publics that produce forms of sociality as a nurturing ground for modes of speculating and imagining. This naturally entails the discussion of terminologies of communication, spectatorship, relationality, and sociality.

Research Hypothesis

The perspective this research develops on curatorial practice (as an activity of knowledge production whose particular modes of hosting, exhibiting, and producing a contention with art have an intrinsic social dimension) entails proposing a "material turn" for curatorial practices. This presents a way to enquire into the epistemology of curatorial practice with regard to how it constitutes the production of sociality, and by what means.

Developing such argument throughout the book focuses not on applying some preconfigured notion of "material" or "materiality" onto curatorial practice, or vice versa, but means to think through the question in what way a material register of curated encounters could constitute a perspective on curatorial practices that is pertinent to contemporary claims made in this field of research focusing on processes of dematerialization, particularly with regard to forms of knowledge production in the curated encounter. Therefore this research develops and describes a material register for the different projects discussed, which allows to critically question the constitution of the curated encounter as a space of knowledge production.

Historically, notions such as "matter," "material" and "materiality" are highly debated terms and concepts, particularly since the modern period. Cultural critic Raymond Williams referred to the often evoked dialectic of form and content, or material vs. ideal, as essentially portraying a class distinction: Material activities are distinguished from spiritual or intellectual activities, to which more value is associated in terms of knowledge production (*Keywords* 164). This, however, can be cast as resulting from a series of misinterpretations of philosophical writings—of Kant and Hegel in particular—who, while maintaining a dialectical approach, do not identify matter or material solely with physical substance regardless of its perceptional experience. Kant refers to matter as substance that has a particular surface value to which our thinking pertains for its perceptional experiences (Eisler, "Materie"). Hegel defines material as that which constitutes reality, as a form that provides a relation between the outer world and the inner self (64-67). While Kant and Hegel do further establish the dialectic of form and content and material vs. ideal, they can, however, also be read as defining "material" as "relational": the moment when material acquires physicality is also always the moment when a relation between reality and perception is produced.

It is such relational understanding of materiality that is fundamental for the purpose of this research, which is to discuss an intrinsic social dimension to the curatorial complex by arguing for a material register of the curated encounter. The call for a subsequent material turn in curatorial practices is a proposition this research aims to make that is responsive to the ways in which issues of materiality determine matters of mediation and knowledge production in contemporary artistic and curatorial practices primarily operating in the discursive sphere.

To pursue a material register of curatorial pratices has at its core an anthropological interest that questions in what ways the material conditions of things and relations transform the world in relation to its cultural, social, and political conditioning. The point of a taking a material perspective on curatorial practices is to avoid reproducing idealistic and rationalistic conceptions of how we perceive the world in our consciousness and extend our thinking beyond familiar divisions between what is and is not "material" for our consciousness to apprehend, interpret, and understand in relation to the production of art.

Throughout the various projects of artistic and curatorial practices discussed in this book—exhibitions, seminars, events, summits, etc.—materiality is argued for as a product of processes and dispositions of materializations that take place in the curated encounter. The analyses of the different projects will reveal that addressing the materiality of the relations produced in the curated encounter can only take place by constituting sociality as a generative force of knowledge production. Such appeal for a material register of the curated encounter should, however, not be misunderstood as a call for greater attention to objects and artworks in curatorial practices. This would represent a restrictive and regressive argument that positions curating as a mere organization of objects. Instead, the proposition for a material turn in curatorial practices carefully and critically serves to question the manifold relationships of knowledge and agency production in the curated encounter for how material things become effective in shaping social relations—neither autonomous of human consciousness by granting intentionality to material things, nor entirely dependent of human agency for deriving symbolic meaning or material things.

Approaching curatorial practices with a perspective on materiality is concerned with what Tony Bennett and Patrick Joyce call a "postrepresentational" logic (5), finding a way of describing semiotic, material and social flows[1] that challenge our forms of perceiving the world into categories of reality vs. fiction, subjectivity vs. objectivity, and representation vs. imagination. It is the notion of materiality itself that gains importance and proves indispensable when articulating a concept of sociality that contains a critique of inherited conceptual dualisms such as material vs. ideal and material vs. cultural, moving beyond the simplistic idea of causal relationships between production and perception upon which a quasi-philosophical theory of change would be found.

Methodology

Methodologically this research aims to move beyond making a distinction between curating and curatorial as manifestations of the realms of practice and theory respectively. A central intention here is to question the validity of the production and further elaboration of such dichotomies—and to move beyond them. Curating can be a production of practice for a reflection on theory as much as it can result in a production of theory for a reflection on practice. In the curatorial, theory and practice are inextricably linked with one another and mutually dependent. It is in this context that claims surrounding the concurrentness of forms of production and reflection in curatorial practices that this research continuously addresses and develops should be perceived.

The methodology of writing each part of the book avoids analyzing exhibitions and other artistic and curatorial projects as mere case studies for a preconceived argument. Instead, each part takes either one project or series of projects as a departure point; they are discussed in order to develop an argument, rather than to prove one. The projects discussed here generate reflections on various forms of artistic and curatorial practices. In turn, these reflections develop new sets of ideas in relation to these practices. The selected projects are looked at in relation to theoretical arguments whose relevance for the discussion emerges from the reflections on practice.

---

1 Bennett and Joyce particularly refer to Gilles Deleuze and Felix Guattari as a key influence for developing a postrepresentational logic, particularly how their account of assemblages denies preconceived models of social ordering (Deleuze and Guattari 22–23 qtd. in Bennett and Joyce 5–6).

The idea of the process incorporating concurrent forms of reflection and production—having theory and practice collapse into one another—is a precise methodological choice. This allows the text to evoke the notion of recursivity, which is an important aspect of claims surrounding the production of knowledge and sociality that this research puts forward.

Each of the projects will be approached individually, however their difference to the other projects in scale, size, visibility and outreach will be taken into account—not so much in an effort to make it comparable to the other project, but for emphasizing the importance to approach each project in the context of the different forms and shapes curatorial and artistic projects can assume. In terms of scale and size the order of discussion of the chosen examples of practices is by no means arbitrary. It follows the idea of constructing an argument that is self-reflexive and in that sense pertinent to evoking and assuming a self-critical potential: The arguments derived from describing and analyzing each project are continuously challenged in the following chapters with regard to the individualities from which they are derived and towards the universalities they claim.

Given the huge number of artistic and curatorial projects potentially available for study, choosing such starting points was a complex endeavour. On a purely pragmatic level, the projects needed to be contemporary in order for me to see them or participate in them as an observer or member of the attending public. It was also important that they should not be limited to a single form of practice, but include exhibitions and projects of a more discursive nature, responding to the many turns (educational, social, discursive, participatory, etc.) that have been proposed in recent decades for artistic and curatorial practices.

The projects also had to represent a somewhat uncharted territory, meaning that they should not, for example, have been discussed at length or in detail in anthologies of curatorial practices. Naturally, over the course of this research a modest number of reviews, critiques, and commentaries did emerge on the projects, many of which I have taken into account. On the other hand, it was essential that the projects not be too marginal in nature, so that they could manifest a relation to contemporary curatorial discourse in the issues they discuss and tackle. The projects ultimately selected for discussion form an interesting constellation of research issues relating to curatorial practices: communication, the dialectics of spectatorship and partic-

ipation, knowledge production, and notions of collectivity and sociality—all of them terms that emerge from the discussion in this research of examples of practice.

The analyses undertaken in this book are centred on, but not limited to, the ever-growing body of texts on curatorial practices from the
late 1980s to current times. Specific emphasis is placed on literature in
curatorial discourse from the early 1990s, when curatorial practices
started to experiment with different forms and mediums of practice.
They questioned the role of the institution and challenged the autonomy of artists and curators through various forms of collaboration.
Curatorial discourse took up these issues and focussed on the ramifications of the changing definitions and strategies of production exercised by curatorial practices. This reserach places the selected examples of practice in the context of the ever-growing discourse specific
to contemporary curatorial practices, and applies this discourse to
contextualize and contrast the practices.

Curatorial discourse can be highly self-referential and sometimes
dangerously self-sufficient. So in order to avoid getting lost in this
labyrinth of jargon, this research takes in key contributions from the
realm of philosophy, social theory, and cultural studies on matters of
collectivity, collaboration, sociality, and knowledge production. This
expands the realm of curatorial discourse to incorporate new perspectives on the matters of concern.

The Communicative
Space of the Exhibition

Formed in and through practice curating is an activity for which the designation of its function is highly contingent upon the parameters by which it is determined (institutional, economical, historical, social, political, etc.). As Beatrice von Bismarck defined it, curating "consists of a constellation of objects, actors, differently defined spaces—aesthetically, socially, discursively, functionally" ("In the Space of the Curatorial" 43). The claims that are made for curating in the following are of an indirect nature. They do not seek to define the term "curating," and neither can the examples discussed in any way be deemed representative of methodologies of practice in the field of the curatorial. To describe the following examples as constellations of objects, images, and actors helps to enquire into the nature of the space in which they are assembled, as well as question the relations that it produces. Are they social relations? Does the materiality of artworks transpire in them? What do they produce? Experience, communication, knowledge?

> The exhibition space, particularly the institutionalized white cube, is an endless source of contention in curatorial discourse. Deemed "one of modernism's triumphs," curatorial practices—particularly in the 1990s—sought to look for alternative ways of making art public in order to escape the ideological nature of the white cube space, especially with regards to how it conditions the artworks it presents. (O'Doherty 79)

The subjugation of artistic production to a frame at once "universal," neutral, ordered, rational, and ultimately problematic for what that so-called universality implies and hides, points to a predicament with which artists and curators have grappled ever since: Exhibitions, by their forms, entangle the viewer in a space at once physical and intellectual, but also ideological. (Filipovic 65)

Together with the deconstruction of modernity and its claims of universality that in large part oppressed and obscured cultural histories and their producers, the exhibition space has been enquired into extensively in curatorial discourse and treated ambivalently in curatorial practices.[2] Less than what the exhibition space is—if that can or should be generalized at all—the question that still has relevance today and remains largely unanswered is what happens or needs to happen in the exhibition space so that it can function as a medium of enquiry rather than representation and be perceived as an arena of significance grounded in the materiality of what is presented rather than of symbolic knowledge production.

If one were to start thinking about what conditions the exhibition space while viewing an exhibition, the questions addressed would presumably primarily concern the grammar of the exhibition, its speech and utterance, and the ways in which it produces meaning and knowledge. These are the pivotal issues this chapter addresses—not in isolation from the politics of the exhibition as an ideological, cultural, and social space, but addressing the politics of the exhibition as an exhibition of politics: "The manner by which a selection of artworks, a tectonic context, and thematic or other discursive accompaniments coalesce into a particular form is at the heart of *how an exhibition exhibits*" (Filipovic 79). The way in which the medium of the exhibition is discussed in curatorial discourse is ambivalent, particularly so in recent times. There are great studies of the exhibition as a form and medium (Misiano et al., "The Grammar of the Exhibition"; Hoffmann, "Overture"), providing detailed analyses of the processes of communication and interpretation responsible for any form of knowledge production in the exhibition space (Ferguson; Poinsot), as well as studies of its social and cultural function (Bennett, "The Exhibitionary Complex" [1996]; O'Doherty; Franke). Some publications forego a discussion of the exhibition space in favour of other spaces, such as the discursive, the performative, or the public (urban) space (O'Neill, "The Curatorial Turn"; Lind, *Performing the Curatorial*), while others directly focus on the notion of the curatorial exploring the conditions of hospitality of exhibitions as communicative spaces with regard to the production of knowledge and meaning that is either generated in them or attributed to them.

---

2 As Elena Filipovic pointed out, it is surprising how many large-scale exhibitions and biennials still favour the white cube model even if aware of its ideological issues and hegemonic claims (68–74). Example of projects that purposely go beyond the exhibition space, such as Manifesta 6, unitednationsplaza, and *Former West*, are analyzed in the subsequent chapters of this book.

The curatorial not only implies a genuine mode for generating, mediating, and reflecting experiences and knowledge developed in artist's
studios and cultural institutions, but also encompasses a whole field
of knowledge relating to the conditions of the appearance of art and
culture and the different contexts by which they are defined. (Bismarck et al. 8)

This description of what the curatorial implies is still fairly conservative in that it hints at a curating practice of exhibiting artists' work
that has been previously produced in their studios or on-site in institutions. But it is nevertheless interesting because it highlights a level
of reflexivity at play that is crucial for the exhibition space to function
as a medium of enquiry, not only regarding what is presented, mediated or generated, but also how its presentation, mediation or generation affects or is conditioned by its materiality, appearance, and contexts of signification.

The intention of this chapter is to develop a notion of practice
applicable to curating. The complex relationships between the experience and knowledge that curatorial practices generates, mediates
and reflects are therefore exemplarily rendered as taking up a position not only of embeddedness, but involvement in how art's political, cultural, and social significance is produced and addressed.

It is for this reason that this chapter discusses two exhibitions:
Michael Fullerton's solo exhibition *Columbia*[3] at London's Chisenhale Gallery and *The Potosí Principle,*[4] a group exhibition conceived
by Alice Creischer, Max-Jorge Hinderer and Andreas Siekmann and
shown at the Haus der Kulturen der Welt, Berlin, both of which took
place in 2010. These two exhibitions are different in almost every
detail. *Columbia* was a relatively small exhibition, showing less than
a fifth of the amount of works presented in *The Potosí Principle.* The
former showed the work of one artist while the latter was a group
show. Chisenhale Gallery, the site of Michael Fullerton's *Columbia*
exhibition, is a medium-sized institution in East London that considers itself an innovative forum for contemporary art focusing on

---

3 The exhibition was on view from 10 September to 24 October 2010 at Chisenhale Gallery in East London.
4 The exhibition premiered at the Museo Nacional Centro de Arte Reina Sofía,
   Madrid, before travelling to Berlin's Haus der Kulturen der Welt, where the
   show was on view from 8 October 2010 to 2 January 2011. Afterwards the exhibition travelled to the Museo Nacional de Arte and Museuo Nacional de Etnografía in La Paz.

artists' solo commissions at an early and formative point in their career. All three institutions hosting *The Potosí Principle* (Museo Nacional Centro de Arte Reina Sofia, Madrid; Haus der Kulturen der Welt, Berlin; Museo Nacional de Arte and Museuo Nacional de Etnografía, La Paz) are well-established large-scale institutions that assume a firm position in a city's and nation's cultural environment and history. Furthermore, walking through Chisenhale's rough metal doors giving way to a small foyer before entering the only exhibition space is a very different experience than crossing the lawn in front of the purposefully commissioned iconic building of Berlin's Haus der Kulturen der Welt in order to enter the large foyer before being guided to one of the many exhibition spaces where the show took place.

Initially, there might seem to be only one thing that *Columbia* and *The Potosí Principle* have in common: both exhibitions were "curated" by artists. However, to point out this apparent similarity is a stretch given that the verb "to curate" is usually not applied when an artist conceives a solo exhibition at an institution. To define whether this or that exhibition is curated is in fact beside the point, as it would be to superficially conflate or a priori differentiate the roles of artists and curators, or to advocate that exhibition spaces, institutions or curators produce the meaning of artistic production. This book renders the latter claim in particular obsolete, since the analysis of both examples will show how processes of meaning production emerge solely from a contention with the artworks in the exhibition space that is dependent on the extent to which the viewer questions the institutional and cultural predicaments of knowledge production in art.

What both exhibitions have in common, and what is, hence, the reason that they are examined here, is a critical attitude towards their own potential for building relations that consciously address their own function as producing knoweldge. Both exhibitions engage with the particular ways in which artistic production and its presentation in the context of an exhibition can begin to enquire into the nature of meaning and knowledge production in order to reveal the complexity of spectatorship and its role in knowledge production. However, the strategies and methodologies the artists employ to construct the exhibitions as communicative spaces and to explore their communicability are at opposite ends of the spectrum. Walking through Fullerton's exhibition *Columbia* was reminiscent of a scavenger hunt in which facts were the prize, but fiction was the means. In contrast to this poetic quality to the politics of communication in Fullerton's exhibition, *The Potosí Principle* confronted the viewer with an abundance of historical facts threatened with omission from cultural history. Their contemporary relevance was subject to the politics of interpretation generated and mediated in the exhibition by various tactics of display. Both exhibitions present an extraordinary challenge to the viewer in terms of perceiving and experiencing the curated encounter from a material point of view, focusing on the question how they exhibit what they exhibit. Both exhibitions conceive of the viewer not solely as a recipient of information or experience but, subsequently, as an agent of knowledge production.

It is precisely this point of view that makes it possible to transgress the stark differences of these two exhibitions in every aspect of scale, size, and outreach, and turn to thinking through the relationships the works produce with each other and the viewer in relation to the social, political and cultural conditions that contextualize their production and exhibition. Therefore this chapter looks at how the strategies of communication and display in both exhibition examples affect and effect relationships between artworks and viewers with regard to forms of agency of spectatorship. The political quality of both exhibitions is to engender a reflexivity upon the matter of communicability of exhibitions—not (or not solely) with respect to the information presented, experience generated, or interpretation provided, but to the relationship between the exhibition space and the reality in which it is situated, which is negotiated by spectatorship as an agency of knowledge production.

In a second part, this chapter reflects on the exhibition's analysis and addresses the question of communication in the exhibition space from a more theoretical point of view by conducting a comparative analysis of two theoretical dispositions: Niklas Luhmann's notion of *communication* and Pierre Bourdieu's concept of *practice*. In this way it seeks to enquire into a notion of practice that provides for a definition of curating: When we speak of activities in the realm of the curatorial, exactly what kind of practice are we considering? What are the particularities of such practice that make it possible for Carolyn Christov-Bakargiev to vehemently oppose Liam Gillick's designation of art and curating as "creative practices alike" (Hiller and Martin 38)? And what conditions of practice would allow for the alignment of art and curating? Bearing in mind the idea of communicability, what particular operations take place in practice when considering exhibition making as involving Joseph Grigely's "doubling of showing and telling" (9)?

The comparative analysis of Luhmann's notion of communication and Bourdieu's notion of practice is based on a conceptual similarity. In building their terminologies and concepts both sociologists foreground an interaction between structure and process, form and formation, and production and reflection that can be applied to how artistic and curatorial practices operate in relation to the social, political, and cultural issues that condition them. Luhmann's and Bourdieu's theoretical concepts help to render the notions of practice and communication as conditioning processes of knowledge production entailing a power of judgement that arises from the social, political, and cultural function of the exhibition space produced by its communicability.

Methodologically, the discussions of the exhibitions intentionally precede the more theoretical elaborations on the terminology of practice. While the exhibitions' analysis centers on highlighting the common desire and aspiration of both exhibitions to conceive of art as a device for knowledge production, the discussion of Luhmann's and Bourdieu's terminology serves to develop the questions necessary for conceiving a notion of practice emerging from an idea of communicability—the potential of an exhibition to function as a space of communication in the context of art as a form of knowledge production. The exhibitions are described with regard to the ways in which the artists display and contextualize their own works and that of others. Thereby two very different models emerge of how an exhibition is defined by the potential of its communicability as a space that produces as much knowledge as it reflects upon. The interpretation of the works in the show and the analysis of their politics of installation develops an understanding of communication that refers to the ways in which processes of interpretation taking place in the space of the exhibition are conditioned by the parameters of communication set up by the artists and curators. This occurs to such an extent that what is primarily produced in communication is a shift in perspective on the part of the spectator from communication to communicability, and from meaning to significance. This paves the way for thinking about how artistic and curatorial practices not only address the position of the viewer in the exhibition space, but also effect a particular social fabric by setting up relations between objects, actors, spaces, and ideas. In terms of communication, these processes are necessarily characterized by a high level of recursivity and sociality, which is not to say that they are entirely self-referential or immanent. Discussing the ways in which Luhmann and Bourdieu structure their concepts of practice and communication as recursive feedback loops will therefore provide an understanding of how curatorial practices are a form of concurrent reflection as well as production of potentialities to produce knowledge, communication, interpretation, spectatorship, and participation.

Communicability

The notion of communicability enables the discussion of the function of knowledge production in curatorial practices in a way that is always integral to the relationship between objects, actors, and agents in a particular space. To think about how an exhibition communicates means to address it as a social, cultural, and political space. Questions about strategies and methodologies of communication go hand in hand with concerns about what it is that is being communicated.

Semiotics, the science of meaning-making, examines the relationship between objects, signs, and subjects on a general level. While it is not specifically concerned with the exhibition space, it is nonetheless worthwhile considering here because of its discussion of the proximity between communicability and significance. For example, Charles Sanders Peirce almost eradicates any distinction between communication and meaning, opposing presemiotic concepts of meaning defined in terms of psychological concepts, and communication in terms of social functions (Parret 33). For Peirce, both terms form part of a pragmatic logic, in which form (meaning) and function (communication) cannot be separated. In a similar way, in order to prevent an essentialist, idealist, and autonomous preconception of meaning, Jürgen Habermas—referring to Ludwig Wittgenstein—asserts that there is no meaning outside communication (107–09). The term "communicability" renders the pragmatics of communication with regard to the use of meaning. In this respect notions of communicability and significance are interrelated. Both are conditions that integrate social, political, and cultural components into the processes of communication and production of meaning to which they refer. Philosopher Immanuel Kant defines communicability as an intersubjective condition of cognitive contents and aesthetic evaluations. For Kant, communicability is a criterion of knowledge in the judgement process in the sense that every form of empirical knowledge is conditioned by its communicability.[5] Furthermore, the *sensus communis* is bound up with the communicability of what is assessed, an element of communality used to overcome individual idiosyncrasies. It presents and represents something to which everyone can connect, and this potential for connection gives judgements an exemplary validity (Kant 107). And although Hannah Arendt dismisses this idea of communicability providing judgements with an exemplary validity, she does explore Kant's notion of communicability enabling the appraisal of judgement as a specific political ability that has an intrinsic public quality (*Das Urteilen*). In her discussion of Kant, Arendt extends the notion of the spectator as the beholder—to which Kant's judgment of the realm of aesthetic was confined—to that of the actor (*Das Urteilen* 73–76). The judgement criterion for spectator and actor alike is communicability, defined here as the faculty of the spectator/actor to appeal to common sense, founded upon "the ability to see things not only from one's own point of view but from the perspective of all those who happen to be present" (Arendt, *Between Pasts and Future* 220). Arendt articulates this as a necessity to conceive of the discursive not as a medium of the political, but as its form and content (*Was ist Politik?* 14).

Applied to the context of the exhibition, my interest in the notion of communicability is not to transfer the way in which it has been described as a criterion of judgement for the role of the viewer. This would imply a superficial equation of a number of concepts, such as perception and aesthetic, or judgement and interpretation. It is from the perspective of curatorial practice as an activity of generating, mediating, and reflecting experiences that the idea of communicability becomes relevant as a criterion for apprehending the exhibition space as a political and social context in which knowledge production takes place.

---

5 Particularly with regard to the notion of taste Kant develops the concept of communicability (106).

From this perspective it stands to reason that one should enquire into the notion of practice, particularly on the background of the importance Arendt gives to action, a *condicio per quam* of the political. The many disputes about how the practice of curators should be defined (whether as "curating" or "curatorial practice," for example)[6] and the efforts to distinguish it from the artistic may call into question many terms and concepts but they rarely address the notion of practice.

Implosion of knowledge—Michael Fullerton's *Columbia* exhibition

The claim for knowledge production in contemporary art has been subjected to much critical examination and reformulation. Emanating from Michel Foucault's definition of knowledge as "that of which one can speak in a discursive practice" (*Archeology of Knowledge*, 201) Sarat Maharaj, Irit Rogoff, and, more recently, Simon Sheikh, amongst others, have all pointed out various problematics surrounding the discourse of art as a site for the production of knowledge. The assumption they question the most is the understanding of knowledge production as an inherent feature and implicit function of an artwork or of artistic research generated in and for the social sphere. It is not so much the relevance of art for society that is the target of their critical examination, but the many ways of uncritically adopted notions of "art producing knowledge" that are advocated by artistic, curatorial, and interdisciplinary research practices, often in a very self-referential fashion.

> The discourse of knowledge production in contemporary art is largely a matter of rhetoric, of branding. In practice, knowledge production in art often amounts to little more than simulation—the "research" in question being little more than advanced browsing that yields hackneyed results. (Lütticken, "Unknown Knowns" 85)

Art historian and critic Sven Lütticken argues along similar lines when identifying rhetoric as a language of branding, and simulation as a methodology that exemplifies the uncritical adoption of the notion of "art producing knowledge." Lütticken concludes his description of the discourse of knowledge production in contemporary art

---

6 See Bismarck and Rogoff 21–41.

by pointing out the apparent function of artistic research "as a par-
ody of instrumentalized academic knowledge production, falling
short of even its eroding criteria" ("Unkown Knowns" 85). But it is
not Lütticken's intention to deny the possibility of or the potential
for knowledge production in art. Rather, his intention is to point out
the ways in which art can produce knowledge in a manner that is
distinct from other ways of knowledge production in the social
sphere, such as academia. Lütticken recommends thinking about
the "symptom in what passes for artistic knowledge production" in
order to wrestle with the question of what modes of production contemporary artistic practices use to produce knowledge and how that
relates to academic research, in which the symptom assumes the
role of "an alternative to the empire of signs created by academic
disciplines—as pointing both backwards and forwards in time, beyond the current order of things" ("Unkown Knowns" 85–86). What
is interesting about the idea of the symptom is that, in contrast to a
sign or symbol, it *simulates* a commonplace rather than reflecting or
producing one. It acts as a "quasi-sign that enlightens by obscuring
and obstructing" (Lütticken, "Unkown Knowns" 107). A sign or symbol enters into communication in order to carry information that
can be related to by all the partners in the communicative relationship as the content of the communicative process. This is where the
symptom obscures: it stands in for the information and thereby
spotlights the lack of the information's significance.

Lütticken argues for symptomatological practices in the realm of
contemporary art and addresses the question of how knowledge is
produced within it. These hold the potential to "turn the main weak-
ness of much artistic 'knowledge'—its complete lack of academic
rigour or accountability—into a strength, critiquing the rhetoric of
knowledge production while beginning to fulfil the promise betrayed
by it" ("Unkown Knowns" 107). He proposes thinking through the
idea of the symptom and its methodologies of simulation in order to
reveal how art contributes to the production of knowledge in the social sphere: An artistic practice can be characterized as symptomatological when its method of knowledge production, such as simulation or appropriation, also offers reflection and critique on the very
subject matter dealt with in its practice.[7] The symptom never func-

---

7 As examples Lütticken refers to Jeff Wall's *Milk* (1984) or *Man with a Rifle*
   (1989), Douglas Gordon's video installation *Hysterical* (1995), and Martha Ros-

tions by itself but only in relation to what it obscures and stands in for. Therefore, establishing a symptom also generates a relationship between the subject matter of the symptom itself and the subject matter of what the symptom is standing in for. This requires a differentiation between what it is that is presented (being-in-itself) and what it is that this presentation stands in for (being-for-another). This differentiation is the condition for the symptom to function as a symptom. In order to be recognized as such it has to differ from the general, the normal, and the expected. Hence, the methodologies of symptomatological practices are the ways in which this differentiation is established through acts of simulation and appropriation that are made visible in their character as hiding something, or pointing to something else, generating not only attention, but also suspicion about the integrity as well as the relevance of the subject matter when it comes to the claim of art producing knowledge.

In analyzing the 2010 exhibition *Columbia*—the first solo exhibition by Scottish artist Michael Fullerton at a British institution—Lütticken's idea of symptomatological practice proves useful when considering the particular function art assumes in relation to knowledge production. Fullerton's artistic practice revolves around the notion of knowledge production, particularly around the question of how much information about their subjects works of art, particularly painted portraits, can accommodate, and how meaning is constructed. As clearly hinted at by the title of his more recent show *Meaning Inc.*[8] at the Glasgow Print Studio in 2014, Fullerton is interested in exploring the relationship between images, knowledge, representation, and power. His artistic practice is not limited to portraiture, and encompasses sculptures, installations incorporating found objects, filmmaking, and printmaking. His oil paintings can, however, be considered the nucleus of his investigations into questions of meaning and knowledge production and are the primary medium in which Fullerton works when exploring a subject matter.

ler's video *The Semiotics of the Kitchen* (1975), amongst others ("Unknown Knowns" 84–107).

8 *Meaning Inc.* was held from 28 June to 15 August 2014 at the first floor gallery of the Glasgow Print Studio in Glasgow.

Accumulating Information

In *Meaning Inc.* Fullerton exhibited several portraits of personalities involved in the technology and communication industries who for one reason or another have crossed paths with justice.⁹ Fullerton previously explored this line of interest in 2010 with *Columbia*, a much more extensive exhibition at Chisenhale Gallery, London, for which he assembled a total of fifteen works: eight paintings, three screen prints, one moving-image work, and three installations.¹⁰ Although the title of this exhibition appears to be less instructive, it does address the exhibition as a whole in a different way. The press release that was handed out at the entrance to the exhibition did not explain what or who Columbia was, but stated that "Columbia serves as a guiding iconic device throughout the exhibition, allowing Fullerton to explore concepts as various as discovery, colonial endeavour, the machinations of power, and the construction of corporate identity" ("Michael Fullerton: Columbia").

At first sight the exhibition space itself didn't look to be much more than an accumulation of many different works not instantly relatable either to one another, or to the proposed "guiding iconic device." The installation directly opposite the gallery doors, the first work one encountered, drew attention to its constant beam of green light circling and hovering over the floor. In gauging the gallery walls it seemed to be trying to scan, monitor, and locate everything else within its scope, assuming some sort of function for configuring and contextualizing all the other works. It is only the title of this installation, *Gothic Version of the Ring Laser Gyroscope Used in Final Flight of the Space Shuttle Columbia STS–107* (fig. 1) that recalls the exhibition's title. The lengthy caption that accompanied the work (Fullerton himself wrote this and all the other captions for the show) explained that the title of the work referred to the Columbia Space Shuttle that was destroyed during reentry into the Earth's atmosphere on 1 February 2003 while returning from mission STS–107. The caption also provides details of the functioning of this light as an inertial guiding sys-

---

9 These included Kim Dotcom, founder of the file-sharing website megaupload. com, for which he was sued for copyright infringement, or Samuel Goldwyn, founder of Goldwyn pictures, now MGM International ("Michael Fullerton: Meaning Inc.").

10 A full list of images and their accompanying captions can be downloaded from Chisenhale Gallery's website ("Archive: Columbia").

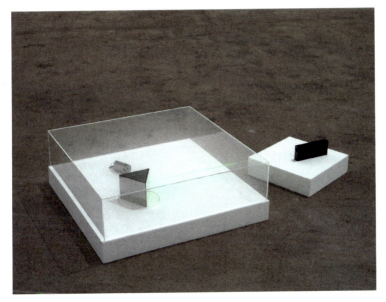

Fig. 1: Michael Fullerton, *Gothic Version of the Ring Laser Gyroscope Used in Final Flight of the Space Shuttle Columbia STS–107*. 2010, mirror, laser, smoke machine, plinth, dimensions variable. Courtesy the artist, the photographer, Carl Freedman Gallery.

tem that uses dead reckoning to calculate the orientation and velocity of a moving object, avoiding the need for external references such as GPS or any other data.[11]

Contrary to expectations one might have of captions and their function in the exhibition space—involving the provision of information about and around the artwork in order to contextualize it—here there was no direct reference to the installation as a work of art, but only to its apparent subject matter. The caption might explain the work's physical and intellectual material, but not why that is presented. The

---

11   The full caption reads as follows: "The Ring Laser Gyroscope is a device that continuously monitors the position, velocity, and acceleration of a vehicle, usually a submarine, missile, or aeroplane, and thus provides navigational data or control without the need for communicating with a base station. This is characteristic of inertial guidance systems. Inertial guidance systems are self-referential and determine location and orientation not from sightings of the stars or landmarks, nor from signals from the ground, but solely from instruments carried aboard a moving craft." ("Columbia: Titles and Captions")

function usually attributed to captions in the context of an exhibition is to help with the interpretation of the information that the artist's work present, transforming information in the work via an interpretation of the work to knowledge about the work (Ferguson 178). With regard to this particular assumed function, captions act as symbols of knowledge production. But this particular caption—and every caption in this exhibition—was completely free of any reference to the artist and his intention with the works. Instead, it read like an excerpt of information from Wikipedia, which rather superficially than substantially satisfied the curiosity of the viewer, who was thereby sidetracked from his or her lack of comprehension of the work.

But if one delves deeper into this work by questioning its modes of appearance and the relation between caption, title, and material, the following question arises: Was this machine locating and monitoring the objects and the bodies of the viewers that moved around? Certainly the sense of being surveilled was triggered every time the green ray of light streaked a visitor's leg. The title raised yet another question: Why was the laser machine described as a "gothic version"? Probably because the components of the installation—a mirror and a smoke machine on a plinth next to the laser—could not possibly have been the real components of a ring laser gyroscope that monitors movement in a submarine, for example. The elements of the installation were props that simulated the functioning of an inertial guiding system, but could not have been be mistaken for the genuine article. Its presence in the gallery space acted within the exhibition as a symbol for a surveillance system as a mode of observation and identification.

What emerges from the contention with *Gothic Version of the Ring Laser Gyroscope Used in Final Flight of the Space Shuttle Columbia STS-107* (fig. 1) as part of analyzing the exhibition are questions that enquire into the definition and role of information in the process of communication between artist, works and viewer, both in relation to the exhibition in general, and to the works in particular. How much do the works represent, or pretend to represent, the associations they have been given in the captions or in the titles? Are the artist (by means of the captions) and the institution (by voicing the artist's intention so prominently in the press release) trying to safeguard the "right" kind of interpretation of the works?

These questions seem ever more cogent when one considers the assumption made above that Fullerton's practice operates symptomatologically according to the terms defined by Lütticken: Artistic practices are symptomatological when their ways of producing knowledge, such as simulation or appropriation, also offer forms of reflection upon and critique of the very same subject matter that their practice engages with. The task now is to define not only what the symptom is here, but also how it functions. Could Fullerton's practice be analyzed as operating symptomatologically when it comes to the way in which the dialogue between works and viewer initiated and developed in the communicative space of the exhibition assumes a knowledge-producing function?

A symptom is an effect caused by something to which it points—something that cannot point to itself. For example, a sore throat points to an infection somewhere in the body. The effect is to a certain extent reflexive since it points to an infection that affects the entirety of the system in which it operates. In the case of the sore throat that system is the whole body and its well-being. In Fullerton's case, the system is the exhibition as a space of and for communication, and it only exists in the process of communication between works and viewer. In order to point at the elements that form this system—information and material in works and texts—and the operations that these elements potentially can initiate, such as dialogue, interpretation and knowledge production—Fullerton employs a symptom as an effect that affects the entirety of the process of communication, and thus points to it.

The malfunction to which the symptom points has thus far been outlined in the analysis of one particular work in the exhibition, but it can be generalized and applied to other works in the show. The malfunction is the distorted relationship between how the works present themselves to the viewer and the information relating to them that is presented by the artist. The confusion regarding the relationship between works and their accompanying information is what disturbs the process of communication that aims to arrive at an interpretation of the work. To stay with the medical vocabulary for a moment, the diagnosis of this malfunction refers to the exhibition as a system. It affects the entire body of the exhibition, and its circulatory system is analogous to the flow of communication relating the different works.

Fig. 2: Installation view of Michael Fullerton, *Columbia*. 2010,
Chisenhale Gallery, London. Photo: Andy Keate. Courtesy the
artist and Chisenhale Gallery.

Fig. 3: Installation view of Michael Fullerton, *Columbia*. 2010,
Chisenhale Gallery, London. Photo: Andy Keate. Courtesy the
artist and Chisenhale Gallery.

Fig. 4: Installation view of Michael Fullerton, *Columbia*. 2010,
Chisenhale Gallery, London. Photo: Andy Keate. Courtesy the
artist and Chisenhale Gallery.

Infection as Affection

The process of communication was confused from the outset and
therefore affected by an act of simulation. Fullerton was suggesting
that the works were about what he wrote in the captions. In doing
so he relied on the codes of conduct generated by so many large-
scale retrospectives and theme-based or historical exhibitions in
museums all around the world: the idea that captions explain the
work. But what the viewer observed in the case of Fullerton was the
symptom, the malfunction of the caption, which did not explain
the information that the work offered in the communicative process to the viewer, but only listed information whose relevance is
still awaiting judgement. What the viewer detected was the symptom that points to the malfunction as an effect that it itself generated.

The process of judgement starts by questioning the very elements
that make for the appearance of the symptom, such as the relationship between form and content of the work. For example, both the

screen print *Using Polish Technology, Alan Turing Devised a More Sophisticated Machine to Crack ENIGMA* (fig. 5) and the painting *Why Your Life Sucks (Alan Turing)* (fig. 6) depict the same person, Alan Turing—as suggested by the title of the painting and explained in the caption of the screen print.[12]

The large wall-mounted screen print on newspaper was a black-and-white photograph of Alan Turing, slightly distorted as it consisted of nine pieces of thin paper, while the painting portrays the figure of Alan Turing in front of a patterned background. Both portraits are of the same person, but the differences in style and kinds of information provided in the captions mattered a great deal when it came to their interpretation. The screen print seemed to tell the story of a man who devoted his life entirely to information as a commodity, its production, as well as valorization. The title and caption of the screen print referred to Turing as the person responsible for cracking the Enigma code used by Germany for top-secret communication in World War II. This information allowed the image on the screen print to be read in a paradoxical fashion: While it portrays a person who mastered the concept of deciphering, the low-res quality of the screen print and the distortion of the facial features associated with the overlapping pieces of paper seem instead to actually encode the image as a representative of a person about whom we know little more than his profession and achievements. The painting is contextualized by its title *Why Your Life Sucks (Alan Turing)* (fig. 6), which gives a more personal account of the man. The caption describes that Turing's apparent professional success was contrasted by a private life that ended in suicide, due to the laws prohibiting homosexuality. Fullerton also tells us that Turing killed himself by taking a bite out of an apple poisoned with cyanide, and that this instant is believed to be commemorated in the Apple Inc. logo. One might read into the

---

12   The caption reads as follows: "Alan Turing is regarded as the father of modern computer science and worked as a code breaker at Bletchley Park, home of the United Kingdom's main decryption centre during WW2. At that time the Germans were using a cipher machine called ENIGMA. They were convinced that ENIGMA could not be deciphered, indeed so confident were they that they used the code for top secret communications. Any deciphered information was so highly regarded by the British that they code-named it ULTRA. Turing was the person that eventually cracked the ENIGMA code." ("Columbia: Titles and Captions")

Fig. 5: Michael Fullerton, *Using Polish Technology, Alan Turing Devised a More Sophisticated Machine to Crack ENIGMA*. 2010, screen print on newsprint, 300 x 220 cm (9 panels, each 100 x 75 cm). Courtesy the artist, the photographer, Carl Freedman Gallery.

Fig. 6: Michael Fullerton, *Why Your Life Sucks* (Alan Turing). 2010, oil on linen, 61 x 46 cm. Courtesy the artist, the photographer, Carl Freedman Gallery.

depiction of the face in the painting the tragedy of his death, and perhaps the blazing background pattern evokes aggression triggered by legal prohibitions that are inexplicable and unacceptable from today's perspective.

The process of encountering the malfunction repeats itself in the viewer's confrontation with the works. If one is to argue that Fullerton's practice is symptomatological—the idea that a symptom confuses the process of interpretation by affecting it—the process of communication must repeat throughout the exhibition as a pattern. As demonstrated with the above example, it is easy to understand the fine line between observing, interpreting, and attributing information. However, the viewer's immersion and investment into turning the pieces of information into a more or less coherent narrative is not solely intrinsic to the work but rather emerges from assumptions personified in the figure of the spectator of art, the person who expects art to be not only informative, but also meaningful. However, as Diederich Diederichsen argued, applying the Marxist theory of surplus value to contemporary art, the "extra quality" that is searched for in art—and makes it art—is essentially a "figure of meaninglessness" because,

> it keeps something going whose constituent parts (labour, the production and distribution of products, exchange) would already be justified in themselves (and only in and of themselves) and therefore have no need for further legitimation or additional constituent parts. (*On (Surplus) Value in Art* 23)

The Discrepancy Between Information and Experience

Fullerton is at once a seeker and a layer of tracks. As much as he provides information and narratives and suggests various different kinds of fragmentary stories, he also seeks to enquire into the very frameworks that surround information and enable their contextualization and evaluation. The veracity of this analysis becomes evident once it is recognized that part of what Fullerton proposes as subject matter—historical incidents, for example—is only symptomatological of what should to be read as an investigation into the politics of information and their distribution in communication.

It is not just the provision of information but also the reliance on its evaluation by the viewer that explains the paradox responsible for drawing the viewer into the process of communication and making him or her complicit in it. What Fullerton presents as information—the materiality of the works, their titles and captions—and how the viewer relates to this information as his or her own experience of the works is not a recipe for a consensual interpretation of the works in terms of "information plus experience equals interpretation." Rather, it is the discrepancy between the informational and experiential components that forms the process of interpretation from which the viewer's enquiry into the works departs. This distinction makes the symptom recognisable as an effect that points to the entire process of communication as a challenge in which the viewer is asked to not simply take the information provided for granted but to question its relevance.

Fullerton develops a rhetoric of branding that simulates and appropriates the function that information assumes as a form of explanation within the medium of the exhibition as a communicative space of interaction between viewer and works.[13] The artist intentionally misdirects the communication between viewer and the works. At first the viewer is oriented by the information provided, but on further analysis of the various elements forming the work—the visual, texts, and the communication that mediates between the two, instigated by the viewer—he or she discovers its symptomatological character.

But what is the purpose of the viewer neglecting to equate the information encountered with the experience made for constituting interpretation, a process that Fullerton actively provokes? On the one hand, the impossibility of determining who or what "Columbia" is and whether there is any kind of narrative to be found in the exhibition relating to this term could generate frustration and disinterest in any further enquiry into the exhibition as a medium in which Fullerton's artistic practice acts as a vehicle of knowledge production.

On the other hand, the denial of the equation between information and experience could itself be regarded as information pertaining to the process of interpretation. The viewer observes the symptom as an effect and feeds back its consequence—the malfunction of the equation between information and experience—into the process of communication. This is when the process of interpretation becomes self-reflexive, when the observations made by the viewer become material for further observations. Consequential to the symptom as an effect that is being recognized as affecting the communicative space of the exhibition, the process of interpretation itself becomes a subject within the process of communication. In communication theory terms the decision of the viewer to feed back the impossibility of determining the subject matter of the exhibition in relation to Columbia is an "operative selection,"[14] a result

---

13 For interactions outside the exhibition space Diederichsen speaks of the nature of advertising as seeking to "eliminate all preexisting assumptions from the act of communication ... in the interest of reaching as many consumers as possible" (*On (Surplus) Value in Art* 25).

14 In communication theory the term operative selection designates a decision that not only forms part of the process of communication, but is formative of it. An operation is a distinction. Operations are what communication is made of, its elements. A selection is the decision to further look at one or the other side of what has been distinguished. An operative selection, then, designates a specification of the process of communication as it reduces the potential of

of being in communication with the work that simultaneously conditions any further communication with and about it. Fullerton conceptualizes the audience by reversing the potential of viewing back to the spectator as a potential of thinking about dealing with information in communication and its subsequent process of interpretation as a production of knowledge. He foregrounds the process of interpretation as being both the driving force for the exhibition and its material, and this process is to be found not only in the works themselves, but also in the processes of communication that are set in motion.

Suspicion as an Attitude of Interpretation

Fullerton himself describes his works as "emphasizing a triangular structure: a relationship between form, content, and the viewer, that can only be communicated as well as interpreted when acknowledging the integrity of this relationship" ("Art Now"). Fullerton makes the integrity of the relationship between form, content, and viewer the subject matter of his exhibition through the symptomatological discrepancy between information and experience for and within interpretation. Form and content collapse into each other as Fullerton configures the element of knowledge production in and through art in the process of viewing as communication, which is not about consuming information, but assuming an interpretive role in its evaluation, reconfiguration and production. The process of communication does not pursue the goal of contemplating the essence of the content that the works might be thought to be proposing. Rather, it acknowledges that any understanding of the works can only come from the relationship between form, content, and viewer, which unfolds symptomatologically in this process.

The artist speaks of a "level of self-awareness" that is necessary for dwelling upon the relationship between form, content, and viewer in order to think about the integrity of the work, about the relationship between what is presented, and how it can be differently interpreted. This self-awareness allows the works "to be read as more

---

misunderstanding, framing the process of transformation from information via experience to knowledge (Schützeichel 379).

than simple symbolic references" ("Art Now"). In the space of communication the viewer assumes a position of understanding and testing the integrity of the work without being subject to it. This position is made possible by an attitude of suspicion that carries the interpretative effort all the way from the initial encounter that questioned the relation between images and captions to distinguishing between form and content, only to acknowledge that these distinctions collapse onto each other.

Suspicion is understood to be an active thought, a subjective idea directed towards a situation and conceived out of expectations and assumptions. It indicates a mind-set, but the premises on which it is based (moral values, truth, integrity, authenticity, etc.) are difficult to dissect. At the same time the suspicion emerges from those same premises, it questions their significance. Suspicion therefore functions as a lens through which one can investigate the very registers it is built upon. This relates closely to Lütticken's initial definition of symptomatological practices as commenting on the relevance of art producing knowledge by initiating a process of its denial in order to refocus awareness on the conditions in which art can be produced ("Unknown Knowns" 85).

Through his works both being about and consisting of the process of interpretation, Fullerton incites suspicion in the viewer on the status of his works. The discrepancy described above between information and experience leads to a questioning of the status of the works. Are they fact or fiction? The value of the information presented is judged by the experience of it. The viewer constantly makes the distinction between fact and fiction, but this process is as fragile as any thinking that attempts to categorize the information provided in the works as true or false. In this state of uncertainty, thinking about the works can unfold in any possible direction, and this generates the complexity of an exhibition whose presentation and contextualization resists the construction of any categorization and remains in a state of communication that dwells not only on what is encountered but, even more so, on how what is encountered is dealt with through interpretation.

One particular work in the exhibition illustrates how that the act of dwelling as an operation in the space of communication is a form of knowledge production that takes into account the possibility of its own failure. *BASF Magic Gold* (fig. 7) is a can of BASF Magic Gold pigment that has partially been spilled next to where the can sits on

Fig. 7: Michael Fullerton, *BASF Magic Gold*. 2010, pigment, plinth, 30 x 32 x 136 cm. Courtesy the artist, the photographer, Carl Freedman Gallery.

Fig. 8: Installation view of Michael Fullerton, *Columbia*. 2010, Chisenhale Gallery, London. Photo: Andy Keate. Courtesy the artist and Chisenhale Gallery.

a plinth (fig. 8). The question of what *BASF Magic Gold* represents can presumably be answered rather quickly: the pigment of the same name. That is what is presented, at least. The accompanying caption further explains the history and usage of this pigment.[15] There is an apparent convergence between how the pigment is presented and how it is contextualized. There is no apparent trigger—in the installation itself, in its title or in its caption—that would prompt any kind of suspicion about the work.

But in order to understand "suspicion" as a realm of enquiry into processes of meaning and knowledge production it is important to comprehend the concept in contrast to other concepts that might seem to operate in the same manner. An example is "doubt," which Descartes defined as the fundamental principle of knowledge production, which functions to reaffirm one's own existence.[16] Later, Heidegger shifted the idea that the purpose of doubt is to reaffirm existence but supposes that any ontological doubt is in itself only an effect of self-concealment: doubt is still regarded as the fundamental principle of knowledge production, but not as affirmation of existence (76). Instead, it is a strategy for being in the world and relating to this world. The idea of an attitude or strategy of suspicion was later established by Paul Ricoeur, who maps suspicion not—or not exclusively—in ontological terms, but in terms of material, themes, images, and registers such as truth, knowledge and significance:

> Over against interpretation as restoration of meaning we shall oppose interpretation according to what I collectively call the school of suspicion. A general theory of interpretation would thus have to account not only for the opposition between two interpretations of interpretation, the one as recollection of meaning, the other as reduction of the illusions and lies of consciousness; also for the division and scattering that differ from one another and are even foreign to one another ... After the doubt about things, we have started to doubt consciousness. (35)

---

15 The caption reads, "Magic Gold°, now discontinued, was part of the Vario-chrome° range of pigments, which represented the cutting edge of BASF's pigmentation technology only a few years ago. It was used primarily in the automotive industry. When sprayed or powder coated, the pigment appears as two different colours: gold or green." ("Columbia: Titles and Captions")

16 Descartes employs the so-called "hyperbolical/metaphysical" doubt, a methodological skepticism that at first repudiates any ideas while subsequently reaffirming them for securing a solid foundation for knowledge production. This methodology, also known as Cogito Ergo Sum (I think therefore I am), makes knowledge production an affirmation of existence (16).

Here, suspicion is not synonymous with doubt in the Cartesian sense. Ricoeur regards suspicion as an exercise of interpretation that circumvents meaning while providing an alternative to its simple restoration or recollection: What is to be witnessed is a composition of ideas that only exist in the format of their exploration, founded in the materiality of the works that incite a form of projection onto the works that is fictional and of a provisional nature in relation to the realm of the real. This proposition can be applied in full to Fullerton's exhibition and the way in which the viewer relates to the works when it comes to testing the character of their contribution to the production of knowledge in the exhibition space. The ideas are projected onto the information (titles and captions) as well as onto the materiality of the works (paint, pigments, paper, etc.) but the exploration they trigger only operates in communication within the discursive sphere of the exhibition.

This circumvention of meaning, which Ricoeur identifies as a methodology of suspicion, is also what Lütticken identifies as a characteristic of symptomatological practices. In this context the production of knowledge is first and foremost the production of a space for thinking, one for which the potential of its unproductivity remains, paradoxically, a characteristic of its productivity. In other words, although we don't know what Columbia is or means, or what it stands for, we know that the interaction with this very question triggers a process of communication that generates knowledge pertaining to the ways in which the medium of the exhibition is a space of communication, and how the process of interpretation sits and acts within it.

Unproductive Production

Investigations into the process of communication in the discursive space of Fullerton's exhibition presented an array of structural concerns for the dialogue between works and viewer, and for the function the artist assumes as a producer and generator within that dialogue. However, the role of the artist as producer and its distinction from the role of the curator as generator or facilitator of modes of production need to be considered further in relation to the claim that art produces knowledge.

In both the art world and academia, thinking and making are often conceptualized as producing a result: A work of art, an exhibi-

tion, or a text is considered a valid outcome that can then be interpreted to produce another outcome in the format of an opinion
whose contingent character is often overlooked. The status of these
examples as results is very questionable—as is their quality, it should
be said. Instead of *results* of thinking or making, they should be regarded as *instigators* of these processes. Critic and curator Simon
Sheikh refers to this structural and functional understanding when
pointing out the condition for knowledge production in, with and
through art:

> We should learn from those structures as spaces of experience, as dis-
> cursive spaces, and simultaneously remain critical of the implementa-
> tion of its productive features, maintaining a notion of unproductive
> time and space within exhibition venues. We have to move beyond
> knowledge production into what we can term spaces for thinking.
> ("Talk Value" 196)

Fullerton's exhibition is just such a space of production, one that unfolds while moving beyond the idea of knowledge production, cir-
cumventing the danger of aligning information with knowledge and
pointing towards the space of communication itself, where thinking
takes the form of doubting—of suspecting the forms of knowledge
that it is expected to produce. But unlike Sheikh I would like to maintain the term "knowledge production" as the element for which the
exhibition generates the conditions by pointing to the communicative space of the exhibition and the functioning of the relationship
between works and viewer within it. Sheikh would negate this approach since for him thinking and knowledge are not equivalent:
"Whereas knowledge is circulated and maintained through a number
of normative practices—disciplines as it were—thinking is here
meant to imply networks of indiscipline, lines of flight, and utopian
questionings" ("Talk Value" 196). Although knowledge may well have
been objectified and institutionalized, the way in which Sheikh characterizes thinking as indiscipline and utopian questioning is no less
instrumentalizing. I therefore argue that knowledge and thinking do
indeed share the same structural conception despite the ways in
which their productivity has been regularized. In structural terms,
knowledge and thinking are processual, yet not unbound; they develop within structures to which they respond, affirming or denying
them. What I am interested in here is the parallel development of
structures and processes of communication, which describes thinking

both as a framework for knowledge production *and* as an activity within and of knowledge production. More precisely, it is a particular material activity in the sense that the thinking process developed not only derives from, but also entirely depends on the relations produced between the different works, their material dispositions and placement within the exhibition. This is a simultaneous process of creation and course of action that requires not only the production of thinking, but also the conscious performance of this production process in the space of the exhibition. This takes place as a dialectical juxtaposition between the information perceived and their contextualization within the sphere of experience of each individual visitor to the exhibition, triggered by the material dispositions of the works and their contextualization by their accompanying captions. These material dispositions are first and foremost relational as they themselves are the material, which is the substance for the thinking process geared towards the production of meaning. In this sense, what characterizes Fullerton's practice is the concurrent formation of thinking as well as of the means by which it takes place. Through an exploration into the myriad different associations with the term Columbia the artist juxtaposes information and experience in such a way that their equation for the process of interpretation becomes impossible. This requires the viewer to direct an attitude of suspicion at the very process of interpretation and its functioning in the communicative space of the exhibition. It allows for a distancing from the specific information and context (which is dealt with differently in each work) and lets this enquiry move towards the essence of the conditions of knowledge production in contemporary art, which are our assumptions and expectations surrounding it. Fullerton's practice is described as symptomatological with regard to provoking a shift from producing knowledge to questioning the conditions of knowledge production. This furthers Lütticken's understanding of symptomatological practices commenting on their own ways of knowledge production as offering forms of reflection and critique over the very subject matter with which it is dealt with.

Exhibition Rhetorics

The subject matter of Fullerton's exhibition is the politics of knowledge production and the communicative space of the exhibition as its medium. Defining the space of the exhibition as a medium, a vehicle of knowledge production, is by no means a new idea. As Bruce W. Ferguson, Reesa Greenberg and Sandy Nairne defined in the introduction to one of curating's most seminal books, *Thinking About Exhibitions,* "exhibitions are the primary site of exchange in the political economy of art, where signification is constructed, maintained and occasionally deconstructed" (2). But Fullerton's exhibition goes beyond pointing to this characteristic of the exhibition space. His practice plays with the fact that fifteen years after *Thinking About Exhibitions* was published, the exhibition as a medium of knowledge production has been internalized and taken for granted, in accordance with a specific rhetoric that institutionalizes the move from the construction to the deconstruction of meaning first discussed by Bruce Ferguson in his 1996 essay "Exhibition Rhetorics: Material Speech and Utter Sense." Fullerton challenges the understanding of an exhibition as the medium of contemporary art "in the sense of being its main agency of communication—the body and voice from which an authoritative character emerges" (175).

My analysis of his exhibition highlights its material register. The way in which the process of communication functions within the exhibition is not one that enables the emergence of authority. Due to the symptomatological character of Fullerton's practice, suspicion emerges as a critical attitude towards affirming any authoritative relationship between the exhibition and the art that it presents, or the viewer. The artist's practice thus impinges on the methodologies of perception and technologies of inspection that Ferguson still argues are the domain of the institution or the curator, and not emerging from the authority of the artist or the artwork itself. While Ferguson proposes conceiving of the exhibition as a communicative space, a "speech environment" (183) that is administered by the institution or the curator, Fullerton reconfigures this definition by showing not only how art serves the exhibition as its very element of speech, but also how speech—communication—emerges from the dialogical relationship between objects, actors, and spaces. In and for this relationship the material dispositions of the exhibition—the works, their placement, their contextualization in captions or accompanying leaflets, etc.—become effective in shaping the social relations that emerge from the curated encounter.

This is what Boris Groys calls the "politics of installation," which in their functioning are independent of their origin in terms of who set them in place; the artist, the curator, or the institution ("Politics of Installation" 51). The politics of installation at stake in Fullerton's exhibition proposed and simultaneously relied on communication as the motor activity of the social sphere. Fullerton draws attention to the space and process of communication in and for the exhibition as a medium of knowledge production. Groys describes the methodology of the creation of such an exhibition space as the politics of installation, which defines the conditions and strategies determining the exhibition in its spatial form and relationship with the public. The installation artwork thereby "installs everything that usually circulates in our civilization: objects, texts, films, etc." It relates directly to the social sphere, operating "by means of a privatization of the public space of the exhibition" ("Politics of Installation" 55). Here, Groys contrasts Ferguson's claims that in instigating and affirming the process of knowledge production in the exhibition space the institution is acting as the representative of the public. On the contrary, believes Groys, writing that the artist imposes his sovereign will upon the space and acts in an authorial way, which has previously been reserved for the role of the curator in placing artworks of all mediums in the eye of the public ("Politics of Installation" 58). The material of which the installation is conceived is already part of or originating in the social sphere, for which a relation to it established by a curator or the institution becomes redundant.

The way in which Fullerton, in Groys' terminology, "designed" the exhibition can be described in such terms—as explored above when discussing Fullerton's imposition of art producing knowledge in the way he intersects texts and images in the exhibition. Fullerton takes absolute control over supposed curatorial arenas, such as the strategic display of the works in the exhibition[17] as a form of their presentation and the simultaneous attempt to offer their explanation

---

17 I am referring here to my earlier description of Michael Fullerton's *Gothic Version of the Ring Laser Gyroscope Used in Final Flight of the Space Shuttle Columbia STS–107* at the entrance to the exhibition space (fig.1).

through lengthy written captions.[18] But Fullerton only takes up these commonly deemed curatorial tasks in order to point to the malfunction of the ways in which we assume knowledge is produced by means of generating art's visualization and visibility.

> The artistic installation—in which the act of art production coincides with the act of its presentation—becomes the perfect experimental terrain for revealing and exploring the ambiguity that lies at the core of the Western notion of freedom. (Groys, "Politics of Installation" 57)

The different kinds of freedom to which Groys points are the "sovereign, unconditional, publicly irresponsible freedom of art-making, and the institutional, conditional, publicly responsible freedom of curatorship" ("Politics of Installation" 58). Although I agree with this distinction, I would like to argue that this is not one that is embedded in the nature of art making or curatorship, but rather a question of what function is attributed to the different practices. Groys himself claims that from the perspective of the viewer the space of the installation invites the visitor to "experience this space as the holistic, totalizing space of an artwork" ("Politics of Installation" 56). The distinction between artistic practice and curatorship is not one to be found within the installation as the exhibition space, but one that determines the installation as a marked space in relation to the unmarked public space. This is the function of the installation, one that applies as much to artistic practice as to how curators work with space, because it is a strategy of display, a methodology of determination incorporating the possibility of its own disruption. Groys' politics of installation have the effect of assisting the viewer in "reflecting upon their own condition, offering them an opportunity to exhibit themselves to themselves" ("Politics of Installation" 63). The viewer assumes ownership over the process of communication, which as an activity is not yet targeted at another form of knowledge production in terms of interpretation as an evaluative judgement of a work, but is set up as a recursive feedback

---

18 Ferguson explicitly describes the function of captions (labels) in an exhibition as "always didactic," instrumentalizing their function of providing "empirical information" to express "an opinion" (178). Fullerton points to this shift while some of his captions do solely provide information but are unrelated to the work on view, and others express an opinion, which makes their supposed didactic function obvious.

loop that independently organizes the way in which art can produce knowledge.

The strategy of communication that Fullerton incited has been found to bring about a particular relationship between artworks and viewers in the space of the exhibition that rests on materializing the relationship between information, meaning, and experience in a way that such relationship generates sociality not as a mere outcome, but as its core substance. This, in turn, demands a complex agency of spectatorship with regard to the ideological realm from which it emerges. This realm was put into question particularly as a source of judgement and interpretation by calling attention to the blurring of boundaries between fact and fiction, causing suspicion to emerge as a critical tool for addressing the exhibition's potential of communicability as a source of knowledge production.

The Heterotopic Quality of the Exhibition Space

The communicative space of the exhibition that Fullerton creates and invites the viewer to partake in can be described as "heterotopic," in accordance with Michel Foucault's explorations of Heterotopias as spaces that reflect the cultural and social structure of society in ways that are neither totally reproductive, nor imaginary. Rather, these spaces "have the curious property of being in relation with all other sites, but in such a way as to suspect, neutralize, or invert the set of relations that they happen to designate, mirror, or reflect" (Foucault, "Of Other Spaces" 231).

In Fullerton's exhibition the blurring of boundaries between fact and fiction results from the back-and-forth feedback loop the viewer uses to deal with the relationships between works, their accompanying captions, and her or his own position as spectator of the exhibition emerging from a particular socially, culturally, and politically conditioned ideological realm. Foucault describes this space as in and of itself heterogeneous, "a set of relations that delineates sites which are irreducible to one another and absolutely not superimposable on one another" ("Of Other Spaces" 231). But Foucault is specifically interested in those sites that can enter a relation with any other (ideological) space by suspecting, neutralizing, or inverting the set of relations they define and by which they are also defined. In this sense the Fullerton exhibition can be described as a Heterotopia. The patterns being suspected, neutralized, and inverted were those of perception, interpretation, and communication through which what is outside of it conditions spectatorship in the space of the exhibition. By generating suspicion regarding the customary rules and forms of behaviour with regard to spectatorship and communication between viewer, works, and their contextualization, Fullerton creates a space that is heterotopic in the sense that it has a self-referential quality. He incites the viewer to perform a blurring of boundaries between fact and fiction, actual and imaginary accounts of history, experience and invention. However, the self-referentiality of this project geared towards the generation and sustenance of suspicion allows one to question whether the penetration of both the concept of the real and of the imaginary in the heterotopic space, a space that is illusionary yet also material, is directed towards the dissolution of one in the other, or if it is merely an example of metafiction. Simply posing such a question fully explores the potential of the exhibition space's communicability, regardless of whether what is communicated is clearly identified as pertaining to an a posteriori constructed or an a priori conditioned ideological realm.

Such distinctions refer not only to the exhibition space's potential for communicability, but also to what is potentially communicable in it. This addresses not so much processes of communication, but matters of interpretation and the question of how meaning is produced in exhibitions in a way that assumes relevance not only in and for the space of the exhibition, but also outside of it. The heterotopic quality of the exhibition space in this sense is that it can dismiss (though not ignore) concepts of linearity and chronology in terms of knowledge production and refer to an experience of the world whose simultaneity can be spatially explored through forms of connections and intersections. As such the exhibition space is a place within society, but simultaneously outside it, countering the structures and patterns social relations rely upon and thus questioning the ideological realms from which it is built.

The Potosí Principle

Discussing *The Potosí Principle* exhibition furthers the investigation into the communicability of the exhibition space in terms of the ways in which meaning and knowledge are produced, and how a relation between the ideological realm of the exhibition and the no less ideological realm outside the exhibition, is built and negotiated in the communicative space of the exhibition, which has a particular material quality.

In the previous analysis of Fullerton's exhibition Sven Lütticken's remarks on the differences between artistic research and academic knowledge production produced a set of questions on the nature of knowledge production in artistic practices versus the academic realm that were fruitful for situating the analysis of Fullerton's exhibition as one concerned with the question how knowledge is produced. *The Potosí Principle: How Can We Sing the Song of the Lord in an Alien Land?* (2010/2011) was curated by Alice Creischer, Andreas Siekmann and Max-Jorge Hinderer at the Haus der Kulturen der Welt (HKW) in Berlin from 8 October 2010 to 2 January 2011.[19] On the one hand it can be discussed as an exhibition whose curatorial proposition furthers this discussion on knowledge production, continuing to dwell on the question of how processes of knowledge production come about within the framework of the exhibition. On the other hand it is also relevant for considering the question why particularly art as a form of cultural production is an important realm for the production of knowledge and the elicitation of meaning, particularly in the context of the "pursuit of not just transdisciplinarity, but really unframed knowledge, where bits of knowledge resingularize themselves with other bits of knowledge in order to produce and constitute new subjects in the world," which is how Irit Rogoff described the virtue of knowledge production in *The Potosí Principle* (Bismarck and Rogoff 31).

The exhibition takes as its departure point the history of the city of Potosí that in the seventeenth century formed part of the Viceroyalty of Peru and was one of the largest cities in the world. At the time it was famous for its extensive silver mining on the local Cerro Rico mountain—the city is still dependent upon this industry to this day. But the history of Potosí as addressed in the exhibition is about much more than silver mining. It explores issues such as colonial rule, exploitation of labour, accumulation of capital, missionary work, and mass production of images, to name only a few starting points that led

19 The exhibition was firstly shown at Museo Nacional Centro de Arte Reina Sofía, Madrid, before travelling to Berlin and then to the Museo Nacional de Arte and Museo Nacional de Etnografía y Folklore, La Paz.

the curators to conceive an exhibition aiming to trace the parallels in the circulation of money and art from the early days of modernity until the present day.

> We originally named the project *Inversión Modernidad*, in order to prompt a revision of the concept of Modernity—long overdue in the art world—and to place this term in its colonial context (in Spanish *inversión* means both inversion and investment). At issue here was whether the historical relationship of artistic production can be projected onto the present as the regalia of a state or as legitimacy for colonial pillage, plunder, and genocide, and whether there is a connection between the function of colonial painting and that assumed by the art system in conferring legitimacy upon globalization's new elites (Creischer et al., *The Potosí Principle* 12).

Together with scholar Max-Jorge Hinderer, artists Alice Creischer and Andreas Siekmann produced an exhibition that takes the production of meaning in the exhibition arena as its subject matter. They articulate their position as curators as

> necessitating a fascinating and exhaustive search in both an academically deformed historiography and in an exhibition industry, which—in the era of event marketing—has outsourced both its responsibility for mediating meaning and context, and its own political memory and archival storage. (Creischer et al., *The Potosí Principle* 12–13)

The exhibition showed a series of colonial paintings originating from Potosí in Bolivia and from other locations in South America, together with especially commissioned works of contemporary art that were conceived in response and reaction to the historical works. These were exhibited within a dense web of curator-articulated explanations, comments and references—both of a literal and figurative nature—to construct an overall interpretative context that confronted the viewer in the exhibition space. The strong relationship between the works and their installation was reinforced by the exhibition guide, which recommended several routes throughout the exhibition, thereby engineering the experience of the exhibition space into a collection of narratives (fig. 13–14).

The Principle of Accumulation

The exhibition was held predominantly in the exhibition hall of Berlin's Haus der Kulturen der Welt, with selected works also being shown outside in the garden and the upper foyer. Upon entering the exhibition hall the notion of disturbance was prominent. From the top of the stairs that lead into the exhibition hall the room appeared to be an amalgamation of images and pictorials covering over every level—hanging from the ceiling, mounted on the walls, pasted on the floor, and installed in the middle of the space. The question of how to engage with the plethora of visual impressions related not only to the exhibition as a whole, but also to the presentation of individual works. While descending the stairs to access the exhibition hall the viewer observes the reverse of one of two large transparent pictures by Quirin Bäumler, silver point drawings modelled on eighteenth century church paintings and engravings (fig. 9–10). Even though the original paintings and drawings were physically absent from the exhibition (one can only begin to imagine the complex and ultimately unsuccessful negotiations for loaning the historic works from South America), their transparent rendering emphasized even more their importance for beginning to understand *The Potosí Principle*. One has to pay close attention and make an effort to decipher what they depict.

The exhibition guide written by the curators describes one as a drawing of a completely preserved painting from the church of Caquiaviri from 1739, part of a picture ensemble depicting *postrimerías*, death, the Final Judgement and hell:

> The picture consists of two highly dissimilar parts. Right at the top, people are depicted strolling through an idyllic landscape in broad daylight and being fished out of it with rods and thrown directly into hell by devils. The legality of torture, the equivalence of torture to sins, the equality in law of cardinals, princes, and popes in the cooking pot—all this is merely a brief distraction from the massiveness of power detached from legality, which without reason can draw people from the landscape into torture. When we look at the picture, we cannot forget that Caquiaviri was a transportation hub of the silver and copper trade, that the cacique, the community authority, held shares in the mines of Potosí 1000 kilometers away. (Creischer et al., *The Potosí Principle* 21)

Fig. 9: Installation view of Quirin Bäumler, *El Infierno de Caquiaviri*. 2010, silver pencil drawing on transparent foil, 317 x 765 cm. In *The Potosí Principle*, 2010, Haus der Kulturen der Welt, Berlin. Photo: Sebastian Bolesch. Courtesy Haus der Kulturen der Welt.

Fig. 10: Detail of Quirin Bäumler, *El Infierno de Caquiaviri*. 2010, silver pencil drawing on transparent foil, 317 x 765 cm. In *The Potosí Principle*, 2010, Haus der Kulturen der Welt, Berlin. Photo: Sebastian Bolesch. Courtesy Haus der Kulturen der Welt.

Fig. 11: Installation view of *The Potosí Principle*, 2010, Haus der Kulturen der Welt, Berlin. View from the foyer looking at the entrance of the Exhibition Hall at the far back. Foreground: Ines Doujak, *Witches*. 2010, sculptures. Photo: Sebastian Bolesch. Courtesy Haus der Kulturen der Welt.

Fig. 12: Installation view of *The Potosí Principle*, 2010, Haus der Kulturen der Welt, Berlin. View from the top of the stairs entering the Exhibition Hall. Photo: Sebastian Boelsch. Courtesy Haus der Kulturen der Welt.

The curators go on to explain that the cacique was held responsible by the Spanish colonial power for recruiting indigenous people throughout the entire region for forced labour in the mines. The recruitment began at the ports, where the slaves were baptized in the presence of depictions of postrimerías.

> Baptism and showing hell thus constitute one and the same moment. The anthropologist Michael Taussig described the role of terror as a mediator par excellence regarding colonial hegemony. It opens up a space in which the arbitrariness of the colonizer prevails as unrestrictedly as the power of hell. These spaces have a long and rich tradition, and their signifiers mingle with those of the conquered. Yet these signifiers do not function correctly, for the arbitrariness of power aims at obliterating meaning. Taussig transfers this destruction of meaning to the same disarrangement between ourselves and commodities. (Creischer et al., *The Potosí Principle* 21)

The reverse of the other drawing features images of a series of etchings that originate from Peru and were made in 1705, inspired by a famous treatise from the Spanish Jesuit Eusebio de Nierembert, whose publication *Diferencia entre lo temporal y lo eterno* (On Death, Purgatory, Hell and the Final Judgement) was an important tool for missionaries in the communities of Peru. The curators compare the methods of torture depicted in the etchings to Naomi Klein's descriptions of the development of shock therapy in 1960s psychiatry to obliterate and erase parts of human psyche in order to reinstall it (Creischer et al., *The Potosí Principle* 20–24).

On many more occasions the curators directly paired historic images with contemporary references in order to demonstrate a relationship between the history of Potosí and today's cultural and economic landscape. This is prolific in two ways: Referring to the problems of neoliberal rule reveals a contemporary relevance to Potosí while the historic images serve to spotlight certain issues in contemporary politics. This practice of storytelling is highly suggestive and works by association, both visually and figuratively. From the perspective of the viewer this practice might initially seem arbitrary and conditioned by a set of political and cultural attitudes that had not been explicitly disclosed. However, the unfolding narrative is no less intriguing and invites the viewer, particularly because of the clashing accumulation of visual impressions and intellectual references, to draw their own references and build associations.

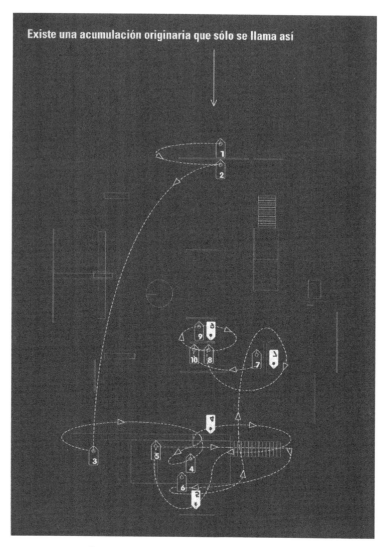

Fig. 13: Graphical illustration of route suggested through *The Potosí Principle* exhibition. In Creischer, Alice, et al., eds. *The Potosí Principle: How Can We Sing the Song of the Lord in an Alien Land?* Verlag der Buchhandlung Walther König, 2010, p. 16.

There is a primitive accumulation that is merely so called

De la diferencia entre lo
temporal y. lo eterno
Juan Eusebio Nieremberg
1705, Jesuit Order Paraguay
Pantere by Gaspar Bocanaz
Antwerp 1684

The Punishment of the Senses
Juan Eusebio Nieremberg
1705
In: Juan Eusebio Nieremberg,
De la diferencia entre lo temporal y
eterno: crisol de desengaños, con la
memoria de la eternidad, postrimerías humanas, y principales misterios
divinos Trad. en lengua guaraní por
Ioseph Serrano, S.I. : Impresso en las
Doctrinas. 1705. Copy from the
Museo Udaondo in Luján, Argentina.
From: Franz Obermeier, Der argenti-
nische Erstdruck Nierembergs De la
diferencia in Guaraní im Kontext der
Bilderzählen in Lateinamerika im
18. Jahrhundert, 2005

If you have not been immediately steered further and have found a seat on a bench somewhere to read (we do not know how long you will be allowed to stay here), then you will now be looking at the reverse of two large pictures. Because they are transparent, you may be able to recognize a few details on the front. Don't go to the front, just take a closer look at the reverse. They depict sadistic and obscene torture scenes, distorted faces symbolizing the senses destroyed by torture. In her most recent book, Naomi Klein describes the development of shock therapy in 1960s psychiatry and its link to neoliberal think tanks and the CIA. Shock therapy grasps the "ill" psyche as a computer program that must be deleted so that it can be reinstalled. The methods of shock therapy were first employed both as torture and as an economic program in the dictatorships of South America. Terror and restructuring programs, paralyzing resistance against antisocial policies by producing fear still belong to the program of neoliberalism.

The engravings you see here were made in the Jesuit province of Paraguay in 1705. They are part of a compendium teaching people how to fear hell and death. What you see here are details of an outstanding pioneering achievement, one of the first self-produced prints translated into Guaraní in the vicercyalty of Peru: That is how important it was to arouse fear.

You deem the leap from the methods of neoliberal politics to these motifs to be too big, too imprecise? You are right. Now let us take a look at the picture from the front and start something we will continue to do along the entire section, namely, to survey the distance of this leap in a more precise way. Please take a look at the first of the two large silver point drawings. They are drawn or duplicating foil and modeled on pictures from the church of Caquiaviri. You can listen to the audio recordings of the five-hundredth anniversary of the church (on January 17, 2010) over the headphones.

The parish refused to lend us these pictures. You can read about the reasons for this on the reverse of the photo which is hanging together with a magnifying glass on the bottom edge of the picture.

17

Fig. 14: Page from *The Potosí Principle* exhibition catalogue including details of graphic design used to guide the visitor through the exhibition. In Creischer, Alice, et al., eds. *The Potosí Principle: How Can We Sing the Song of the Lord in an Alien Land?* Verlag der Buchhandlung Walther König, 2010, p. 17.

Staying on the recommended first course through the exhibition (fig. 13–14) the viewer was led to a wall of documents, drawings, and photographs resting above a series of washing machines documenting the cultivation of genetically modified soy in Argentina, an activity that grew exponentially following the country's economic crisis in the late 1990s and early 2000s. The *Soy Children* installation (fig. 15) by Argentinian artist Eduardo Molinari focuses especially on the role of local children that are hired to run between the plants and wave flags that signal to the planes where they should drop more pesticides in order to maximize the soy production. While the soy business, not just an Argentinian phenomenon, but a transnational industry across Argentina, Brazil, Bolivia, and Paraguay, brings wealth to the region and employment to the parents of these children, the long-term effects of exposing families to the highly toxic chemicals used to cultivate the soy, which have polluted the entire area, are just beginning to show. Here, the artist is responding to *Imposición de la casulla a San Ildefonso*, an anonymous painting from the seventeenth century that at its bottom shows an immaculate garden cared for by monks, who, looking up, imagine themselves in a heaven guarded by Mary, who is depicted giving an embellished coat to Saint Ildefonso, a defender of the dogma of Immaculate Conception. Apart from the fact that one can draw a direct parallel between the exposure of children in Argentina to chemicals and the indigenous workers who had to walk directly on the on mercury poured over pulverized mountain stone to speed up the amalgamation process, the parallel that Molinari draws is that the end product is loved and valued beyond all else, including life itself. The curators present this work in a narrative around the status of the commodity. Next to Molinari's installation there is a small booth in which extracts from Karl Marx's *Capital* are read out in English with a strong Russian accent.

> The discovery of gold and silver in America, the extirpation, enslavement, and entombment in mines of the aboriginal population, the beginning of the conquest and looting of the East Indies, the turning of Africa into a warren for the commercial hunting of black-skins, signalized the rosy dawn of the era of capitalist production. (Marx; ch. 31)

In the installation, perhaps every second word was interrupted by American pronunciation corrections, and at one point a heated discussion on the contemporary political relevance of the text gets so loud that a picture hanging outside the little chamber starts to trem-

Fig. 15: Eduardo Molinari, *The Soy Children*. 2010, installation, drawings, collages, photographs. At the centre of the installation is the anonymous painting *Imposición de la Casulla a San Ildefonso*. 17th c. In *The Potosí Principle*, 2010, Haus der Kulturen der Welt, Berlin. Photo: Sebastian Bolesch. Courtesy Haus der Kulturen der Welt.

Fig. 16: Lucas Valdés, *Milagroso de San Francisco de Paula*. ca. 1710, Museo de Bellas Artes, Sevilla. *The Potosí Principle: How Can We Sing the Song of the Lord in an Alien Land?*, edited by Creischer et al., Walther König, 2010, p. 161.

ble. *Retratro Milagroso de San Francisco de Paula* is a work by the Spanish painter Lucas Valdés and dates from around 1710 (fig. 16). It shows an artist's atelier in which the artist is lying potentially dead or unconscious on the floor while an angel has taken his seat in front of the painting of the cleric in order to finish it.

> This painting, which comes from Seville and not from the viceroyalty of Peru, was an initial spark as well as an ongoing provocation in our project. We speculated that the painter was just receiving a visit from an officer ordered by the government of the heavens to supervize the accuracy of the depiction and correct the work. It shows an impotent artistic praxis that can no more oppose divine power than it can take a stand against a historical process—such as, for example, that of primitive accumulation. (Creischer et al., *The Potosí Principle* 117)

The audio installation *The Rosy Dawn of Capital* (2010) (fig. 17) located in the small chamber is a work by The Karl Marx School of English Language initiated by David Riff and Dmitry Gutov, and was conceived to relate directly to the painting. In a letter to Dmitry Gutov, David Riff interprets the role of the angel looking at the dead or unconscious painter in the image as follows:

> The angel is a censor, but more, a figure of art's total desubjectification: a divine agency, a totality, an utterly foreign force. ... The individual—even when he or she is stripped bare of everything—still has possession of his "soul" and his innate capacity to work in a virtuosic manner, which he can then alienate or sell to some passing angel who will suck him dry, consuming and disposing of him as material, but material has a name, a slave recognized by his master. A slave with the basic human right to be expended. (Creischer et al., *The Potosí Principle* 118)

Describing some of the works and their contextualization serves first of all to give an impression of the exhibition, even though it is near impossible to put into words the experience of the juxtaposition of colonial images with contemporary works, surrounded as they were by the graphic design the curators chose and developed to accompany the images in order to indicate their place in the exhibition and reference in the guide. There were barely any plates or captions directly accompanying the images anywhere in the exhibition, reflecting a conscious choice made by the curators. Instead, cards resembling hotel "Do Not Disturb" signs were used for numbering works. Each colonial work got a black number on a white background while each contemporary response got the same number in white number

Fig. 17: The Karl Marx School of English Language, David Riff and Dmitry Gutov, *The Rosy Dawn of Capital*. 2010, installation in a closed space with oil paintings on canvas and audio installation. View of the small chamber in which the reading from Marx's *Capital* was streamed. In *The Potosí Principle*, 2010, Haus der Kulturen der Welt, Berlin. Photo: Sebastian Bolesch. Courtesy Haus der Kulturen der Welt.

on a black background. The whole sign is turned upside down. The works were thus tagged to indicate their placement in the various narratives outlined in the exhibition guide to be followed as routes through the show. The guide provided the actual details of the works (title, artist, and place of origin) within a pictogram of a suitcase on a conveyor belt (fig. 14). This icon can be interpreted as referring to both the status of the work as a travelling object and of having been "packaged" into a certain context.

It is possible to interpret in a variety of ways the initial impression of the exhibition as an endless accumulation of juxtaposing visual sensations cast in a dense framework of references—historical and contemporary, aesthetic and intellectual. From the perspective of what the visitor to the exhibition is given to work with *The Potosí Principle* could not differentiate more from Fullerton's exhibition. There is no doubt as to how the various pieces of information fit together. There is no necessity to construct narratives—in fact, their presence is so strong that a large amount of the viewer's investment

Fig. 18: Left: Gaspar Miguel de Berrío, *Descripción del Cerro Rico e Imperial Villa de Potosí*. 1758, oil on canvas, 182 x 262 cm. De Berío's painting is installed on a freestanding wall whose reverse side is used to project Harun Farocki's *The Silver and the Cross* (2010, multimedia installation) which directly relates to the De Berío painting. Right: Alice Creischer, Andreas Siekmann and Christian von Borries, *Dubai—Expanded Horizons: The museums create a new public sphere*, re-enactment of a press conference/ music performance, 2009. Copyright VG Bild-Kunst, Bonn 2017. In *The Potosí Principle*, 2010, Haus der Kulturen der Welt, Berlin. Photo: Sebastian Bolesch. Courtesy Haus der Kulturen der Welt.

in the exhibition goes into comprehending them. The combinations of different artworks in the context of their installation producing different narratives might appear as equally fragmentary, yet they all have a common denominator: the Potosí Principle. More evident in the Spanish than the English translation, the title *Principio Potosí* hints at the complexity of the different levels of interpretation that the viewer is confronted with and invited to partake in. The Spanish word *principio* means both "principle" and "beginning." The silver from Potosí contributes significantly to the primitive accumulation made possible by the emergence of capitalism in Europe. In this respect, Potosí is not only a beginning but also a principle that defines our society. Especially the colonial images fulfil a dual function in terms of their role in the process of communication with the viewer. They are simultaneously carriers and generators of meaning. On the one hand they depict something very specific and are interpreted on their own terms of production and derivation. On the other hand,

Fig. 19: Installation view of *The Potosí Principle*, 2010,
Haus der Kulturen der Welt, Berlin. At the right hand side,
the reverse side of the wall on which Berrío's painting is hung,
functions as a projection booth for Harun Farocki's *The Silver and the Cross*
(2010, multimedia installation). Behind and above: Alice Creischer,
Andreas Siekmann and Christian von Borries, *Dubai—Expanded Horizons:
The museums create a new public sphere*, re-enactment of a
press conference/music performance, 2009.
Copyright VG Bild-Kunst, Bonn 2017. Photo: Sebastian Bolesch.
Courtesy Haus der Kulturen der Welt.

particularly for the contemporary artists who produced works in response to them, they generate a process of interpretation that goes far beyond their historical context.

This process of interpretation is twofold. The meaning of the work that is derived from its historical context is overshadowed by a production of meaning attributed to the historical work by the artist that chooses this work as a form of inspiration for the production or installation of his or her own contemporary work. However, in the process of communication unfolding between works and viewer in the exhibition this meaning is solely communicated in the form of the contemporary work. Only when consulting the catalogue's interviews or text was it on occasion communicated in a more direct way, either by quoting the artist or describing his or her intentions. To better understand in what way the historical works were both a generator as well as carrier of meaning, it serves to look at one additional example. Gaspar Miguel de Berrío's 1758 painting *Descripción*

del Cerro Rico e Imperial Villa de Potosí is exhibited on the rear of a
wall onto which Harun Farocki's eighteen-minute film *The Silver and
the Cross* (fig. 18–19). Their proximity in the exhibition installation at
the far back of the exhibition hall is only a first indication of the high
level of proximity that Farocki spent familiarizing himself not only
with Berrío's work but also the whole history of Potosí and the subject of colonialism. Even when looking back and forth between the
painting and the projection, the detailed level of observation that
Farocki gained while having spent days with the painting can never
be gained by the viewer. As such the viewer is intended for failing to
interpret the painting with the same scrutiny. Such failure is precisely the very subject matter of Farocki's work. The painting shows
a top view of Potosí and its surrounding mountain landscape. The
industrial city's blocks of houses at the foot of Cerro Rico Mountain
are meticulously painted. Street life is depicted between the houses,
with a wedding, a funeral, an animal being slaughtered, and other
scenes. The clothes worn by the figures hint at their social status.
What the painting doesn't show is the mining, let alone any sign of
the severe working conditions in the mine. Instead it shows only the
wealth of the industrial city in the midst of the barren mountainous
landscape—its infrastructure—not its source. Farocki's film worked
against this invisibility, the curators claim, and also contextualized
the picture through its reference to Adam Smith's *The Wealth of Nations*, which describes how an invisible hand creates wealth. It was
first published in 1776, eighteen years after the picture was painted
(Creischer et al., *The Potosí Principle* 36). The film is a video essay in
which the artist both handles the painting itself and uses a detailed
analysis of what it does and—especially—does not show to explore
the European colonization process and the ways power was exerted
over the indigenous population. The film was shot on location at the
Museo Colonial Charcas in Sucre, home to Berrío's painting, and in
Potosí. In long shots Farocki focuses in on the painting to reveal the
meticulous details, enabling the viewer to appreciate the painting in
far more detail than would be possible by viewing at the original.
Farocki's work is at once an interpretation of the painting and an
interpretative tool for approaching it—with the process of interpretation being the very subject matter of the work. The viewer's gaze is
somewhat anticipated by Farocki's approach to investigating the
painting in great detail, particularly because the film never reveals
an overtly explanatory, interpretive attitude. Exemplarily for the

whole exhibition the relation between the two works and their contextualization by the curators reveals an interpretative process in which the viewer is by no means the final link in the chain. Quite the opposite, the viewer acts as an agent for establishing a process of communication via a material register of the exhibition, which can transgress the dichotomy between form and material, theory and practice, as well as fact and fiction. This has an enabling potential towards the role with which history is approached from a contemporary viewpoint: not so much as a linear series of events whose cultural function is fixed by their chronological order, but as an accumulation of experiences that shape today's understanding of culture as a process of materialization and symbolization of sense within the production of knowledge as a continuous work in progress.

As in the Fullerton exhibition, in terms of communication in *The Potosí Principle* exhibition the process of interpretation is the common denominator for everything and everyone involved in the exhibition: artworks, curators, artists, and, of course, the visitors. Given the almost dictatorial style in which the curators wrote the accompanying guide, one might assume that there is not much room for interpretation when it comes to the tight weave of references that the curators proposed in order to contextualize the artworks. I would argue that the opposite is true: The high density of historical information and intellectual references provided by either the curators or the participating artists (Farocki, for example) when juxtaposed with the ever-present question about the contemporary relevance of this information, turns the viewer's investigative interest onto the process of interpretation itself, which is certainly motivated by the curators' and artists' own interpretive processes (Creischer et al., *The Potosí Principle* 3).

Even though in a totally different context and by very different means, the analysis of the role and function of the communicative process in Fullerton's exhibition also holds true for *The Potosí Principle*: Both the curators and the artists seek to enquire into what surrounds the information presented to them in the colonial works, for example, and enable their contextualization and evaluation by employing the material forces an exhibition can put forward through mechanisms of display, including the juxtaposition of different narratives. In a similar way to Fullerton, the narratives surrounding historical incidents are symptomatological of what is in fact an investigation into the politics of interpretation and their production of meaning. Different levels of interpretation therefore emerge from the works and the exhibition as a whole, contributing to a process of meaning production that generates the contemporary relevance the curators speak of in their introduction to the exhibition guide:

> You have left the security of your contemporary context, and are now located in a historic space, which, we would claim, is not linear, but simultaneous and never of the past. (Creischer et al., *The Potosí Principle* 3)

The curatorial methodology of the exhibition is one in which juxtaposition and accumulation have a disturbing and somewhat disorientating function, effected by focusing on the question how the ordering of things affects the ordering of people and what makes up the production of sociality as a condition for processes of knowledge production in the first place. In case of *The Potosí Principle,* the idea of conflict is very much inherent to this process on two levels. One concerns the aforementioned complexities of institutional politics, particularly in the context of getting colonial paintings to be exhibited in the formerly colonialist country. This affects the way in which the curators perceive their curatorial responsibility in conflict with the national and ethnic identity politics at play during the process of putting the exhibition together. Consequently, notions of conflict, disturbance, and interference, were central to the way in which the exhibition was perceived by the viewer with regard to the relationship between works and viewer and to the contextualization the curators provided in their efforts to guide the viewer through the exhibition. The viewer entered into a process of continuous self-reference accompanied by an abundance of efforts supposed to help the viewer orientate: the guide with its proposed routes throughout the exhibition; the pictorial signs; the artwork numbering system; display elements such as magnifying glasses hanging in the exhibition; a stepladder provided to reach a better viewing position of artworks; and so on. The excess of information presented to the viewer and the limited time available for processing it in the exhibition space actually produces a lack of orientation on the historical matter. This favoured a level of interpretation addressing the contemporary significance of the material presented. To give an example, in their communication with the viewer in the guide and in general communication about the exhibition in the catalogue, the curators always flip back and forth between different levels of interpretation, as evidenced by the captions for some of the artworks. In this respect they express the duality of the Potosí principle to the full: they show it as a beginning, but ultimately seek to arrive at an understanding of it as a principle of contemporary societies.

From the Politics of Display to the Display of Politics

The preceding analysis in parts described the nature of the exhibition's display in an attempt to visualize it and recount the process of interpretation from it. However, its particularities should be considered in the context of theories of display central to curatorial discourse. It is in relation to this discourse that the importance of the exhibition as a communicative space and vehicle of knowledge production becomes apparent.

Discussions of mechanisms and strategies of display in curatorial discourse focus on the enunciative function of the artwork, its simultaneous vitality and historicity in time and space. Conceiving of the nature of display not just as the means of presenting artworks, but as a form of action to render them visible, to point to their social, cultural, and political relevance, became important again for curatorial discourse after Mary Anne Staniszewski's published *The Power of Display*, in which she discussed exhibition design as a discipline in its own right, integrating the installations of the international avant-gardes within the discourse of modern art. She also pointed to the similarities of commercial sales strategies and institutional exhibition practices with regard to how the gaze of the viewer is directed through display mechanisms.

Notions of display in curatorial discourse are characterized by how their discussions bring together practical and theoretical aspects of forms of visibility and processes of visualization. For example, German artist Stefan Römer expands the notion of the display to include the choice of themes for an exhibition: the content that will be made public (Schade et al. 195). Questions of display can thus be regarded as addressing the politics of how and what is made public, an area addressed in practice early on in the twentieth century. Architect, artist, and set designer Friedrich Kiesler realized designs for exhibitions that required an active dialogue with the viewer. For his *International Exhibition of New Theatre Techniques* at the Konzerthaus in Vienna in 1924 Kiesler conceived of a mobile installation structure that was freestanding and therefore independent of any spatial setting that the room provided. The mobile display units extended the space of affect of what was shown in them—in this case, drawings, photographs, posters and architectural models—into the exhibition space. Kiesler's design concepts merged the work with the space and the viewer, making him an agent in the reception of the work. This way of working should be viewed in the context of, and in connection to, the contemporaneous practices of Herbert Bayer and designers, artists, and architects at the Bauhaus (O'Neill, *The Culture of Curating* 11).

Contemporary discourse on display strategies largely credits artistic practices for discussing ways of presenting and exhibiting as processes of visualization that, often in a critical fashion, relate to and point to the ways in which institutions exert a signifying function through their strategies of display (Beck; Bismarck, "Display/Displacement" 71). In this sense the display mechanisms operating in *The Potosí Principle* can be treated as a method rather than merely as a means of production. For example, colonial paintings from Potosí were not mounted directly on the walls. They were instead suspended from the ceiling or shown on purpose-built temporary surfaces with the intention of pointing to the fact that these pictures never had an allocated place in European art history. The exhibition's display mechanisms deliberately dispense with traditional object-oriented practices and with chronological orders. This serves to draw the viewer's attention to the politics of presentation and focus the interpretation process on how the exhibition addresses its central themes by means of a detailed contention with the materiality of display.

Creischer, Siekmann, and Hinderer articulate the aim of the exhibition as being to, "illuminate the parallels between colonial and neoliberal regimes" (Creischer et al., "1000 words" 302). The production of art plays a specific role in this process—both in contemporary times and in the particular case of Potosí. The curators cite an essay by Bolivian art historian Teresa Gisbert in which she lays interpretative connections between colonial and neoliberal systems of power.

> Gisbert argues that there is a definitive link between the pictures produced in the Andean region and the labor in the mines, one that can be read on a formal level as an expression of class struggle—that the

pictures show traces of both oppression and resistance. At a certain point, the indigenous artists in the workshops—who were expected to paint up to three hundred pictures a month—defied the pressure of the workplace. They refused to take academic examinations, ceased to adhere to the rules of central perspective. With these interrelations between the economy, art, and resistance in mind, we use the term *principio Potosí* to describe the way in which cultural "surfaces" are subtended by material reality, and how cultural production function-ally relates to economic mechanisms and technologies of power. These kinds of connections are key, since our project is not to exhibit cultural or art history but to look at the history of colonialism and to ask how the *principio Potosí* manifests itself today. (Creischer et al., "1000 words" 302)

The curators interrogate the institutional speech that the exhibition itself is an expression dependent upon, but not incapable of acting against, its institutional staging. The multiplicity and complexity of meaning at the centre of art is thus not balanced out or resolved, but upheld, and encouraged.

The idea that meanings are *impossibly unstable* is embraceable be-cause inevitable. With works of art, meanings are only produced in context and that is a collective, negotiated, debated and shifting con-sensual process of determination. (Ferguson 186)

If we, as artists and writers, responsibly and independently conceive and curate exhibitions, that is because they give us an opportunity to critically examine how meanings are made. (Creischer et al., "1000 words" 303)

The curators are very much aware of their institutional depen-dence and do not seek to articulate the difficulties of working on the exhibition with their partner institutions. Particularly with re-gard to identity politics, the curators struggled to find a position that neither supported a national-identitary representation nor affirmed indigenous alterity to legitimize their curatorial endeav-our, for which they chose to occupy a "decidedly internationalist and anti-identitary position" (Creischer et al., *The Potosí Principle* 13). How that position was articulated in the exhibition itself is, however, questionable. It might only be rendered in the ways with which the curators avoided any articulation of a specific identity—whether colonial, national, or ethnic—and chose to visualize the institutional representations of relationships, particularly those in which the process of loaning works from South America to Europe, and vice versa, failed.

The question of how such positioning was received by the partnering institutions can be answered by looking at how they articulate their own positioning in the matter, for example in the various forewords to the catalogue. Manuel J. Borja-Villel, Director of the Museo Nacional Centro de Arte Reina Sofía in Madrid, understands the curatorial endeavour of the exhibition as building a feedback loop. "It reflects a situation of exploitation and increasing labour insecurity, of which culture is art and part, while at the same time *problematizing* this through the very same art" (Creischer et al., *The Potosí Principle* 3). Borja-Villel does not explore what particular repercussions such a problematization would cause and how this would affect the institution. He chose instead to contextualize this double articulation of the exhibition and its defiance of notions of origin and linearity as a critique of modernity. The director of the Haus der Kulturen der Welt Bernd M. Scherer also praises this emancipatory potential of art and goes so far as to render the whole exhibition as an artwork in the tradition of the *Gesamtkunstwerk*, or total work of art.

> The most important creative moment of *The Potosí Principle* as a *Gesamtkunstwerk* is the transgression of boundaries, and consequently a number of the core categories with which Western Modernity imposes order on the world have been consciously deactivated. (Creischer et al., *The Potosí Principle* 4)

To define the exhibition in terms of a Gesamtkunstwerk is not only questionable, but an ill-considered and superficial approach that neglects the complexities in the relationship between different works of art from different periods of art history that also reflect different functionalities of art in their respective historical social contexts. To perceive the exhibition as a Gesamtkunstwerk would entail collectivizing everything that is displayed and subject it to a form of interpretation that does not originate in the process of communication the exhibition sets up between works, viewer and their contextualization, but that is externally conditioned. Even though many of the references the curators make in order to contextualize the works seem far-fetched, they nevertheless stem from a line of associations in which the works of art originate the dense web of references that contextualizes their installation. In an essay in the catalogue for Harald Szeemann's 1983 exhibition *Der Hang zum Gesamtkunstwerk* at Kunsthaus Zürich, art historian Bazon Brock defined the Gesamt-kunstwerk as a fictional dimension that in its totalizing character—disregarding the aesthetic or epistemological differences and partic-ularities of the materials involved or presented—has an ultimate claim for truth. For Brock this kind of claim must be historically grounded if it is to avoid the political, social or cultural aspirations becoming mere myths (24).

According to Scherer, the Gesamtkunstwerk that is *The Potosí Prin-ciple* exhibition is founded on a methodology that transgresses a num-ber of temporal, spatial and intellectual boundaries: it "compresses the temporal strands from the sixteenth and seventeenth centuries and the present to form one temporal layer"; it conceives of a dissolution of territorial boundaries, abandoning the concept of the nation-state for a global perspective; it "transgresses the boundaries of the category of art, itself a product of Modernity, and of its segmentation into social subdivisions" (Creischer et al., *The Potosí Principle* 4). Consequently, the claim that the exhibition pursues is to "reveal the mechanisms and representational strategies of a self-globalizing economy" so that the parallels of exploitation of human relationships between the times of Potosí and nowadays become apparent (Creischer et al., *The Potosí Principle* 5). The way Scherer outlines the curatorial methodology is precise and the claim it aspires to make is certainly truthful, however the contextualization of the exhibition as a Gesamtkunstwerk renders it powerless. Perceiving the exhibition as such would entail the viewer foregoing any involvement with the different layers of interpretation.

Looking at how Alexander Alberro addressed the process of inter-preting the show by constructing his own narrative and casting his own web of associations, is a good example for how much attention to detail the process of interpretation requires. Alberro meticulously describes different works in the show in order to reveal the meaning of the juxtaposing installation of the works and the way this accen-tuates specific issues in the history of Potosí as well as in contempo-rary cultural production. Only in the second part of the review does Alberro begin to evaluate the show.

The main provocation of the show lies in the parallels it draws be-tween the operation of colonial painting and the function that con-temporary art serves in legitimizing the new elites of globalization. ("The Silver Lining" 169)

Focusing on describing the relations between the artworks and in so doing presenting the dense web of associations the exhibition fosters—generated by the viewer's interaction with the artworks as well as teased by the references the curators provide—Alberro's description of the exhibition ponders on the manifold relations between colonial and contemporary works. Unlike Scherer, he does not generalize this contention *for* perceiving the exhibition as a transgression of boundaries, but—at the very end of his review—highlights the boundary that this contention sets up:

> The show makes the powerful point that the interpretation of images is never entirely in line with the technology of power—that even the most subservient art can offer messages of resistance to future generations. ... In close readings and critical interpretations of art such as these, the curators see the glimmer of present and future hope. ("The Silver Lining" 172)

The boundary that Alberro refers to is the limited capacity of an artwork to act as a carrier of meaning that does not only not emerge from a contention with its own materiality but is also ignorant of its production process. Instead, the previous quote from Alberro's review, which is also the closing argument of the whole article, recognizes the curatorial methodology of the exhibition as one in which the interpretation process involving the many different elements oscillates between historical, social, and political contexts of the production of art and economic wealth—two things that have historically always been linked.

Hence, the exhibition cannot be perceived as a Gesamtkunstwerk, since this would preclude the spectator from engaging in manifold interpretative processes and disguise the function of interpretation as not only a reflexive, but also productive practice of signification. This applies as much as to how the relation between colonizer and colonized are represented in art history, as well as to how parallels between the colonial and contemporary neoliberal regimes can be drawn. It also refers to how the teleological understanding of modernity, particularly in the context of art history, can be revisited and countered.

According to Christian Kravagna, any productive postcolonial exhibition cannot be content to analyze and denounce forms of violence founded in colonial racism and economic ideologies, but must present historical and contemporary forms of resistance. Postcolonial forms of exhibition research and practice are thereby always also linked to critical perspectives on historiography (Kravagna 60). The exhibition with its critically reflexive attitude is itself a form of cultural production. The curatorial methodology can therefore be described as provoking a process of critical interpretation that addresses the very question how knowledge is produced.

Interpretation as the Material of Communication

The argument was that the meaning of an exhibition resides neither "in" the artworks not in the arrangement of the display, nor even in the texts written to accompany the show. Meaning is constructed by the spectator in a space that includes all of these, as well as the discussions and reviews the show generates. ... Art becomes socially meaningful only within the discursive contexts, explicit or implicit, in which it is experienced. (Alberro, "The Potosí Principle" 33)

This quote refers to *The Potosí Principle*, but could equally be applied to Michael Fullerton's exhibition *Columbia*. The juxtaposition of pictorial languages, sculptures, text, and moving images recall the ways in which Fullerton set up the communicative space of the exhibition as a framework of enquiry into the process of communication. Here, the notion of "suspicion" arose questioning the definition and role of information provided in the process of communication between artist, works and viewer, both in relation to the exhibition in general and to the works in particular. In the case of *The Potosí Principle*, however, suspicion was directed not at what was shown in the exhibition, but at how that material—both historical and contemporary—could be interpreted for reconfiguring an alternative cultural history.

In very different contexts, and by very different means, both exhibitions request the viewer to actively engage self-reflexively with the exhibition. The mechanisms and strategies of display and presentation of artworks and narratives within the exhibition as a set of utterances were not simply communicated to the viewer as a task to be completed, but instead emerged from engaging with the exhibition in a way that requires an understanding and appreciation of its materiality as a constitutional element of sociality produced in the curated encounter. Fullerton's presentation of artworks with their at times factual and at other times fictitious narratives primarily defined the space of the exhibition as a communicative space in which meaning is produced via different modes of suspicion over the assumptions, opinions, and concepts on which meaning is generated. *The Potosí Principle's* mechanisms of communication were far more straightforward and compelling. They do not blur the issue of fact or fiction, focusing instead on the matter of presentation as a way to critically engage with meaning production and its political, social, and cultural repercussions.

With regards to the issue of knowledge production, both exhibitions are conceived as spaces that defy knowledge production as a form of identification with what is presented. Rather, they challenge processes of identification starting with the very notion of what the material is that constitutes the curated encounter: first and foremost artworks, their presentation, contextualiation and interpretation. Informed by the specific materialities of the curated encounter, its staging as well as infrastructural frameworks, the artists and curators devise forms that engender suspicion and that invert and neutralize passive spectatorship. Therein, not only material things, but also the material constitution of the ideologically predetermined communicative space of the exhibition becomes effective in shaping social relations. Instead of following a representational logic whereby artworks are employed to directly invoke aesthetic and ideological forms of interpretation, often supplied by their art historical context, both exhibitions set in motion processes of production of further and more complex relations between the materiality of art production and their epistemological qualities and functions.

The Practice of Communication

Both exhibitions enquire methodologically into the ways in which information, meaning, and knowledge is displayed, communicated and produced in situ in such a way that it demands active engagement on the part of the spectator. The conglomeration of such modes of production cannot be allocated solely to the position of the viewer, the artist, or the curator. It takes place in the relationships built into the site of the exhibition when recognizing the distinction between the space of the installation of works, the space of the exhibition surrounding and contextualizing the installation, and the unmarked public space that includes the exhibition space, relating the exhibition space to that which is outside of it. This distinction is one that anyone partaking in the process of communication must perform prior to any form of interpretation. This process of communication is the element of practice in which preconceived notions and traditionally defined assumptions or prejudices become renegotiated, "delocalized and deterritorialized" (Groys, "Politics of Installation" 63).

Looking further into this distinction serves to determine how the exhibition space can be defined differently from other realms in the social sphere in terms of knowledge production, particularly given that in recent years discursive and performative modes of practice (seminars, talks, conferences, educational programmes) are coming out of the shadow of the exhibition now that formerly peripheral elements of museum programmes are assuming a more prominent position. Before discussing these and other examples in detail in the subsequent chapters, it is important to comprehend the particularities of a dialogical understanding of exhibition making. What makes the exhibition space a prevalent site for negotiating processes of knowledge production is its ability to express "connective possibilities." In this context, curator Hans Ulrich Obrist described the changes to their social function that exhibitions have undergone in recent decades: Where once they emphasized order and stability in order to educate bourgeois citizenry, exhibitions are now sites that disrupt order, favour fluctuation and promote "relative and not absolute truth" (25–26).

In the processes of communication determining exhibitions as sites of knowledge production, the role of art is self-referential. "In order for art to be art, its function is to communicate how specific impressions are rendered as perception" (Baecker, *Studien zur Nächsten Gesellschaft* 15). The intentional foundation of an artwork is conveyed to the spectator whenever she or he differentiates between communication and perception while looking at the work. This differentiation is the choice of the viewer to accept any kind of signal or information (perceiving it) and then to question or refuse it (communicating). Referring to the social systems theory as developed by Niklas Luhmann, in which this distinction is grounded, German sociologist Dirk Baecker further argues for a differentiation between art as communication and the individual subject as agent and producer of perception. This differentiation is highly important because, in contrast to communication, perception cannot be negated, since any negation of perception would by definition necessitate entering into a process of communication with the work. Baecker claims that such perplexity of individual consciousness with respect to its own perceptive abilities manifests itself in the illusionary assumption that perceptions appear to be information that should be accepted as facts belonging to the sphere of things, rather than as an act performed by the individual self. To abolish, or rather to negate, this illusion is the function of art as communication.

The communicability of both *Columbia* and *The Potosí Principle* can be understood in these terms. Both exhibitions first of all communicate their potential for setting up communicative, dialogical spaces for the production of knowledge. The very first element of knowledge production is the distinction between art as communication and the viewer as agent and producer of this communication while perceiving art as art. Communication is therefore primarily a production of further and more complex relations. To address the social dimension of knowledge production means to investigate into how art in general and exhibitions in particular are sites in which communication is communicated. Curator and critic Simon Sheikh attests to art being "a place 'where things can happen' rather than a thing 'that is in the world'" (Sheikh, "Talk Value" 195). As Baecker argues, from a sociological perspective art functions as communication in that it not only forms part of the social sphere but is, more importantly, a production of what constitutes the social—politics, culture, moral values, opinions, etc. ("Die Adresse der Kunst" 83). The forms of the social, which communication itself produces, also condition communication. This simultaneity of form and formation is the subject for the following analysis of concepts of communication and practice that are determined by the ways in which their processual undertakings are a form of self-organization.

This is a necessary prerequisite for conceiving the curatorial as a radical epistemic practice producing sociality as a result of its recursivity. Starting by disambiguating terms such as "sociality" and "recursivity" we enter the field of sociological theories of action, accompanied by an abstraction from the field of art theory and other writings directly associated with artistic and curatorial practices. In keeping with the indirect approach to discussing curatorial practice outlined at the beginning of this chapter, this abstraction will generate a notion of practice that emerges from contentions with issues of curatorial practice—such as the exhibition as a communicative site—while also addressing those processes of knowledge production that take place in the exhibition space that are constitutive of the social sphere rather than different and isolated from it.

From Communication to Practice:
Niklas Luhmann and Pierre Bourdieu

"If the definition of a system of communication is not substantial, but relational, two other features are essential. We can call them 'recursivity' and 'sociality'" (Baecker, "Systemic Theories of Communication" 92). While the first term defines communication as a principle of operative selections, the second refers to the web of dependences and interdependences in which these selections are cast. Recursivity is based on the idea that the number of messages to be communicated is indefinite, as is the number of units perceiving it. The term refers to the element of self-referentiality necessary for communication to occur in that the understanding of any message can only happen in relation to the memory of previous messages and the anticipation of coming ones. Without recursivity it is not possible to identify a message as a message. Sociality, in this context, is a particular scope of relationality and refers to the interplay of those participating in communication, and the ways people tend to build structures as modes for anticipating and cultivate cultures as forms of evaluation of what is communicated.

The following study enquires into communication as a form of practice that operates within the principle of recursivity and on the basis of sociality, using the theories of Niklas Luhmann and Pierre Bourdieu to work out their structural similarities with respect to how relations are built. This is in response to questions first raised in the analyses of exhibitions about what the self-referential feedback loop in communication serves and what—besides more relations— it produces. In the last forty years both Bourdieu and Luhmann have highly influenced any discussion on epistemic practices and their role within and for the social sphere. At the core of their respective theories is an interest in sociality and in the structures and functioning of societies. The social is both the premise and the subject of their interests and research matters. When Bourdieu speaks about social structures and Luhmann about social systems, both are interested in naming the relations between groups, generations, sexes, and classes, the forms these might take and the processes through which they are generated (Bourdieu, *The Logic of Practice* 95; Luhmann, *Social Systems* 15). Both dedicate their thoughts to sociality as a condition of the social, which they believe unfolds and is describable in some form, whether it is structure, or system. The question that looms over this analysis providing for a reconfiguration of the notion of practice, is whether sociality can be understood as a condition that unfolds and further develops as relations in practice or as a mere product of practice.

I will be mainly referring to a set of written works that are centred on the enquiry into the social and discussing the approach both theorists chose with respect to the subject matter (Bourdieu, *Outline of a Theory of Practice*; *The Logic of Practice*; Luhmann, *Social Systems*; *Theories of Distinction*). The state of research in the field of sociology and cultural anthropology at the time these works were written, and the references made to them, will be taken into account. It is necessary to look into the departure points of both theories in order to articulate their concepts and reformulate their interests, references, methodologies, and strategies. But alongside paraphrasing the most important concepts in both theories and highlighting their differences, similarities and possible points of agreement, the primary question on a metalevel is what kind of issues and problems they face when developing their own theoretical structures. I will outline the specific approaches that both theorists chose to address the social as a matter of research within the dichotomies of theory and practice, observation and action, and of objectifying tendencies versus context-oriented interpretation of social action, a dichotomy that was very prevalent at the time when the theories were developed (from the late 1970s to the mid-1990s). Preliminarily it can be said that what Luhmann and Bourdieu have in common is that they aim to transcend those dichotomies and find a way in which the social can be enquired into as a phenomenon incorporating both poles. In order to test this assumption the following analysis will concentrate on the difference between structure and system, the terminological foundations of Bourdieu's and Luhmann's respective theories, and on the difference between the operations that generate communication and practice and in so doing focus on the methodologies and models of thinking that both theories employ in order to analyze the social. To conclude, the comparative effort will reveal the different ways in which Bourdieu and Luhmann address the social as their subject of enquiry, and focus on what kind of sociality those theories might constitute. Their respective conclusions provide for developing a new model of concurrently thinking and producing the social that serves to ground the notion of curatorial practices in a definition of practice that is both productive and reflexive with respect to its material and subject matter of social relations.

Towards a Theoretical Habitus

A comparison of theories is in general a challenging undertaking, particularly if those theories emerge from different realms of thinking within the same discipline, as they do in this case. One might want to start with the conclusions that each theory draws, or compare the most well-known arguments. However, this might not be a valid comparison of theories, given that it would not start from the basic assumptions the theory is built upon, and would thus fail to consider how abstract thoughts become articulated using a specific vocabulary that is employed to formulate differences and devise distinctions with previously elaborated ideas and concepts in a way that has never been done before in this particular way. The key area of interest might not be exclusively, and certainly not primarily, the subject of the theory, but the construction of its arguments and logic.

The French ethnographer and anthropologist Pierre Bourdieu also became known as a sociologist when his questions regarding the social changed from asking about the nature of human behaviour to questioning the relations that form and perform this nature within the broader system of society (*The Logic of Practice* 3). In this he was very much influenced by the ideas of Claude Lévi-Strauss, the most distinguished representative of French Structuralism.[20]

20 Structuralism is a term that Claude Lévi-Strauss coined in the mid-twentieth century foregrounding an approach to the human sciences that attempts to analyze a specific matter of interest (field) as a complex system of interrelated parts. The emphasis is laid on the relational aspect between the actions of practice of human beings and its underlying structures. The French linguist Ferdinand de Saussure is considered to have initiated this approach when he introduced the distinction between language as an act (parole) and its underlying system (langue) whose structures could only be studied through the examination of the act. This initial distinction and the acknowledgement of ac-

Bourdieu sees the "essential novelty" of this approach in that it introduces a structural method, "a relational mode of thought which, by breaking with the substantialist mode of thought, leads one to characterize each element by the relationships which unite it with all the others in a system and from which it derives its meaning and function" (*The Logic of Practice* 4). The central terminologies that allow for a characterization of the elements that form the social through the relationships within them are structure, disposition, habitus and, most importantly, practice. But while constructing this set of terminologies in order to formulate his theory of practice, Bourdieu is also extremely critical of Structuralism, criticising its methodologies for assuming that everything that is observable is also classifiable or distinguishable in structures and systems. According to Bourdieu, classifications would not say much about the subject of interest, but only overdetermine it in theoretical terms.

> [Anthropology] has to make a second break and question the presuppositions inherent in the position of an outside observer, who, in this preoccupation with interpreting practices, is inclined to introduce into the object the principles of his relation to the object, as is attested by the special importance he assigns to communicative functions (weather in language, myth, or marriage). (*Outline of a Theory of Practice* 2)

Bourdieu directed his attention to the methodologies of research and the conditions that frame it. The phenomena he was primarily concerned with in the two works that are of interest to this comparison, *Outline of a Theory of Practice* (1977) and *The Logic of Practice* (1990), are language, myth and marriage, and their rituals, rules and strategies. His research in Kabylia (Algeria) is an investigation into the mechanisms and dispositions that are employed when fighting over positions and functions within hierarchical societies. This led to his later research on the field of cultural production and education in France looking into the power structures and mechanisms of capital in French society (*The Field of Cultural Production*, 1993). But despite all this research—for which he is most often credited when it comes to evaluating his contribution and his influence on the study of social

---

tion being based on some kind of structures or systems led to the development of a structuralist method with which many phenomena could be considered, not only in linguistics but in all fields of research concerned with the social, such as anthropology, philosophy and psychoanalysis (Schützeichel 16–22).

sciences—for this comparison it is particularly interesting to see how Bourdieu reconfigured the methodology with which to approach research in the first place.

> The science of practice has to construct the principle which makes it possible to account for all the cases observed, and only those, without forgetting that this construction, and the generative operation of which it is the basis, are only the theoretical equivalent of the practical scheme which enables every correctly trained agent to produce all the practices and judgements of honour called for by the challenges of existence. (*Outline of a Theory of Practice* 11)

Prior to even embarking on his analysis of his observations of what social structures suggest about their own formation, Bourdieu's most immediate concern is the dichotomy between theory and action, between theorization and empiricism, between reflection and production, and between objectivism and subjectivism.

> The critical break with objectivist abstraction ensuing from inquiry into the conditions of possibility, and thereby, into the limits of the objective and objectifying standpoint which grasps practices from outside, as a fait accompli, instead of constructing their generative principle by situating itself within the very movement of their accomplishment, has no other aim than to make possible a science of the dialectical relations between the objective structures to which the objectivist mode of knowledge gives access and the structured dispositions within which those structures are actualized and which tend to reproduce them. (*Outline of a Theory of Practice* 3)

In pointing out the limits of objectivist knowledge, instead of turning towards an analysis purely determined by empirical experience Bourdieu builds a theory that does not theorize in order to anonymize the observer's standpoint and erase any sense of consecutiveness or temporality from the set of actions that are at stake in practice. Rather, and this is a first hypothesis around Bourdieu's theory of practice as well as the lowest common denominator for the following comparison with Niklas Luhmann, he tries to picture the empirical in theory without theorizing it (Nassehi and Nollmann 85). Bourdieu's contention with the theoretical, the objectivist standpoint, the role of the observer, is actually a contention with its opposite—the subjective, the practice of everyday life, the immediate. It is a contention with the conditions that make theory possible. Those conditions are the actions that are preliminary to their observation, but that can only be studied in relation to them. A study of actions leads to a study of their observation, the methodologies, strategies and methods that are involved in it, and the structures and dispositions they produce (Bourdieu, Out*line of a Theory of Practice* 72).

Niklas Luhmann was not overly concerned with the role theory plays in the study of actions. His interest lay instead in the subject of how actions become instrumentalized for the formulation of a theory: "Sociology is stuck in a theory crisis" is the first sentence in *Social Systems* (xlvi), originally published in German in 1984, in which the German sociologist presented his systems theory for the first time. Defining this crisis as the incapability of empirical research producing a "unified theory for the discipline" through successfully "increasing knowledge," Luhmann enquires into the relationship between theory and empiricism as well as the role of theory in general. He questions what theory can do in a science (social science, in this case) that he classifies as of "empirical nature," verifying "hypotheses about relations among data," conceptualizing "in a broad, somewhat indeterminate sense" (*Social Systems* xlvii). This question defines his entire systems theory. *Social Systems* was not Luhmann's first book, but the first chapter in a proposition to sociology that he made in 1968 when he started his professorship at Bielefeld University: "My research project will be a theory of society" (Gripp-Hagelstange 4). Over the following 30 years he published a series of books on different areas of the social—economics, science, law, art, politics, religion and education—culminating with *Theory of Society* (*Die Gesellschaft der Gesellschaft*) shortly before his death in 1998, which has been translated into English in 2012. Unlike his teacher Talcott Parsons, with whom he studied in Harvard in the 1960s, his aim was to leave behind a body of work that is very concise and speaks for itself not as a mere series of thoughts but as a single, dense theoretical endeavour (Lutz 29). This endeavour was built on a set of theoretical premises with which Luhmann identified: systems and action theory. Systems theory stems from the premise that there are complex structures (systems) in nature, society, and science, that are formed of objects or things related to each other and that produce some result in their interaction.[21] This can be an organism, an organization, or a part of society. Systems theory is neither a

---

21 Ludwig von Bertalanffy, an Austrian biologist who introduced the terminology of General Systems Theory (Allgemeine Systemtheorie), first used the term

theory about a specific field, nor a definite discipline. Rather, it is a methodology with which to approach various problems and questions shared by different disciplines such as ontology, philosophy, science, biology, political science, psychotherapy, etc. Systems theory acts as a device with which to shed light on the organization of knowledge. Talcott Parsons was the first to use the term "system" in order to study structures in society (Parsons and Shils 16). Structures, for Parsons, present a form of social reality. Its operations are actions, moments of dissolution in a continuous process of selection that the actors face. These selections result in the development of systems that can be observed and studied according to the conditions under which they were constituted, taking into account behavioural, evolutionary, biological, normative and psychic parameters (Parsons and Shils 22). The term "system," for Parsons, relates various aspects of a matter under a selective viewpoint. Actions perform the distinctions generated from that selective viewpoint and constantly reassess the development of the viewpoint when differentiating it from its environment, either withdrawing or adjusting. Luhmann's ideas emanated from that basic principle of a system having an environment and relating to it via the process of distinction and selection.

> Systems are oriented by their environment not just occasionally and adaptively, but structurally, and they cannot exist without an environment. They constitute and maintain themselves by creating and maintaining a difference from their environment, and they use their boundaries to regulate this difference. (*Social Systems* 17)

For Luhmann, systems theory is not simply one device amongst others with which to analyze the social system next to other theoretical models, such as Structuralism, for example, with which Parsons affiliates himself in his later writing. Rather, it is the general theory of social systems: "Every social contact is understood as a system, up to and including society as the inclusion of all possible contacts" (*Social Systems* 15).

The operative principle of social systems is communication. All different forms of communication combined constitute the entity of society. In that sense, society is marked by a method of functional

---

system to describe the principles that are common to most organisms, and with which behaviour patterns might be explained.

differentiation: Within the overall system of society various other and smaller, but nevertheless self-sufficient, systems operate—economics, law, art, love, etc., that filter communication by means of specific codes. These sub-systems determine what processes of communication link and convert improbable communication into probable communication. "Only communication can communicate" (*Social Systems* 188). Communication is the principle of all social action, it is not an action performed by an individual, a subject, or by means of language, but the overall condition for all action. It is a selective process, understood as a synthesis of three different selections: "the selection of information, the selection of utterance [*Mitteilung*] of this information, and the selective understanding or misunderstanding of this utterance and its information" (Luhmann, *Theories of Distinction* 157). Within the process of communication, systems are forced to select pieces of information from the complexity of an environment. For each communication their goal is always to provide one that follows up on the previous distinction between information and utterance. This has a stabilizing effect on the growth of a social system. In turn, while social systems operate using communication as their code or method for selection of what is relevant for them or not, psychic systems (individuals, organisms) operate on the basis of perception, a different mode of selection that will be discussed at a later point when it will be necessary to point out whether and how social and psychic systems—individuals and society—interact. However, what both have in common is the principle of selection.

This all-encompassing notion of how a society is formed technically through differentiations as selective processes enables Luhmann to cut across the sociological controversies that he analyzed at the beginning of *Social Systems*:

> The general theory of social systems claims to encompass all sociology's potential topics and, in this sense, to be a universal sociological theory. Such a universal claim is a principle of selection ... accepting bodies of thought, ideas, and critique only if and insofar as these make this principle their own. (15)

Here, Luhmann is not trying to pose his claim for universality as a claim to correctness or demand exclusivity. It is not about what the claim to universality serves for but rather how it can be recognized and valued: "Theories that claim universality are easily recognized by the fact that they appear as their own object" (xlvii).

Luhmann and Bourdieu both develop their ideas from an observation of the methodologies at stake in their field and the subsequent analysis of a problematic relationship between theory (an observatory and objectivist standpoint) and empiricism (a strategy focusing on processes rather than structures, on production rather than reflection, and on subjectivity and individuality rather than objectifying principles and common patterns). The concerns that articulate the ways in which research and theoretical analysis are undertaken convey a great deal of reflexivity over Luhmann's and Bourdieu's own positioning as researchers and theorists. Both put their own analytic position into question in the first place. This leads them—prior to any definition of conditions of sociality or determinations of social structures—to reconsider the matters and methodologies of sociological research and to find their very own self-reflexive way of dealing with them. In the following this research attitude will be further looked at as methodologically intrinsic to the notion of practice.

From Objectification to Observation

Before enquiring into how Luhmann and Bourdieu define the limits of objectivism and the objectivist standpoint from their perspective as researchers, it is important to clarify how both thinkers understand objectivism or what is deemed an objectivist approach.

> The knowledge we shall term objectivist ... constructs the objective relations (e.g. economic or linguistic) which structure practice and representations of practice, i.e., in particular, primary knowledge, practical and tacit, of the familiar world. (Bourdieu, *Outline of a Theory of Practice* 3)

Bourdieu's first definition here is not directly negative about objectivism as a method for generating knowledge of social structures, but it does immediately make clear that if one is to be critical of objectivist knowledge, it is because it implies a hierarchical order of structures over different modes of knowledge as ways of relating to social experiences made. By "objectivist knowledge" he means classifications gained over the observation of so-called "primary knowledge," which is not mediated by structures, but which is gained from immediate experiences in the social world, that which "gives the social world its self-evident, natural character" (*Outline of a Theory of Practice* 3). In contrast,

> objectivism constitutes the social world as spectacle presented to an observer who takes up a "point of view" on the action, who stands back so as to observe it and, transferring into the object the principles of his relation to the object, conceives of it as a totality intended for cognition alone, in which all interactions are reduced to symbolic exchanges. (*Outline of a Theory of Practice* 96)

For Bourdieu, this danger of objectivism lies in the distance and hierarchy that it generates with respect to the matter of interest: social structures and the ways they manifest in social actions. This distance is achieved through a process of reflection that has a negative effect of rationalizing about the social, often referring to alien structures rather than to the conditions and characteristics of the practices and practical modes of knowledge present (*Outline of a Theory of Practice* 4). The erroneous consequence of objectivism lies in the misrecognition of structure. It obscures the "distinction between 'the things of logic and the logic of things.' ... It presents the objective meaning of practices or works as the subjective purpose of the action of the producers of those practices or works" (*Outline of a Theory of Practice* 30). To look into the structures of the social through research is a matter of distinctive selections, and it is precisely this process and manner of selection of which Bourdieu is so critical.

In the first of his highly acclaimed lectures introducing the subject of systems theory[22] Luhmann described his own research practice as a form of ironic alienation from the subject matter in order to constantly return to it. The failure of an all-encompassing method of observation from the standpoint of the observer was not a problem for Luhmann, but the central condition to the complexity of his theory. The search for the blind spot within observation as a methodological study of social phenomena was a motivation for Luhmann to develop a theory that incorporates an analysis of action and, on another level, also its observation.

Unlike Bourdieu, Luhmann does not see the danger of objectivism rooted in observation and reflection. For Luhmann, these do not exemplify a determination of rigid structures going hand in hand with

---

22 *Vorlesungen zur Einführung in die Systemtheorie*, which Luhmann held in the winter of 1991–92 at Bielefeld University (Baecker, *Niklas Luhmann*).

a dismissal of the processual character of actions. Rather, he points to their processual character and their embeddedness in their immediate context; they can never be extracted in an objectivist manner from the practices in which they are invested. Observation is,

> a matter of events or processes that are not immediately under pressure from a situation. ... Free of the pressure of having to produce results, observation can afford a more complex view of the system. ... This is possible because action and observation do not necessarily exclude each other. Chances for action and observation constantly fluctuate; both occur together and collaborate as soon as observation is communicated or even observed. (Luhmann, *Social Systems* 300)

The observation of an observation is not only an operation, but also a process, constantly referencing itself. As such, it is self-referential, which for Luhmann—as pointed out earlier—is a defining characteristic of any system. The purpose of observation as an operation is a matter of distinction, of determining differences, and of generating reflections. "Difference is the functional premise of self-referential operations. ... Without difference from an environment, there would not even be self-reference" (*Social Systems* 17).

If Luhmann defines observation, a system's operation, as a necessity to self-referentiality, a system's function, this also indicates that the basic principle that allows for both to occur is selection. "Difference does not determine what must be selected, only that a selection must be made" (*Social Systems* 32). Whereas Bourdieu is critical about the manner in which selections are made, Luhmann provides us with the opportunity to focus on the process of how selections are made as an operation that serves as a specific function for the development of a system, and therefore of sociality. Luhmann allows us to step back from any determination regarding the value of those selections and emphasizes the process of their generation. This provides for an understanding of a relationship between reflection and process, and between theory and practice, that is neither dichotomous nor dialectical, but of an interdependent and interactive nature. It allows for understanding observation as not necessarily objectifying. With the help of Luhmann we are able to shift the emphasis from the classification of observation as a tool for objectifying practice, to observation as a basic distinctive operation that is necessary in order to generate the possibility of social structures as systems. While for Bourdieu the danger of objectivism lies in the distance and hierarchy that it generates from and for practice, for Luhmann "hierarchization is only a specific case of differentiation" (*Social Systems* 18). Observation and objectification are not necessarily equal, just as reflection and theorizing are not always on the same plane.

Hence, the problem of objectivism is not rooted in observation and reflection as basic operations of social systems, but in the fact that they often misrecognize social structures. Bourdieu and Luhmann complement each other and reveal this problem. With Luhmann providing a different use of the same terminology we can now look differently into Bourdieu's thinking around social structures without getting entangled in the relationship between theory and practice. If we really want to look at how the social is constituted and formed—as is the aim of bringing these thinkers' thinking together—we must keep an operative distance from the idea of an always-hierarchical relationship between theory and practice, and between observation and action. It is necessary to think strategically and technically about these theories and intersect Luhmann's emphasis on sociality as a set of operations in and between systems with Bourdieu's view on social structures and the dispositions that engender them. Only then can a formulation of theory and practice, of action and reflection, be established that is not automatically caught up in the dialectics of theory and practice (as suggested by the anthropological and sociological debate briefly referred to above) but instead emphasizes a mutual process that is technically nothing more than differentiations and distinctions.

To a certain extent this articulation disregards Bourdieu's claims surrounding the distinct structural dispositions of action and reflection. But I do not intend to discard the politically conflictive ramifications of Bourdieu's theory of practice and the role distinction plays in it as a methodology for establishing systems of power. However, for now the intersection of Bourdieu and Luhmann focuses strategically on the structures and dispositions that their terminologies determine and set in motion, which is a mechanism of distinctions. Both theorists aimed at a relationship between actions and their observation and subsequent reflections as processual and alternative to the hierarchical logic of structuralism, without the danger of the reflections falling into objectifying tendencies. The following study of their concepts of "structure," "process," and "disposition" will therefore provide vital grounds for the development of a notion of practice as generating social formations by treating sociality as its material in constant production and reflection.

Structure and Process (Luhmann) as Dispositions (Bourdieu)

For Luhmann, structure and process mutually presuppose each other: "structuring is a process, and processes have structure" (*Social Systems* 44). The only way in which they differ from each other is through their relation to time. However, the difference is not merely that structures are atemporal and processes temporal, but that the difference between structures and process "reconstructs the original (=environmentally conditioned) difference between reversibility and irreversibility" (*Social Systems* 44). Structures capture the reversibility of time as they offer various possibilities for choice, whereas processes are composed of irreversible events. Again, for Luhmann these are descriptions of modes of selection:

> Structures comprehend the open complexity of the possibility that every element could be connected with every other one, in a narrower model of relations that are "valid," customary, predictable, repeatable, or whatever is preferred. By means of this selection they can instruct further selections by reducing the constellations that can possibly be surveyed at any moment. Processes (and this defines the concept of process) result from the fact that concrete selective events build upon one another temporally, connect with one another and thus build previous selections or predictable selections into individual selections as premises for selection. (*Social Systems* 44)

Luhmann is describing how decisions are made within social systems or, in other words, he is giving various accounts for the generation of habits, of behaviour, and of conditioned actions with respect to the inherent goal of increasing probability for the operations of social systems. Structure and process are two forms of reflexive selection, meaning that the distinctions necessary to arrive at their constitution always take into account their own conditioning as forms of practice.

> A system that controls its own structures and processes can assign *all* the elements that it produces and reproduces to these forms of amplifying selectivity. ... The gain in order here lies in that the system can orient itself to these differences and adjust its operations to them. (*Social Systems* 45)

Both structure and process are reflexive selections that enable a system to produce and reproduce itself with its decision-making patterns: "the preselection of what can be chosen is experienced as validity in the case of structure, but as the sequence of concrete events in the case of processes" (*Social Systems* 46).

Luhmann's terminology of structure and process differs from how Bourdieu defines structures as relations.[23] It is important that for Luhmann structure consist of "how permissible relations are constrained within the system" (*Social Systems* 286), but the structure is not the entirety of these relations. Rather, they are what enable structures to form and to develop. What Luhmann thus terms "preselections of what can be chosen" (*Social Systems* 45) is to be found in Bourdieu's concept of disposition functioning as "an internal law relaying the continuous exercise of the law of external necessities" (*Outline of a Theory of Practice* 82). This, as with Luhmann's structure and process, is a form of distinction that takes into account its own conditionings. It is temporal in that it is constituted by a selection of events but at the same time it provides the preselection for the selection of those events, generated by a continuous process of distinctions.

Habitus (Bourdieu) and Double Contingency (Luhmann)

If structure and process, and disposition, are methodologies that enable selection while they are themselves selections and distinctions with respect to the environment, then we should examine how they become implemented and affect the functioning of systems and structures. Here, Bourdieu and Luhmann provide us with the most prominent and important concepts within their research: "habitus" and "double contingency." These are also particularly relevant for the wider context of sociology and anthropology addressing the question of how the social is generated, how it operates and develops.

> Habitus is the system of durable, transposable dispositions, structured structures predisposed to function as structuring structures,

---

23 As previously mentioned, Bourdieu defines structures as "relations between the groups, the sexes, or the generations, or between the social classes" (*The Logic of Practice* 95). This comes rather close to Luhmann's definition of a social system built out of communications as relations. "Every social contact is understood as a system, up to and including society as the inclusion of all possible contacts" (*Social Systems* 15).

that is, as principles of the generation and structuring of practices
and representations. (Bourdieu, *Outline of a Theory of Practice* 72)

These acquired dispositions function as categories of perception
that are at the same time also the organizing principle of action
(Bourdieu, *Distinction* 108). As an operationalized set of expectations and understandings based on the collection of experiences,
the habitus is a "durably installed generative principle of regulated
improvisations that produces practices which tend to reproduce
the regularities immanent in the objective conditions of the production of their generative principle" (Bourdieu, *Outline of a Theory
of Practice* 78). The habitus is both the result of and the condition
for social practice. Methodologically, it is the central element of the
social and cultural theory that Bourdieu developed in order to analyze the relationship within and functioning of social groups and
their divisions and classifications. These are placed in relation to a
system of potentialities associated with the situation in which the
interests of those involved are defined (Bourdieu, *Outline of a Theory of Practice* 76). This is a reciprocal event, unlike the establishing
of rules that solely function as objectifying principles.[24] Formed as a
system of dispositions, the habitus does not assume the character
of a rule because rather than being static, it is a "strategy-generating
principle enabling agents to cope with unforeseen and ever-chang-
ing situations" (Bourdieu, *Outline of a Theory of Practice* 72). Bourdieu emphasizes the recursive and reflexive character of the formational process of dispositions:

> Any "habitus" is only effectively realized in relation to a determinate
> structure of socially marked positions; but conversely, it is through
> dispositions, which are themselves more or less completely adjusted
> to those positions, that one or another potentiality lying inscribed in
> the positions is realized. (*Rules of Art* 256)

Habitus is a principle used to generate objectively classifiable judgements. It is a structure that structures and organizes practices, but is
also itself structured as the principle of division into classifications
that organize the perception of the world.

Such an organizing principle for actions that is determined by its
own conditioning, outlining the way in which systems operate and

---

24 Bourdieu is referring to Max Weber and his definitions of rules as principles for
    interactions in the systems of economy and society (Weber 246–49).

reproduce themselves, is also to be found in Luhmann's concept of "double contingency." This term is taken from Parsons' anthology *Toward a General Theory of Action* (1951), in which Parsons establishes double contingency as fundamental for all interaction.

> On the one hand, ego's gratifications are contingent on his selection among available alternatives. But in turn, alter's reaction will be contingent on ego's selection and will result from a complementary selection on alter's part. (Parsons and Shils 16)

For Parsons, the problem of double contingency is not a matter of mere agreement or a behavioural pattern, but the condition for social action. This circle of mutual dependency and of self-referential determination needs to be solved in order for social interaction to occur. Parsons chooses to solve this problem within the concept of action by making a "shared symbolic system," a normative orientation assuming consensus, a feature of action (Luhmann, *Social Systems* 104). It is on this point that Luhmann vehemently disagrees with Parsons, given that he does not believe in a normative code for interaction as a solution or as an elimination of contingency. Luhmann criticizes Parsons for presupposing that behavioural patterns (e.g. culture) are handed down in society and that every social action always uncovers these patterns (*Social Systems* 104). Rather, the effect of social structures in communication is a stabilizing one that comes from within the system, not from the outside. The "social dimension" (*Social Systems* 116) of communication is that it constitutes a set of processes that necessarily include as much contingency as selection. Luhmann reformulates double contingency in that it shifts from being a problem to being a condition for social structures. Double contingency provides much of the impetus for the evolution of social systems, but no preordained value consensus is required for double contingency to occur. The concept refers to the generation of meaning and knowledge in social interaction, which for Luhmann is always communication. If double contingency is understood as a condition,

> the concept thus describes something given (something experienced, expected, remembered, etc.) in the light of its possibly being otherwise; it describes objects within the horizon of possible variations. ... It enables the differentiation of a particular world dimension for socially distinct meaning perspectives (the social dimension). ... The social is then accessible in all meaning as the problem of the similarity or discrepancy of interpretative perspectives. (*Social Systems* 106)

Both Luhmann and Bourdieu develop concepts aimed at analyzing the selective patterns used in social situations to generate understanding and knowledge. Semantically, the two concepts of habitus and double contingency are quite similar. Whereas Bourdieu defines the habitus as a system of dispositions that tends to "reproduce the objective structures of which they are the product," and that "are determined by the past conditions which have produced the principle of their production" (*Outline of a Theory of Practice* 72), Luhmann similarly defines a self-referential relation to the conditions of production of double contingency:

> The autocatalysis of social systems creates its own catalytic agent: namely, the problem of double contingency itself. ... The self-reference built into the circle of reciprocal consideration becomes negative—and, with that, productive. (*Social Systems* 121)

Luhmann's and Bourdieu's concepts of double contingency and habitus investigate the formation of order within the social, an order defined as producing a self-referential and recursive relation between structure and action (form and formation) which is not imposed on the process of communication in which the formation of order is negotiated, but is actually a product of it. These concepts do not operate dialectically, but recursively as a continuous mode of self-organization.

Temporality and Connectivity: Formation of Practice

It is now necessary to point out why the concepts of structure and process as dispositions (double contingency and habitus) gain relevance for the formulation of practice and communication, which as stated at the beginning of this enquiry implies a Möbius effect, or recursive feedback loop, with respect to its portrayal of how social order is generated and how its patterns and logics operate. Both theorists discuss the matter of time and temporality to introduce the idea of consecutiveness of social activity. As soon as temporality comes into play, the reciprocity of concepts such as habitus and double contingency is confronted with the issue of reversibility and irreversibility in interaction.[25] For Luhmann, systems not only repro-

---

25 The element of the difference between reversibility and irreversibility was already shortly introduced when clarifying Luhmann's concepts of structure and

duce through selections that are made according to mutual expectations (as in double contingency), but also according to experiences. The concept that brings experiences and expectations together in order to place emphasis on the selective process is culture, which Luhmann defines as a,

> supply of possible themes that is available for quick and readily understandable reception in a concrete communicative process. ... Culture is not necessarily a normative content for meanings; perhaps it is more like a limitation of meanings (reduction) that makes it possible to distinguish appropriate from inappropriate or even correct from incorrect uses of themes in theme-related communication. This terminological simplification of complex theoretical deduction makes it possible to formulate questions dealing with the relationship between culture and system structures on societal development. (*Social Systems* 163)

Luhmann characterizes culture's relevance for society as a social memory that is maintained for the purpose of communication. Culture is thus first and foremost understood as a process of formation that consists of a constant balance of reflection on the past in order to grasp the contemporary. The operation of "grasping," though, does not arise from a decision that follows an external norm, because, as with any other selection, it can only take place within the system; it cannot be determined from the outside. "The generalized result of constant operation under the condition of double contingency is finally the social dimension of all meaning, namely, that one can ask for any meaning how it is experienced and processed by others" (*Social Systems* 112). The moment of asking is when "expectations acquire structural value for building emergent systems" (*Social Systems* 110), which is a connective value. Connectivity presupposes temporality. In communication as in interaction the supply of themes (i.e. culture) can only manifest itself in a constant oscillation between experience and expectations (i.e. double contingency) in which selections are made that aim for the highest possible degree of connectivity.

When it comes to Bourdieu, it might appear as obvious to first equate the concepts of culture and habitus. However, I choose to point out similarities between the concepts of culture and double contin-

---

process. Here, however, it is not limited to clarifications about Luhmann but shifts towards a necessary characteristic for both theories.

gency because they are both thought of as conditions of practice and communication, rather than their results. If one were to equate habitus with culture, this would presuppose that culture is something external or even superior that predetermines communication and practice. Bourdieu relates to Saussure's concept of the constitution of linguistics in order to criticize the formulation of culture as a code.

> Saussure constitutes linguistics as a science by constructing language as an autonomous object, distinct from its actualizations in speech, in order to bring to light the implicit presuppositions of any mode of knowledge which treats practices or works as symbolic facts, finished products, to be deciphered by reference to a code (which may be called culture). ... It would not be difficult to show that the construction of the concept of culture ... similarly implies the construction of a notion of conduct as execution which coexists with the primary notion of conduct as simple behaviour taken at face value. (Bourdieu, *Outline of a Theory of Practice* 24)

More precisely, Bourdieu calls this a "detemporalizing effect" that is imposed on practice. For Bourdieu, the dismissal of temporality in social science[26] has the effect of totalizing situations when analyzing them, disregarding the embeddedness of the situation in a temporal context. Instead, he claims "to restore to practice its practical truth, we must therefore reintroduce time into the theoretical representation of a practice which, being temporally structured, is intrinsically defined by its tempo" (*Outline of a Theory of Practice* 8).

> Practice unfolds in time and it has all the correlative properties, such as irreversibility, that synchronization destroys. Its temporal structure, that is, its rhythm, its tempo, either acceleration or slowing down, subjects it to a destructuration that is irreducible to a simple change in an axis of reference. In short, because it is entirely immersed in the current of time, practice is inseparable from temporality, not only because it is played out in time, but also because it plays strategically with time and especially with tempo. (*The Logic of Practice* 81)

There is an element of linearity in both theories, although their very rigid structural outlines might suggest that. But this is not a linearity that unveils a hierarchy of social order or a chronology of its evolu-

---

26 Here, Bourdieu directly contradicts Max Weber who thinks that time is not important for the analysis of a situation when arriving after the situation occurred (Bourdieu, *Outline of a Theory of Practice* 9).

tion (this would be counterproductive to their common understanding of the social as being able to reproduce itself continuously), and the linear component I would like to highlight is that of consecutiveness of events, of occurrences.

Bourdieu and Luhmann set out from the idea of linearity when it comes to how consciousness deals with the complexity of social structures. Luhmann introduces the fundamental distinction between social and psychic systems in order to differentiate between society and social groups communicating according to their roles and functions and the self with its consciousness and individual modes of perception. "The social system places its own complexity, which has stood the test of communicative manageability, at the psychic system's disposal" (*Social Systems* 272). The individual consciousness has to deal with the relationship between structure and process within social systems, which is a continuous process of selection that constantly reduces, but also produces complexity. In relation to that, the psychic system reacts in "temporalizing the society system's complexity" (*Social Systems* 271). Something only becomes visible and graspable for the psychic system when there is a process of distinction, differentiation and selection. Bourdieu similarly defines the nature of practice as "an essentially linear series" (*The Logic of Practice* 83) when it comes to its meaning production. However, it is important to point out that linearity is not analogous to chronology: It consists of "practical time, which is made up of islands of incommensurable duration, each with its own rhythm, a time that races or drags, depending on what one is doing, that is, on the functions assigned to it by the actions that are performed in it" (*The Logic of Practice* 84). It is a quality of linearity that a perspective can be generated from any perceivable moment. This forms part of the production of the social. Bourdieu and Luhmann's formulation of the social and its formation are tightly bound up with time, with actuality and with ongoing events. There is as much a process of production involved as there is of reflection, of observation and action, and of presentation and representation.

Communication as a Form of Practice: the Möbius Effect

I have outlined the theoretical dispositions of Luhmann's and Bourdieu's articulations and explorations regarding the emergence of the social. Now it is time to ask what the ramifications are of bringing the two theories together. They display similarities not so much in their terminologies as in their approach to the conditions and possibilities of the production of the social. Both highlight the proximity between the production of the social and the conditions that enable it. This "recursive and reciprocal process," as I characterized it earlier, employs a Möbius effect: While structures and systems provide the framework for distinctions and selections, those distinctions and selections are (in accordance with the concepts of the habitus and double contingency) reproductive of the structures and systems.

To apply such a description of practice to curating as a structural and processual disposition sheds light on the function curating assumes within the field of cultural production. Before looking into how this disposition also affects the curatorial as a form of knowledge production, the terminologies of practice and communication will be clarified in order to show their mutual dependency for curating.

For Bourdieu, practice,

> always implies a cognitive operation, a practical operation of construction which sets to work by reference to practical functions, systems of classification (taxonomies) which organize perception and structure practice. Produced by the practice of successive generations, in conditions of existence of a determinate type, these schemes of perception, appreciation, and action, which are acquired through practice and applied in their practical state without acceding to explicit representation, function as practical operators through which the objective structures of which they are the product tend to reproduce themselves in practices. (*Outline of a Theory of Practice* 97)

For Luhmann the,

> elementary process constituting the social domain as a special reality is a process of communication. In order to steer itself, however, this process must be reduced to action, decomposed into actions. Accordingly, social systems are not built up of actions, as if these actions were produced on the basis of the organico-psychic constitution of human beings and could exist by themselves; instead social systems are broken down into actions, and by this reduction acquire the basis for connections that serve to continue the course of communication. (*Social Systems* 139)

Bourdieu and Luhmann define practice and communication as operations intrinsic to how the social comes about. Both communication and practice reproduce their own structures every time they are performed in action by means of double contingency and habitus. These concepts have a very important function in that they provide connectivity and probability. For Bourdieu, the habitus "functions like a self-regulating device programmed to redefine courses of action in accordance with information received on the reception of information transmitted and on the effects of produced by that transformation" (*Outline of a Theory of Practice* 11). Similarly, for Luhmann, double contingency "founders upon the problem of complexity and the necessarily selective reduction of complexity that is steered self-referentially within the system" (*Social Systems* 107). The fact that both models have a self-referential and recursive character makes them different from almost any other dialectical model. The idea of result as something that puts an end to a process is absolutely abandoned. The self-organization of this model of practice is assured through the endlessness of communication.

The notion of practice exemplifying a Möbius effect, a recursive self-referencing loop, first emerged as a subject for analysis when exploring Michael Fullerton's exhibition *Columbia*, suggesting that the relationship between works and viewer is conditioned upon such a feedback loop as a principle of self-organization of communication in the exhibition space as a device for the production of knowledge. The analysis of the process of communication that was installed by Fullerton through the different elements that constituted the exhibition (i.e. text, images, the process of communication itself as material in the dialogue between viewer and artwork) provided for a claim around knowledge production in which knowledge is defined not as a thing or a series of facts, but as a network of relations that are built and negotiated in the communicative space of the exhibition. In particular, the artist negates the direct transformation of information to knowledge by implementing the element of suspicion, which initiates a process of knowledge production that is not a result of interpretation, but is conditional upon it. For Fullerton, suspicion functions as a self-regulating device for pursuing knowledge production as a composition of ideas, works, materials, etc., constituting the exhibition as realm in which knowledge production emerges through the condition of sociality.

The Potosí Principle exhibition is a similar case, even though the means used to arrive at a production of knowledge are quite different. It might appear that the abundance of information on the history of Potosí is a realm of knowledge imposed on the viewer. But the curators of the exhibition framed the works and installations with a critical and suspicious attitude towards the cultural conditioning of knowledge production in systems of power (government, religion, etc.). They invited the viewer to partake in critically addressing the production of meaning. Absolutely central to the exhibition was the question of how meaning is constructed and how it assumes a relevance that is not only a result of specific relations and connections, but also conditional upon sociality as a requirement for knowledge production.

In Luhmann's and Bourdieu's definition of communication and practice the motor of sociality is not something that can be added in order to make communication and practice function, but is implicit in the way these concepts have been constructed, relying as they do on the self-reference of double contingency and the habitus. With the help of Luhmann's and Bourdieu's theoretical concepts it is possible to define a process of formation as practice that is concerned with knowledge production inclusive of structure and process, observation and action, and production and reflection. However, a concurrentness of production and reflection constituted by recursivity does not imply that such a model of practice is entirely immanent and only serves to reproduce itself. Its generative function towards the production of sociality on the conditions of its reflexive nature provides for a perspective on artistic and curatorial practices having a transformative function that results from an understanding of the materialities that effect the production of sociality in the curated encounter. If we understand curating as a practice responding to the oscillation between structures and actions set up in the exhibition space, then any transformative function of the knowledge it produces is not a matter of the application of something within the exhibition space to what is outside of it, but a matter of negotiating the materialities involved in processing it. Sociality, in such intellectual conception, is understood to be performed and thereby produced in terms of "path building" or "order making" activities (Bennett and Joyce 4), not determined by otherwise predetermined structures, but of all those involved in building relations and communicating via the building of relations in the curated encounter. Beyond any artworks and their contextualizations, sociality is the material with which curating as a practice of communication deals. The forms of sociality that it produces and administers through its processes of knowledge production are not bound to their place of origin but exist in the ways their communicability and connectivity acquires a new structural value for a further building of relations that can—in other social contexts—reassume a generative function via their materiality towards the production of sociality. To constitute this material register as an important dimension for exploring the curated encounter, and specifically here the communicative space of the exhibition, serves to appreciate a hitherto under-theorized dimension of the curated encounter as a space of social ordering and form of cultural production.

However, in this context it would be farfetched to derive a definition of curatorial practices from these observations, particularly because the corresponding concepts of spectatorship and relationality have not yet been discussed. But from having looked at particular examples in which artists and curators not only actively engaged the viewers and participants at their exhibitions in processes of knowledge production, but also made them the source of processes of knowledge production, there emerges a concept of epistemic practices based on a system of organization and manifestation that is generative of its own social, political, and cultural conditions. Such system of organization through processes of communication can thus attempt to manifest a relevance of what is produced beyond its specific politics of installation, which is to conceive of art as a device for knowledge production and the curated encounter as a medium for the production of sociality by shedding light on its material dispositions in terms of the relations that are being produced in and by them.

The Discursive Model of Practice

Enquiring into the function of communicative processes taking place in the exhibition space remains an unfulfilled task if there is no discussion of the notion of spectatorship. While the analyses of exhibitions in the previous chapter looked at the ways in which objects, actors, and spaces are brought together into a relation and also determined the functioning of these relations referring to theories of social action, spectatorship was not addressed in any more detail than through a description of its active and participatory role in the process of knowledge production. In isolation, however, this concept is subject to a series of debates, particularly in relation to artistic and curatorial practices that dismiss the exhibition space with the intention of preventing passive forms of spectatorship and linear modes of knowledge production.

This chapter discusses a series of projects that purposely move away from the exhibition space in order to differentiate from, circumvent, and subvert the ways in which spectatorship is conditioned, often restrictively, by the confrontational relationship between viewer and works customary to the exhibition space. The selected works are Manifesta 6, unitednationsplaza, and *Night School*, a series of independent yet consecutive projects between 2006 and 2010 initiated by American Russian-born artist Anton Vidokle in collaboration with artists, theorists, writers, etc. The dismissal of the exhibition as a communicative space in the examples discussed entails an exploration of dematerialized media in contemporary artistic and curatorial practice that transform form, content, and modes of presentation of art, altering the roles of institutions, their political agendas, and their social function. The analysis further refines the notion of the communicative space by looking at how the discursive provides a model of practice and a concept of space.

From Communication to Interaction

The selected projects are mainly concerned with the transformation of the role of the spectator from observer to participant, an active stakeholder in processes of communication and interpretation in the space of contention with art. This is no longer the exhibition space, but might be a seminar room, a bar, an office, a kitchen, or any other space in which people meet to talk, discuss, and debate. Nonetheless, the exemplarily formulated opposition of observers and participants must give way to a much more nuanced consideration of the nature of spectatorship, particularly in view of the numerous debates pertaining to curatorial and contemporary art discourse in the recent decades surrounding "discursive" (Wilson), "educational" (Rogoff, "Turning"; O'Neill and Wilson), and "social" (Bishop, "The Social Turn"; Bang Larsen 92–95) turns. Especially with regard to the previous chapter, which described artistic and curatorial strategies and methodologies of inciting the viewer to become an active partner in the communicative situation created, selected concepts of spectatorship, audience formation, and public are here subjected to further discussion in order to situate the examples described in the complex discursive formations to which they belong, and which they reflect and produce in their practices.

A consideration of Jacques Rancière's *The Emancipated Spectator* will be followed by a short introduction to the argument surrounding Nicholas Bourriaud's *Relational Aesthetics* (Bishop, "Antagonism and Relational Aesthetics"; Bishop, "The Social Turn"; Kester, "Another Turn"; Bishop and Gillick 95–107) that brought the debate on socially engaged artistic practices to broad public attention and further discussion. Manifesta 6, unitednationsplaza, and *Night School* are addressed as examples for discussing the social dimensions of knowledge production. Conditions of sociality as emerging from the projects will be contrasted with how art's social dimension is articulated in contemporary curatorial discourse. Emphasis is placed on different forms of defining the relationship between what is often, superficially, called "the social," on the one hand, and artistic practices, on the other, in order to look into claims of public engagement and the production of collectivity in discursive practices. Much of the discussion around a social function of art is directly related to investigations into forms of political agency that can be assumed by not only the artists, but all participants in the processes of communication set out in discursive practices. For this reason, the analysis contains references to Bruno Latour's notions of "gathering" and "reassembling the social" in the context of actor-network theory (ANT) with the purpose of advancing the idea of knowledge production emerging on the conditions of sociality.

The Emancipated Spectator

In his recent publication on contemporary curatorial thought Terry Smith asserts that "spectatorship is the next major category of agency in the art world" (236). This claim is not, however, the beginning of an enquiry into what kind of agency spectatorship would entail. Rather, it is the conclusion to a general review on activist curatorial practices that directly reshape the viewers' role as "prosumers," "consumers of art becoming participant producers" (Smith 237).[27] Although my approach to disambiguating a notion of spectatorship follows a reverse order of argument to Smith's, it also affirms a correlation between spectatorship and agency. However, my interest lies in a more nuanced definition of the condition for knowledge production that the prosumer concept would entail.

Jacques Rancière's *The Emancipated Spectator* became widely discussed for its redefining of spectatorship, particularly with respect to participatory and performative artistic practices. The essay was first published in Artforum (2007) before appearing in a publication of the same name alongside further investigations into the political efficacy of art and imagery (2009). The French thinker elaborates on a notion of emancipated spectatorship by discussing models of engaged spectatorship (that with which the spectator is confronted) in theatre, such as Bertolt Brecht's *epic theatre* (Brecht 13–29) and Antonin Artaud's *theatre of cruelty* (Artaud 89–101, 122–33) as well as with the notion of the spectacle itself (Debord 12–17). Rancière articulates a paradox here: There is no theatre without spectators, but the spectator is "separated from the capacity of knowing just as he is separated from the possibility of acting" ("The Emancipated Spectator" [*Artforum*] 272). Brecht, Artaud and Debord defy understandings of theatre as forms of representation that the passive spectator merely consumes. Instead they proclaim theatre as a forum for active participants. Rancière, however, calls into question a number of presuppositions based on these theories from the field of Marxist social and cultural critique. He casts doubt on the equivalence of theatre and community; seeing and passivity; mediation and simu-

---

27 Smith reviews a number of examples of what he calls "engaged, activist curating." For example, *The Interventionist: Art in the Social Sphere* (2004), co-curated by Nato Thompson and Greg Sholette at MassMoCa, or *This is What Democracy Looks Like!* (2011), curated by Keith Miller at New York University's Gallatin Gallery (232–37).

lacrum; and the opposition of collective and individual. And most importantly of all, he casts doubt on the idea that spectatorship is a form of passivity that should be "turned into activity" (Rancière, "The Emancipated Spectator" [*Artforum*] 272). Instead, "it is our normal situation" (279). Rancière sees a fundamental foundation of inequality in how Brecht and Artaud try to convey forms of equality by conceiving of theatre as a pedagogical realm for the transmission of knowledge. The radical instructions that force an active engagement of the spectator only serve to further manifest an insurmountable distance between the schoolmaster and the ignorant, even though "in the pedagogical process the role of the schoolmaster is posited as the act of suppressing the distance between his knowledge and the ignorance of the ignorant" (Rancière, "The Emancipated Spectator" [*Artforum*] 274).

Rancière does not discard the idea of the spectator's participation and performativity, instead arriving at its realization by different means, namely by recognizing distance "as the normal condition of communication ... dismissing the opposition between looking and acting and understanding that the distribution of the visible itself is part of the configuration of domination and subjection" (275). Here, the activity of looking has a modifying capacity in the sense that its processes of interpretation are already means of transformation and forms of reconfiguration of such distribution. Rancière specifically addresses the dramaturge's intention for the spectator to see, feel and understand particularities of what is presented, and sees this position as aligning with that of the master who conceives of his realm of practice as one of "equal, undistorted transmission" (277). For the role of the curator or organizer Rancière's proposal of emancipated spectatorship means to not presuppose that the processes of communication entail forms of knowledge transmission or a cause-and-effect principle of learning.

Equally problematic, in Rancière's view, are those forms of practice that, subsequent to an understanding of the realm of the theatre as a space of production of affect, have thought of forms of active participation on the part of the viewer that result in a "gathering of an unseparate community" (278). Rancière is skeptical of the idea of theatre as a specifically communitarian place, since "the collective power that is common to these spectators is not the status of members of a collective body" (278). Instead, their collective power is their ability to translate what they are looking at in their own way. According to Rancière, emancipated spectatorship is a capacity external to viewing—but also its "normal situation"—which works through "unpredictable and irreducible distances" and a "play of associations and dissociations" (279).

The emancipatory effect of this concept of spectatorship becomes obvious when acknowledging that Rancière is writing from the perspective of class distinctions; the agency of spectatorship belongs to everybody, and not to a particular class. That which is seen and interpreted can lead to a "redistribution of the sensible," which is an a priori law that conditions the possibility of perception according to its social, political, and cultural predicaments (*The Politics of Aesthetics*), blurring "the opposition between those who look and those who act, between those who are individuals and those who are members of a collective body" ("The Emancipated Spectator" [*Artforum*] 279).

The idea of emancipation as a process of "collectivizing our capacities invested in scenes of dissensus" (Rancière, *The Emanicpated Spectator* 124) becomes important when examining the function of spectatorship in relation to its social, cultural, and political conditioning as explored in discursive practices. They can be viewed as analogous to participatory forms of theatrical practices that Rancière describes as interested in disrupting the traditional distribution of places ("The Emancipated Spectator" [*Artforum*] 278). A question that Rancière only touches upon is in what way a collective body can be produced with an element of communality inherent to it rather than prescribed to it.

This chapter dwells in detail on this question throughout the analysis of unitednationsplaza. Rancière's conclusive proposition of emancipated spectatorship issuing a "community of storytellers and translators" ("The Emancipated Spectator" [*Artforum*] 280) is, however, far too vague. It does not further define the processes of translation referred to or discuss what function stories assume for the production of knowledge. It is in the conditions that Rancière formulates for art to assume a political and social function that his work is important for how different actors relate to each other in communicative space. His "aesthetic break" is a condition for art to produce political effects, a condition that entails a rupture of artistic cause and political effect. Another condition for emancipatory spectatorship is a level of indeterminacy of the image. The "pensive image" generates thinking processes that cannot be attributed to the intention of its producer and have an effect on the viewer without establishing a fixed relation to a particular object (Rancière, *The Emancipated Spectator* 107).

Introducing Rancière's notion of emancipated spectatorship to discursive practices that do not rest upon the production of images makes tangible a certain level of paradoxicality in Rancière's thinking. On the one hand, Rancière outlines forms of direct relationing between spaces of experience and what is installed in them, while on the other, he argues for an intrinsic element of rupture between the aesthetic and political regime. This becomes particularly apparent when looking at how Nicholas Bourriaud responds to Rancière in the context of how his conception of relational aesthetics has met criticism from the French philosopher and other intellectuals.

Relational Aesthetics

In 1998 Bourriaud published the widely discussed essay "Relational Aesthetics," in which he describes the work of artists such as Rirkrit Tiravanija, Liam Gillick, Vanessa Beecroft, Philippe Pareno, and Douglas Gordon as concerned with the changing systems of social relations, taking as their horizon "the realm of human interactions and its social context, rather than the assertion of an independent and private symbolic space" (*Relational Aesthetics* 14). From a contextualization of these works, specifically regarding their "form" as encounter, or as Bourriaud prefers to say, "formation" (structures with independent sets of inner dependencies that resemble typical features of everyday life), the French curator derives a particular characteristic that sparked controversy amongst many in the fields of art theory, curatorial discourse, philosophy and sociology.

> As part of a "relationist" theory of art, inter-subjectivity does not only represent the social setting for the reception of art, which is its "environment," its "field" (Bourdieu), but also becomes the quintessence of artistic practice. (Bourriaud, *Relational Aesthetics* 22)

Critiques of Bourriaud's concept of relational aesthetics coincide in the accusation directed at Bourriaud that he did not differentiate between what the work emphasizes and what it produces, meaning that even if a work emphasizes the role of dialogue and negotiation this does not presuppose that those relationships also define the work's content. Rancière criticizes Bourriaud for confusing the realm of production with that of reception, which consequently entails the dissolution of inter-subjectivity in communality. This criticism comes on the back of Rancière's own account of the political effectiveness of art and its ability to issue social transformation. For Rancière, the radical autonomy of the "aesthetic regime" of art is that is has no utilitarian or representative function (Rancière, *The Politics of Aesthetics* 23). Relational art is problematic to him, since it conflates political forms of collective actions with punctual and symbolical subversions of the system, which is how Rancière characterizes the artistic practices Bourriaud discusses. Bourriaud, in turn, criticizes Rancière for overlooking the formal dimensions of works such as Tiravanija's installations of soup kitchens, and accuses the philosopher of arguing on the basis of a conservative notion of art that locates an emancipatory potential only in its difference and distance from activist tendencies (Bourriaud, "Precarious Constructions" 22).

The particularities of their respective critiques obfuscate the core question and problematic that both theories discuss. How does art configure a relationship to the world in such a way that its production constitutes its reception but does not determine it and, in turn, have its reception respect the particularities of the work but not depend on them? This question addresses the degrees of autonomy produced in communicative spaces for all stakeholders involved in partaking in the production of discursive formations. It also serves to differentiate between levels of individual and collective autonomy, particularly with regard to how the latter is proclaimed as a product of a transformative social function of art.

For discursive practices, the category of the work needs to be rethought and reformulated in a way that accords with its dematerialized status, which is crucially important for situating the curated encounter in the context of the commodification of knowledge production.

Simon Sheikh gives a precise account of the double process at stake:

> Since the 1960s, with the advent of minimal sculpture, conceptual art and site specific practices, art institutions have had to take the double process of dematerialization of the art object on the one hand and the so called expanded field of art practices on the other, into account. Which, in turn, has led to the establishing of new public platforms and formats, not just exhibition venues, but also the pro-

duction of exhibitions in different types of venues, as well as creating venues that are not primarily for exhibition. The crucial shift that cannot be emphasized enough is accurately best described as "art conquering space" by Chevrier, who has written of how this conquest has facilitated a shift in emphasis from the production and display of art objects to what he calls "public things." Whereas the object stands in relation to objectivity, and thus apart from the subject, the thing cannot be reduced to a single relation, or type of relation. (Sheikh "Objects of Study")

To perceive the product as a thing introduces processes of constant renegotiation of the positionalities assumed by stakeholders in the discursive formations built into the process of communication. In addition to such renegotiations of positionalities (spectatorship, audience conceptions, public address) the ethical and political quality of the discursive as a model of practice is in need for deliberation. Sheikh sheds light on the conflictive situation confronting dematerialized artistic practices. Their intention to reflect on the meanings of art—its social and political responsibility and function within the sphere of cultural production—led to forms of discursive practices that seek to evade processes of commodification while simultaneously caught up in them.

> We can then, perhaps, talk of a linguistic turn, meaning that language and (inter)textuality have become increasingly privileged and important, in art practice, the staging of the discourses around art, the aestheticization of discourse, and the new knowledge-based industries such as marketing, PR and services. Similarly, and also simultaneously, as art has become dematerialized and expanded, labour itself has become dematerialized and expanded, we could say, and production shifted towards a cultural industry and the so-called knowledge economy. (Sheikh "Objects of Study")

What is subject to processes of commodification in the knowledge economy is not a particular relation that is produced in discursive formations, but the element of relationality itself, which lies in the recursivity intrinsic to processes of relation-building in discursive art practices.

However, Claire Bishop refers to such recursivity as the political quality in relational forms of artistic practices. "Rather than suggesting that the only good art is political art, the essay was moving toward what I understand Rosalind Krauss to mean by 'recursivity' (i.e. a structure in which some of the elements of a work produce the rules that generate the structure itself)" (Bishop and Gillick 107). Bishop seeks to more precisely define the functioning of relationality. She criticizes Bourriaud for perceiving the quality of relational art as solely bound to its environment of production. "Relational art sets up situations in which viewers are not just addressed as a collective, social entity, but are actually given the wherewithal to create a community, however temporary or utopian this may be" ("Antagonism and Relational Aesthetics" 54). Instead, she locates the political quality—the socially and culturally transformative function of a work—in the interdependency of the structures that enable the building of relations with the processes that condition it. Bishop is critical of how Bourriaud defines the spatial and temporal constellations of an artwork as the basis of its political significance, since this conception not only disregards any level of recursivity between production and reception, but also ignores the level of reception entirely. This in turn identifies participation not as an active engagement in the realm of reception (formerly the environment of spectatorship) but as part of the artist's practice. Futhermore, she accuses Bourriaud of equating "aesthetic judgment with an ethicopolitical judgment of the relationships produced by a work of art" as Bourriaud fails to address the quality of the relationships established by relational art (Bishop, "Antagonism and Relational Aesthetics" 56–63).

The following discussion of examples from the realm of discursive art practices—primarily unitednationsplaza—is situated in a complex and paradoxical landscape. Given the way in which recursivity was articulated as a condition for the emergence of sociality, in the context of artistic practices fostering relation-building processes recursivity assumes a dual function—both positive and negative. While Bishop refers to recursivity as a condition for a political quality of relational art practices, Sheikh defines its dematerialized status as particularly responsive to forms of co-optation by the knowledge economy.

This chapter addresses this conundrum associated with practice and discusses the examples from both perspectives, particularly in the context of ultimately proposing a material turn for artistic and curatorial practices for finding ways to counter forms of co-optation and recuperation in and by the knowledge economy. Therefore discursive art practices are examined in the context of the interrelations and interdependencies of the history of artistic practices and their social and political function and relevances, institutional politics, the commodification of immaterialities in contemporary cultural production and the knowledge economy. However, the notion of materiality is not being proposed in clear opposition to the immaterial, but as a mode of thinking through and negotiating the complexity of how artistic and curatorial practices can produce sociality and thereby issue political relevance for cultural production within the increasingly dematerialized knowledge economy.

Particular attention is paid to the demise of the exhibition space and claims of its loss of political affect. Hence, the preceding introduction to the notion of emancipated spectatorship served as a transition from discussing the role of the viewer in the communicative space of the exhibition in the previous chapter to taking the element of recursivity into a context of dematerialized discursive art practices that foster a social and political engagement of art with the world that is otherwise neglected.

Unitednationsplaza—From the Exhibitionary to the Discursive

Unitednationsplaza is a highly complex example in that it reflects on cultural, social and political issues while challenging many assumptions that underlie the contemporary discourse surrounding artistic and curatorial practices. These include the disambiguation of the roles of curator and artist, the exhibition space, institutional practices, the notion of the public, and art as a medium of critique and social transformation.

Unitednationsplaza was an independent event-based programme of talks, lectures, workshops, and screenings set up in 2006 by e-flux, a collective publishing, artistic and curatorial enterprise with Anton Vidokle acting here as its main protagonist in collaboration with Boris Groys, Jalal Toufic, Liam Gillick, Martha Rosler, Natascha Sadr Haghighian, Nikolaus Hirsch, Tirdad Zolghadr, and Walid Raad. It was an experimental series of seminars lasting twelve months and involving around one hundred artists, writers, philosophers and audience members. Hosted in a building on Berlin's Platz der Vereinten Nationen (United Nations Plaza), the project gained its name when Liam Gillick placed the lettering unitednationsplaza upside down on the outside of the building (Uchill 33; fig. 20). Inside the former supermarket office building various spaces were furnished with a modlar system by architects Nikolaus Hirsch, John Lau and Michel

Müller, whose elements could be configured to facilitate all sorts of different activities: talking, listening, showing, reading, looking, cooking, drinking, dancing, etc. "The spatial concept of unitednationsplaza investigates the ambivalent character of the contemporary art institution," presenting different models of institutions such as galleries, theatres and schools ("Unitednationsplaza"; fig. 21–22). The audiences—sometimes large, sometimes small—were mostly made up of international artists or art world figures living in Berlin.

The project itself can neither be analysed outside of the context from which it emerged, nor without taking into account how it transformed after the session in Berlin during 2006 and 2007 and its condensed, one-month version in Mexico in March 2008. It is therefore important to consider unitednationsplaza as one project in a string of events that took place between 2006 and 2010, starting with Manifesta 6, the biennial curated by Mai Abu El Dahab, Anton Vidokle and Florian Waldvogel—which was scheduled to take place in Cyprus in 2006 but never happened—and ending with *Night School*, a version of unitednationsplaza realized at the New Museum in New York in 2008 and 2009.

Manifesta 6 School

> The Manifesta 6 School is a pretext, an excuse and an opportunity. It is a pretext for questioning and possibly challenging the methods of the institutionalized art world. It is an excuse to bring together inspiring thinkers and cultural producers to invigorate the position of art, and cultural production at large. It is a great opportunity for a wealth of critical endeavours: looking at the role of art institutions as participants in cultural policymaking; questioning the role of artists as defined by the institutional climate in which they practice and produce; revealing the power positions that legitimize the prevailing elitism; looking at culture's entanglement with the pressures and demands of corporate globalization. And, finally, asking what kind of education do we as art professionals need today in order to play an effective role in the world? (El Dahab 2)

The idea of initiating an art school instead of curating an exhibition took centre stage right from the beginning, when, in early 2005, curators Mai Abu El Dahab, Florian Waldvogel, and artist Anton Vidokle responded to the open call initiated by the Manifesta Foundation in Amsterdam for appointing a team of curators for the 2006 biennial

Fig. 20: View of the unitednationsplaza building by day,
with addition by Liam Gillick, at Berlin's Platz der Vereinten Nationen.
Berlin, 2006. Courtesy e-flux.

Fig. 21: Unitednationsplaza's modular architecture inside the former
supermarket office, designed by Nikolaus Hirsch and Michel Müller.
Berlin, 2006. Courtesy e-flux.

Fig. 22: Concept of modular architecture for unitednationsplaza proposing different forms of use. Architecture by Nikolaus Hirsch and Michel Müller. Team: Nikolaus Hirsch, John Lau, Michel Müller. Photo: Michel Müller.

scheduled to take place in Nicosia, Cyprus. The Manifesta 6 School was envisioned as a temporary institution comprising three departments[28]—each led by one member of the curatorial team—and the plan was for it to take place in both parts of the divided city of Nicosia, in both the Greek and Turkish sectors. Various activities were set to take place over the twelve-week duration of the biennial: lectures, screenings, performances, publication launches, exhibitions, radio and television programmes, symposiums, workshops, and so on. Alongside members of the local or general public, those involved was to include 90 people who had been selected for each department following an open call that was widely published by the Manifesta Foundation and advertised on e-flux. The "exhibition-as-school" concept articulated a desire to move away from the space of the exhibition towards the more discursive space of the school. The reasons with which all members of the curatorial team manifested this desire—and thereby elaborated on the concept of the school as a discursive medium—either focused on the school as a medium for an enhanced educational experience, or on the element of the discur-

---

28　The first department was overseen by Mai Abu El Dahab and was set up to look at different forms of agency and modes of participation within the cultural field, with particular interest in the power structures of public institutions, academia, media, and other forms of organizations that operate on a socio-political scale. The second department was led by Anton Vidokle and centred on topics such as the entanglement of cultural production with politics of progress and the ethical/aesthetic value of incorporating subjectivity into the classical Marxist equation (this was supposed to happen in a school in the Turkish part of Nicosia). The third department was set up mainly to operate online. Florian Waldvogel supervised its intended focus on the production of knowledge and meaning in the context of Cyprus as a complex political reality and specific location, both on a social, and individual level.

sive as a different mode of production for art practices.[29] What unit-ednationsplaza inherited from the Manifesta 6 School concept was not the structure of the school with its three departments, its themes or its realization within a three-month timeframe. Rather, it took from it an ambition and an intention to explore alternative ways to the framework of the exhibition as a construct for thinking about art as a catalyst of the cultural, social and political histories that condition its production and reception.

> But what precisely does it mean, the desire that art should enter all aspects of social life? Is it a desire to bring art out of rarefied and privileged spaces, or is it merely a move towards the further instru-mentalization of art practice? Perhaps the exhibition is not the place to start. One must begin at the beginning. The Manifesta team pro-posed going back to school. (Vidokle, "Exhibition as School" 8)

Vidokle saw the potential of this proposal in that it offers much more than a process of learning.

> An art school is not concerned solely with the process of learning, but can be and often is a highly active site of cultural production: books and magazines, exhibitions, new commissioned works, semi-nars and symposia, film screenings, concerts, performances, theatre productions, new fashion and product designs ... these and many other activities and projects can all be triggered in a school. I say "trig-gered" rather than "located at" or "based in" to draw attention to the danger pointed out by Paulo Freire, who wisely cautioned against po-sitioning school as a privileged or an exclusive site of "knowledge pro-duction," which only reaffirms existing social inequalities and hierar-chies. The activities of the Manifesta 6 School are an attempt to infiltrate the space of the city, to transform it and be transformed by it. ("Exhibition as School" 4)

---

29 I am referring here mainly to a set of writings by Vidokle ("From Exhibition to School") together with various collaborators (El Dahab et al.; Rosler and Vi-dokle; Vidokle and Zolghadr) or presentations of unitednationsplaza and *Night School* at symposiums (Vidokle, "Art Without Artists?"; Vidokle, *New York Conversations*), in which Vidokle recalled his intentions, described the project and responded to its critics. Shortly after the end of *Night School* in 2009, Vi-dokle commissioned a selection of essays by Liam Gillick, Maria Lind, Monika Szewczyk, and Jan Verwoert reflecting on unitednationsplaza and *Night School* as well as on his artistic practice in general (*Produce, Distribute*).

The divided city of Nicosia on Cyprus, however, never saw this transformation take place. The school's plan to hold events in both parts of the city led to a number of political conflicts that drew in the biennial's organizer Nicosia for Art Ltd. (a nonprofit organization owned by the Municipality of Nicosia and set up to run the project) and the International Manifesta Foundation based in Amsterdam. In a press statement published on 6 June 2006 on e-flux, the curators stated that their contract was terminated by the Mayor of Nicosia on 1 June 2006, effective immediately. This decision was taken due to a variety of alleged breaches on their part, including their apparent unwillingness to mediate the conflicted situation of the school taking place in both parts of Nicosia so as to reach an amicable compromise allowing the project to be realized. The curators defended themselves by making clear that any form of disagreement should not be resolved by compromising and thereby obstructing the dissemination of ideas and impeding artistic production. While acknowledging the politically conflicted situation of organizing a project in a divided city (the contractual agreements made with the local authorities had always defined the project as bicommunal) the curators felt that the opportunity to realize Manifesta 6 in only one section of the city would mean a profound change to the initial concept that they would not and could not accept. Manifesta 6 was therefore cancelled.

The debates sparked during the process of cancellation and in its aftermath concentrated on the reasons behind the biennial being cancelled, on how the conflicted political situation came to affect the realization of the Manifesta 6 School. But they also engaged with the subject of the concept of the school's potential for becoming a problem-solving strategy for political conflict. It is curator Mai Abu El Dahab who takes a self-critical stance here, judging the project's intention to work bi-communally to be a "naive problem-solving strategy that ignores similar contrived attempts that have always fallen short as they repeatedly underestimate the complexity of this longstanding reality" (3). Behind this argument lies the understanding that the local context needs to be the matter from which any conceptualization of an international biennial emanates. Therefore the conflicted political situation of the divided city of Nicosia as the location for the biennial is a situation that for Vidokle demands not "commentary, but involvement and production" ("Exhibition as School" 9).

This demand is not exclusive to the Manifesta 6 School, but a central concern to Vidokle's artistic practice. In a collection of essays, editor Brian Sholis puts forward two parameters that characterize Vidokle's artistic practice:

> The first characteristic is the self-effacing nature of his endeavours. Not only are many of his projects subsumed under an anonymous/ sounding corporate identity, e-flux, but they are also nearly always collaborative. ... The second quality is his relative freedom from the network of institutions that is generally believed to confer legitimacy upon individual artistic practices. (Sholis 7)

Anton Vidokle was one of the founders of e-flux, a collective publishing enterprise, artistic project and curatorial platform, which started as a newsletter information service for the art world in 1998. Today, e-flux is much more than a news feed, it functions as a framework for an online platform incorporating the e-flux Journal, and e-flux Projects realizing exhibitions and other projects such as *Time/Bank* all over the world and in cooperation with major institutions, including Documenta 13. The e-flux news service derives revenue from the fees paid by institutions to have their press releases or announcements mailed out to about 70.000 members of the art world. This is often used to fund the projects, amongst them unitednationsplaza. This institutional self-sufficiency is often at the centre of debates around Vidokle's role as an artist/entrepreneur. As Tirdad Zolghadr summarized: "e-flux sparks debates that are heated and polarized. ... To some, e-flux represents the ultimate model of artistic emancipation; to others, a culmination of art-as-business." Conceptually, Vidokle frames his projects through his role as an artist rather organizer, a position that Zolghadr finds "cogent."

Unitednationsplaza is an example of Vidokle's independence from institutions when financing and disseminating his artistic practice, enabling him to create a public discourse that serves to critically address, interrogate, and validate his practice. The aforementioned demand of involvement and production can thus be understood in another way: as the process-based form of self-reflexivity with which Vidokle makes his own involvement in every aspect of production the subject of his artistic practice. It should be noted that what might be interpreted as a form of control mania is paired with an emphasis on the collaborative nature of his practice.

The Discursive Model of Practice

Unitednationsplaza created a communicative space for relationships to develop over time with a set of different roles and responsibilities involved that can nevertheless all be incorporated in the notion of "the participant." The project was conceived in opposition to what Ferguson calls the "standard story" (176), a straightforward definition of the institution or the curator being the host of an exhibition in which the art object is as much a guest as the viewer, with no or only little agency. Vidokle explores the discursive model of practice as an alternative to the framework of the exhibition with regards to how art can function as a catalyst of the cultural, social, and political histories conditioning its production and reception. Vidokle saw the potential of the discursive model of practice as "a highly active site of cultural production" ("Exhibition as School" 9). He emphasizes the idea of space triggering processes of transformation rather than being viewed as a secluded and privileged site for knowledge production. It is with regard to the potential of discursivity as a spatial activity that Vidokle wants unitednationsplaza to be a transformative project. This prompts the question of how relations between participants are spatially configured and what processes of transformation take place in them or are subject to them.

Revised Relations

The relationship between space, people, and things that Vidokle configures in unitednationsplaza is first and foremost a proposition to leave behind the communicative space of the exhibition. Maria Lind paraphrases unitednationsplaza's intention and ambition in the form of a question: "How can we think things differently, form the points of view of formats and protocols, methods, and procedures?" ("Dilemmas" 22). Vidokle points to a loss of the potential of the exhibition as a communicative space. Somewhere in the process of the institutionalization of the exhibition as a medium for knowledge production the "possibility of the audience having an active stake in the situation" is lost, or at least severely diminished ("From Exhibition to School" 198). In contrast, curator Anselm Franke believes that the taking over of exhibitions' responsibility for generating the conditions for viewers to assume agency is a framework that entails "a sort of atmospheric, all-around dynamism in which entire subjects, if not worlds, are animated ... creating zones of contact between subjects and 'worlds'" (8). These zones of contact follow certain scripts and rules in which behaviour is prescripted, and thus largely predictable. Seldom does the contact zone come to fully represent the meaning that Mary Louise Pratt gave the term:

> an attempt to invoke the spatial and temporal co-presence of subjects previously separated by geographic and historical disjunctures, and whose trajectories intersect" in an interactive and improvisational dimension. More so, the contact zone symbolize the frontier at which "accounts of conquest and domination" are fought out. (Green 24)

This generates not a production of subjectivities, but a "subjectifying magical circle waiting, like negative forms, to be filled in" (Franke 8). The function of the exhibition is being reduced to an "economy of negation and the affirmation of conditions" (Franke 11), and falling short when it comes to continuing the enquiry into processes of production that could stem from communicative exhibition spaces.

Hosting Relations

Vidokle's interest in experimenting with different discursive formats is an attempt to model an alternative pattern of hospitality for the relationship between institution, artist, and public. Jan Verwoert identifies a relational quality in Anton Vidokle's authorship: "To authorize also means to inhabit the space you open up through your voice, your discourse, to spend time in this space, furnish it and turn it into a place for living" ("Gathering People" 12). For Verwoert, the kind of authorship that Vidokle assumes is that of a "contemporary host" who is "called forth to conjure up names of saints, seasons or rites of passage to celebrate and themes to interpret in order for guests to be invited, audiences to be invoked, thought to be gathered and works to be created" ("Gathering People" 16). Verwoert describes Vidokle as a facilitator, generating the conditions for engagement and functioning as a commissioner, programmer, and editor. Vidokle never adopts the role of presenter, never discloses the hospitable condition as an authorial gesture. Rather, at most of the events held by his friends and collaborators—writers, artists, or curators—he is one guest among many. Vidokle's authorial position as the initiator and organizer of unitednationsplaza is somewhat concealed by the collective nature of the project. But—and here comes the twist to an otherwise common articulation of curatorial responsibility—the position from which Vidokle speaks is not one in which various forms of engagement are already mapped out in his mind. Furnishing the communicative space of the discursive means to assume the "role of being a keeper of the building" as well as "one of the voices that it houses" (Verwoert, "Gathering People" 16).

Over the course of unitednationsplaza a series of events challenged the understanding that the host primarily becomes a guest to the discursive condition that has been created. Writer and curator Tirdad Zolghadr challenged such an authorial position using different formats, complicating the ways in which the communicative spaces of the discursive are devised. In a series of seminars titled *That's Why You Always Find me in the Kitchen at Parties*, which ran from 12 to 23 March 2007, Zolghadr sought to "pursue this possibility of new forms of discussion as rigorously as possible," and "apply the analytical rigor customarily reserved for ideological, infrastructural or art-critical concerns to the very material format in which these discussions are embedded."[30] Zolghadr expressed an interest in testing Vidokle's call for active productive engagement, investigating the discursive as an infrastructure that can maintain a certain quality of ambivalence towards an authorial positioning in relation to the participants. The specific target of the intervention was a format that dominated unitednationsplaza: the seminar and the lecture. Even when not held in an academic or otherwise institutional setting, these open spaces for conversation always entail the allocation of roles: speaker versus audience. Zolghadr was interested in pointing to how the degree of participation Vidokle imagined was actually hindered by the rather conventional academic format. Zolghadr therefore changed the format of his contribution to the programme every night, inviting other colleagues and artists to come up with new and different formats. An intervention by artist Chris Evans set off a debate about how strategies of exclusion control the discursive—even when the intention is to provide possibilities for inclusion. Evans, in turn, also invited several other participants, including

---

30 Invited guests were Stefanie Wenner, Adrienne Goehler, Florian Schneider, Jackson Pollock Bar, Chris Evans, Jörg Heiser, and Jennifer Allen ("Seminar 4: Tirdad Zolghadr").

Fig. 23: Seminar with Diedrich Diederichsen during the opening
conference "Histories of Productive Failures: From French
Revolution to Manifesta 6" of unitednationsplaza on 29 October
2006. Courtesy e-flux.

Fig. 24: Discussion with Martha Rosler during
unitednationsplaza's Martha Rosler Library lecture program on
19 June 2007. Unitednationsplaza, Berlin, 2006. Courtesy e-flux.

Zolghadr himself, to sit down at the kitchen table for a discussion that was broadcast via video to the seminar room. The divide between those in the kitchen and those in the seminar room was unintentionally widened by a technical failure preventing the broadcast from taking place. The audience in the seminar room could not hear anything—they thought this was part of the performance, assuming that this was an intentional strategy for alienating them from the discussion. In response, some people in the seminar room decided to form their own discussion—buying their own drinks, and eventually using the modular furnishing to barricade the kitchen with the performers inside. Later, the participants in the kitchen asked why nobody had communicated with them about the technical failure, wondering to what extent the other participants' response of using the blockade to further the agonistic separation was a reinforcing of conventional hierarchies (Hadley + Maxwell 22).

This controversy surrounding Evans' intervention points to the economies of attention that determine levels of participation and engagement when the discursive is employed as a medium for interaction aimed at generating different (predominantly more informal and less didactically governed) conditions for knowledge production. Despite its intentions, unitednationsplaza did not articulate the relationship between the degrees of freedom provided by means of unconventional formats of presentation and those provided by traditional frameworks (the exhibition space, the lecture, the seminar). Instead, the project manifested this relationship in ambivalent, at times paradoxical, and certainly conflictive terms.

Rebecca Uchill attests that even though unitednationsplaza points to "limits of open engagement in knowledge production," its various formats—employing forms of exhibiting, instructing or governing relations—are indicative of discursive practices that "even at their most experimental, have regulating capacities" (36). The conflictive pattern of hospitality rendered by the project can be described thusly: While aiming to point to the limits of discursive procedures it in fact acknowledged and accepted them. For Uchill this forces "both producers and produced publics to determine their willingness to operate within them" (36).

Collective Authorship

Unitednationsplaza never produced a limitless space in which authorship could be given up entirely. Rather, authorship was collec-
tivized. Verwoert starts by defining the relational quality of authorship as being "founded through the creation of a voice" whose job
it is to "follow through and conclude a discourse" that is a "stream
of words, thoughts, stories, ideas or images, a series of articulations
or manifestations unfolding (according to) a pattern, structure, or
choreography that allows for ideas and emotions to take shape"
("Gathering People" 12). This produces a body of work "that offers
something for others to share," and which becomes "a resonating
body that makes the voices of many others resound" (Verwoert,
"Gathering People" 12). The collective surrounds the authority of
the host. The very format of bringing people together by generating
a space for the fathoming of relationships and associations is a
definition of collectivity that "manifests itself in some kind of subjectivity that would make the multiplicity of its voice resonate"
(Verwoert, "Gathering People" 13).

    The constitution of collective subjectivity is a moment of experi-
ence, for which individually "one material trace [is] produced in the
course of the signifying practice of unfolding authorship" (Verwoert,
"Gathering People" 13). Sharing the experience of many individual
voices coming together and authorizing the experience they have
produced together makes for the realization that this process "has an
effect on—and in this sense acquires a certain authority/credence
in relation to—the way people experience themselves" and their immanent togetherness (Verwoert, "Gathering People" 15). The continuous deliberation over one's individual role in a collective event creates a loop, an indefinite process of negotiating the individual in
relation to the collective and the collective in relation to the individual. Hence, the production of collective subjectivities appears as a
manifestation of a "twist" on how collective subjectivity is a form of
consciousness produced through particular forms of material practice. In the case of unitednationsplaza, these particularly include
the modular furnishing that is used differently in each case to influence the behaviour patterns of guests, hosts and participants.

    As with the example of the Chris Evans performance, the materi-
ality of the furnishing can assume an authoritative character that
produces different forms of subjectivities as both individual and col-

lective forms of experiences. Understanding the modular furnishing as a form of material production also makes it possible to render the role of Vidokle as resting on the ambivalence between inclusion and exclusion, individuality and collectivity. It is the production of collective subjectivities for which Vidokle ultimately receives credit as a host in the pursuit of autonomy, or better "the dream and demand of autonomy" inherited from modernity, "the hope and claim that the power of a cultural practice to truly make a difference was inseparable from the freedom to determine its own conditions" (Verwoert, "Gathering People" 17–19). The curated encounters that unitednationsplaza produced can be described as situations of hospitality in which the host sought to escape the hospitable condition and joined the experience as a guest. This, however, established a type of authorship that was a form of governance, despite its relational qualities. The collective functioned as a disguise for the host's authorial role, but did not replace it.

In this context Vidokle's understanding of artistic practice should be read as a "demand ... to engage with society in order to create certain freedoms, to produce the conditions necessary for creative activity to take place at all" ("From Exhibition to School" 193). Curators also subscribe to this demand as a form of curatorial responsibility, producing a communicative space and thereby *facilitating* a context for argument, debate, and the generation of art as a product of the social, political and cultural factors that condition it. On the face of it, this shared demand seems to be blurring the categorical distinction between artist and curator. While appearing to be his own guest, making art about creating the conditions for art production, the host Vidokle assumed and exercised power when making decisions about whom to invite as speakers or not. In running as an artist-run independent project in the larger framework of e-flux, he even obliterated the one condition writer J.J. Charlesworth claimed was necessary for the categorical distinction between artist and curator: "It may be that an artist can curate and that a curator can make art, but—until all artists are in charge of their own personal art space—the categorical distinction between artist and curator remains an institutional one, governed by an inequality of access to resources."

My intention is by no means to define Vidokle as a curator, but to describe unitednationsplaza as a particularly interesting example of a curated encounter within the discursive as its medium of production. I respect the many ways in which Vidokle disavows the practice of curating as well as the role of a curator and positions himself against those forms of practice as an artist ("Art Without Artists?"). However, I would suggest that Vidokle intends unitednationsplaza to complicate the ways in which we think art is produced, what art can produce, and how artists, curators, critics, institutions, and the public have a stake in art. Unitednationsplaza is, therefore, not only an interesting proposition for the curatorial, but also exemplary for its condition as practice.

The Discursive Model of Practice

Unitednationsplaza creates a communicative space in the realm of the discursive. The project did not, however, introduce the discursive as a realm of production to the art world—the discursive is a highly contested ground that unitednationsplaza adopts, taking on the many complexities that define it. Many examples can be found that explore the discursive as a sphere of knowledge production and a medium foregrounding artistic practices that abandon the exhibition space,[31] and there are many more theoretical concepts that contextualize it.[32] While I will return to some of these at the beginning of the next chapter on curatorial discourse, at this point I will focus on discussing the notion of the discursive in direct relation to unitednationsplaza, closely examining the way its initiators, participants, and critics addressed it as a model of practice.

One of Vidokle's most frequent collaborators is artist Liam Gillick, who played a central role in unitednationsplaza and *Night School*. His many contributions were all concerned with the notion of the discursive challenging the exhibition space as a predominant mode of knowledge production by foregrounding improvised and self-organized structures rather than aiming to infiltrate institutional mechanisms. Gillick describes the discursive as analogous to forms of artistic practice that are "indebted to conceptual art's reframing

---

31 For example, Documenta 11 (2002), directed by Okwui Enwezor, and *Utopia Station* (2003), curated by Hans-Ulrich Obrist, Molly Nesbit, and Rirkrit Tiravanija for the 50th Venice Biennial.

32 For example Foucault, *Power/Knowledge*; Shermann and Rogoff; Bourriaud, *Relational Aesthetics*; Kester, *Conversation Pieces*; Bishop, "Antagonism and Relational Aesthetics" and "The Social Turn"; Sheikh, *In the Place of the Public Sphere*; Möntmann, *Art and its Institutions*.

of relationships." The discursive is a "model of production in its own right, alongside the production of objects for consideration or exchange." In speech and writing it takes the form of statements, conversations, discussions and debates, and it is "the basis of art that involves the dissemination of information." In this context it can take the form of either an infrastructure (a seminar, a workshop, a publication) or a medium (spoken or written word). (Gillick, "The Discursive")

Whenever Gillick speaks about the discursive as a model of practice, his description is echoed by his own involvement in unitednationsplaza (fig. 25).[33] In the many short texts that he read out or talked about in his brief lectures, followed by rather lengthy discussions in the seminar room, auditorium or bar, the discursive was not only the medium of choice, but also itself the subject matter of the discussion. It is this doubling of the function of the discursive that Gillick explores with regards to the role of the artist and public address within the broader framework of cultural production. The subjects of his presentations and discussions dealt with the problematics and ambivalences as well as with the potentialities with which he characterized the discursive as a model of practice. In early 2009, following his many participations in unitednationsplaza in Berlin and Mexico,[34] and during *Night School* in New York,[35] Gillick gathered his thoughts in a collection of two texts subsequently published on e-flux, titled *Maybe It Would Be Better if We Worked in Groups of Three*. The first text was subtitled "The Discursive," and the second "The Experimental Factory." These texts are a consolidation of his

33 Gillick spoke in the very first conference at the start of unitednationsplaza on 28 October 2006, for which the subject of discussion was "productive failures," followed by a response from Maria Lind. Later, he gave five 30-minute lectures followed by discussions at the bar on 7, 8, 9, 10 and 11 May 2007 ("Seminar 5: Liam Gillick").

34 On 1 and 2 March 2008 Gillick presented *Two Short Texts on the Possibility of Creating an Economy of Equivalence* (Day 1: "The day after closure of an experimental factory of Equivalence"; Day 2: "Reoccupation, recuperation and PRECISE renovation").

35 As part of the third public seminar of *Night School* on 27, 28 and 29 March 2008, Gillick presented a series of three one-hour lectures titled *Three Short Texts on the Necessity of Creating an Economy of Equivalence*. The lectures themselves were subtitled, "The night before closure of an experimental factory," "Redundancy following the promise of infinite flexibility," and "Reoccupation, recuperation and pointless renovation."

Fig. 25: Detail of Liam Gillick's presentation during his program series
"Five Short Texts on the Possibility of Creating an Economy
of Equivalence," 7–11 May 2007. Unitednationsplaza,
Berlin, 2006. Courtesy e-flux.

presentations during unitednationsplaza and *Night School*, and they
should be viewed in this context, even though they were published
almost a year later. Relating Gillick's analysis of the discursive to
unitednationsplaza seeks to evaluate its qualities as a producer of
alternatives to the exhibition space, and points to the problematics
of the discursive as both infrastructure and medium. In relation to
unitednationsplaza Gillick is a participant, an observant, but also
acts as a critic. This serves to illustrate just how difficult it is to analyse unitednationsplaza, due the ceaseless shifts of roles and perspectives: from viewer to participant, from artist to curator to critic,
and from participant to activist to observant. The different interests
that come to the space of communication in order to claim their
place and their stake in discursive practices are many and varied.

Going to the Bar

> The use of the word discursive includes the following considerations: first (a technical definition), the movement between subjects without or beyond order; second, a set of discussions marked by their adherence to one or more notions of analytical reason. (Gillick, "The Discursive")

This preliminary division between a rather technical and a more intellectual definition of the discursive helps to enquire into how unitednationsplaza employs a discursive model of practice. What first comes to mind when thinking about the "movement between subjects without or beyond order" is quite literally the flow of people in the Berlin building, frequently moving around the seminar room, kitchen and bar. Gillick incorporated this flow of people into his participation in the programme as a strategy of displacement. Each of his half-hour lectures was followed by a discussion at the bar (fig. 26). In so doing he disrupted the traditional relationship between speaker and audience that was prevalent during his more formal lectures and used the informal space of the bar to continue the discussions on a either one-to-one basis or in small groups, inviting people to assume an active part in the discussions.

For Vidokle, the informal character of these conversations was derived from the openness of the project, in that "everyone who came could participate to the degree that they wished" ("From Exhibition to School" 198). The possibility "of the audience having an active stake in the situation" serves to negate, abandon, subvert and displace the traditional roles of speaker and audience (197). Challenging the roles and responsibilities of artists, curators, artworks, and spectators enabled "the kind of productive engagement that is still possible, if spectatorship is bypassed and traditional roles of institution/curator/artist/public are encouraged to take on a more hybrid complexity" (198). In order to overcome the limitations of the exhibition as a space of production (understood to be inherent to the predominant passive forms of engagement in spectatorship, which result in the loss of agency of artists in social and political terms) the discursive is employed as a model of practice investigating the potential of mapping a space of production in which more active forms of engagement and interaction can develop.

"The discursive is what produces the work, and in the form of critical and impromptu exchanges, it is also its desired result" (Gillick,

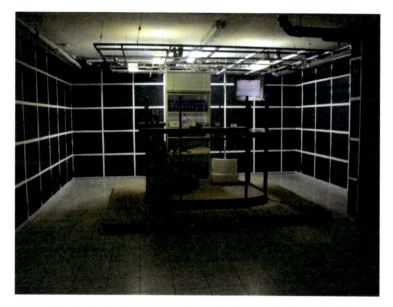

Fig. 26: Bar at unitednationsplaza by Salon Aleman, a project by
Ethan Breckenridge, Julieta Aranda, Eduardo Sarabia, Danna Wajda,
and Willi Brisco. Berlin, 2006. Courtesy e-flux.

"The Discursive"). Analogous to the nature of the discursive—as
founded upon the dissemination of information as an alternative to
the studio or exhibition space—the element of speculation opens
up spheres of experimentation and risk. It functions in this context
as a mode of construction that is "in flux," designating the discursive
as a continuous movement. Furthermore, the positionalities behind
the statements and texts are of an equally incomplete nature. With
regard to the question of authorship, their individuality can only be
viewed in the context of their collectivity, which generates a "sense
of reclaimed speculation" (Gillick, "The Discursive").

> At no point does my use of the word [discursive] really imply coher-
> ence with notions of "discursive democracy" as posited by Habermas
> and others, yet within the cultural terrain it does have some connection
> to the idea of melding public deliberation while retaining the notion of
> individual practice within the "group." (Gillick, "The Discursive")

Although Gillick does not tap into a discussion of the Habermasian notion of communicative action as a democratizing tool, the relationship between the individual and the group supplies a protective mechanism to the element of speculation:

> The discursive is a practice that offers one the opportunity to be a relatively unexamined, free agent within a collective project. ... It allows the artist to develop a set of arguments and individual positions without having got to conform to an established model of artistic or educational quality. Incomplete projects and partial contributions are central to an effectively progressive, critical environment, but in the discursive they are not expressed—rather, they are perpetually reformed. (Gillick, "The Discursive")

In this sense, artistic practice produces a curated encounter in which the relation between host and guest seemingly fades in favour of a collectively produced and shared experience, which in turn, however, is the very result of the artists' positioning in the collective project. The collectively shared experience is no longer just something that can potentially emerge from the curated encounter, but is its product, the result of a process in which the artist proceeds to designate the public realm he created "as art or like art" (Vidokle, "From Exhibition to School" 192). Vidokle's own position as an artist in relation to the pattern of hospitality he creates is not that of a host, but of a guest becoming the parasite to the collective condition created.

From Vidokle's perspective, unitednationsplaza not only addresses concepts and terminologies of art, publicness, and sociality, but also produces them. Vidokle regards these notions as intrinsically linked. Definitions of art, publicness and sociality form a horizon of ambition for unitednationsplaza within their realm of production: the discursive. Their entanglement is at the heart of Vidokle's argument: He regards the curated encounter as an artwork, which by means of the discursive as its sphere of production designates a public realm. This, in turn, is posited as a condition for a production of sociality as a form of active engagement with and within the public realm.

Social Space and Public Engagement

Vidokle is fundamentally critical of the exhibition space as a place for public engagement, the constitution of audiences, and the condition of spectatorship. He detects in large-scale international exhibitions "a strong desire on the part of the organizers and participants ... to see their work as transformative social projects rather than merely symbolic gestures,"[36] going on to question this desire by asking whether "an exhibition, no matter how ambitious, [is] the most effective vehicle for such engagement?" (Vidokle, "From Exhibition to School" 191). From the context it remains unclear to what kind of engagement he is referring, however. Is it a form of engagement with reality, requiring active participation in addressing political and social struggles of our time? Or perhaps a commitment towards attempting to resolve responsibilities on the part of curators, artists, writers—in short, all those in the realm of cultural production? The kind of engagement for which Vidokle claims that the exhibition is no longer an effective vehicle is explored as a form of political agency in discursive practices. According to the artist, this is impossible to assume in the social formations to which exhibitions are geared: "audiences" rather than "publics." Expressing agreement with observations Martha Rosler made in the 1980s,[37] Vidokle and Rosler write that "the spectators of art have largely lost their political agency as such" and have "no necessary means or particular interest in affecting social change" (Rosler and Vidokle 70–77). While these observations do not impede the potential to continue to "produce a critical art object ... there seems to be no public out there that can complete its transformative function"; therefore Vidokle looks to the discursive sphere as a way to "recuperate the agency of art in the absence of an effective public" (Vidokle, "From Exhibition to School" 191–93).

In 2005, the exhibition *Making Things Public*, curated by Bruno Latour and Peter Weibel at the Center for Art and Media (ZKM),

---

36 Vidokle mentions the examples of *Critical Confrontation with the Present* as part of Documenta X (1997), curated by Catherine David, and *The Production of Cultural Difference* as part of the 3rd International Istanbul Biennial (1992), curated by Vasif Kortun.

37 Martha Rosler's project *If You Lived Here...* (part artwork, part curated group show, part discursive series on and around the subject of homelessness) took place at Dia Art Foundation, Soho, New York, in 1989. e-flux presented the archive of this project in 2009 at their New York space on Ludlow Street.

Karlsruhe, Germany, enquired into possibilities of public representation. It proposed a reconfigured engagement with politics by means of public engagement, revolving around a central question: "What would an object-orientated democracy look like?" (Latour, "From Realpolitik to Dingpolitik" 14).

> We might be more connected to each other by our worries, our matters of concern, the issues we care for, than by any other set of values, opinions, attitudes or principles. ... Objects—taken as so many issues—bind all of us in ways that map out a public space profoundly different from what is usually recognized under the label of "the political." It is this space, this hidden geography that we wish to explore through this catalogue and exhibition. (Latour, "From Realpolitik to Dingpolitik" 15)

This geography could be described as the premise on which the notions of "public," "democracy," and "representation" and the ideas surrounding them are questioned in relation to each other. Representation is itself understood to encompass three ideas that have been kept separate but need to be taken in to account in relation to each other. The first disposition, the political, "designates the ways to gather the legitimate people around some issue" (Latour, "From Realpolitik to Dingpolitik" 16). The second, scientific disposition presents the concerns, issues and topics for representation. The third, the artistic, translates directly into the curatorial concept in that it presents a model of practice, "a third meaning of this ambiguous and ubiquitous word 'representation,' the one with which artists are more familiar, had to be called to solve, this time visually, the problem of the composition of the 'Body Politik.'" (Latour, "From Realpolitik to Dingpolitik" 16). The Body Politik is a strategy for assemblage, a form of composition in which Latour includes everything from "clothes to cities, technologies of meeting, gathering" ("From Realpolitik to Dingpolitik" 16), the latter deriving from the Heidegerrian understanding of "thing" as not only having properties, but also accounting for its own history in form and matter (Heidegger and Krell 148–51). The relational is a conditional circumstance for all kinds of gatherings around matter-of-concerns such as "what forms the Body Politik"? For Latour, this serves to register "a huge sea change in our conceptions of science, our grasps of facts, our understanding of objectivity" with the aim of imagining "a new eloquence" that entails a consideration of its formational process, exercised through an object-orientated democracy that "should be concerned as much by the procedure to detect the relevant parties as to the methods to bring into the centre of the debate the proof of what is to be debated" ("From Realpolitik to Dingpolitik" 18). This is what Latour calls *Dingpolitik* (politics of things), a term that he uses to describe the refocusing of political thought.

> Thus, long before designating an object thrown out of the political sphere and standing there objectively and independently, the Ding or Thing has for many centuries meant the issue that brings people together because it divides them. (Latour and Weibel 10)

Curator Katharina Schlieben uses this concept in the context of discursive practices to "examine collective forms of collaborative work in terms of social constellations of actors" (16). Schlieben looks to Latour for thinking about the motivations behind attending collectively to the discursive sphere and for rethinking the ways in which people gather around issues. She refers for example to *Collaborative Practices, Part 1* at Kunstverein Munich (2004) and *Vielstimmigkeit—Collaborative Practices, Part 2* at Shedhalle, Zurich (2005), both of which she was involved in as a curator. According to Schlieben, they represent "a strong call to address the question of collective work processes, group constellations and collaborative practices, in order to differentiate and to examine them under the lens of societal, cultural and political inquiries" (17). This also holds true for unitednationsplaza.

The first ever event held at unitednationsplaza was a conference[38] that discussed and reflected on the non-occurrence of Manifesta 6. The main subject of debate was the notion of the school, with reference to historical predecessors such as the Bauhaus, the Black Mountain College of Art or the Copenhagen Free University. Examining how these examples presented forms of gathering around matters of concern sparked a debate about what kind of gathering the notion of the school provides and whether it is truly free and independent from the constraints characterized the communicative exhibition space. In this sense Diederich Diederichsen criticizes an indepen-

---

38 The conference was titled *Histories of Productive Failures: from the French Revolution to Manifesta 6* and took place as unitednationsplaza's opening conference from 27 to 29 October 2006. Guests invited to make presentations included Anselm Franke, Anton Vidokle, Haris Pellapaisiotis, Mete Hatay, Pavlina Paraskevaidou, Rana Zincir Celal, Liam Gillick, Maria Lind, Diedrich Diedrichsen, and Tirdad Zolghadr.

dent artist-run discursive space as creating a "quasi-academic space" (*On (Surplus) Value* 24) that seeks to institute processes that contradict the disciplines of academia but at the same time operate on the very premise of academic knowledge production. This criticism is based on a functional form of judgement, one that Katharina Schlieben criticizes as "ill-equipped to convey the multi-layered and complex nature of the work processes involved" (17). Instead, Schlieben suggests looking more closely at the premises upon which collaborative art projects operating in the discursive sphere are predicated upon, paying attention to their "polyphonic lines" (18). The notion of polyphony refers to how language, as a medium, can include a variety of voices, and how those become communicated.

Applied to unitednationsplaza, this entails the question how the identity that unitednationsplaza creates for itself is made up from the voices that it houses. Latour's concept of gathering provides Schlieben with a form of negotiation, a possibility for defining identification in the sense of group formation as a process-oriented practice allowing for polyphony, disagreement and antagonism. Recalling Verwoert describing the collective as environing Vidokle's identity as the project's host, Schlieben considers the ways in which the actors involved partake in the process of negotiating the individual and the collective. This applies both to the ways in which the invited collaborators took an authorial role (in contrast to Vidokle, who himself never gave a presentation during unitednationsplaza) and to the ways in which the participants engaged in the communicative processes that took place. A case in point, cited earlier, is the Chris Evans performance, staged by Tirdad Zolghadr.

> Many collaborative constellations of actors could be ascribed to a culture of practice because the component of gathering is indeed integral to social practice. ... At the outset of these practices lies a fragmented, incomplete knowledge or a limited palette of methods that motivate the actors involved to engage in a dialogue that may be transformed into joint social action. This presupposes generating contact zones or interfaces, and may be formulated as a social moment that focuses on the "in-between" as productive opportunity, avoids reproducing dichotomies, acknowledges diverse speaker perspectives, and reflects on the dynamics and paradoxes of translation. (Schlieben 20)

Art as Social Space

Nina Möntmann enquired into the social function of art by looking into propositions of art as social space, analysing different forms of spatiality that artworks suggest or with which artists work (*Kunst als Sozialer Raum*). Following various analyses of relationships between space and place beyond the framework of the studio, gallery or museum—into the urban, discursive, and cultural sphere—Möntmann locates the potential of art deliberating social spaces, under the condition that it,

> discards inside/outside dichotomies in favour of a reciprocal dynamic process between issues immanent to the institutional art world and public issues(those publicly discussed in institutional, cultural, urban and consumption and action-specific discourses). This process produces a new social space that incorporates the recipients—authorized as social subjects—into the discursive artistic process. This realm of production—concrete, distinguished and coupled with an analytical interest—presents a model function for the handling of a place as a platform for the production of social spaces. (Möntmann, *Kunst als Sozialer Raum* 166, author's translation)

As a result of this process, art deliberates social space in that it can provide a context for reflection, and speculation, on the possibilities that arise upon references to space, to people or to things and their relation to other spaces, people, or things. The curated encounter functions as a platform for the production of social space. This requires ensuring what Schlieben calls the "in-between," speculation as simultaneous reflection and production, which per se constitutes a relational activity (18).

For Vidokle, however, unitednationsplaza is not a curated encounter as a platform for the production of social space. He expects the project, in the context of artistic practice, to "play an active part in society" following the "paradigm of critically engaged art practice that we are still following today" ("From Exhibition to School" 192). Furthermore, Vidokle seeks to reformulate this expectation. He is interested in rescuing the premise of contemporary art practice from being rendered "futile or, at the very least, severely reduced in its transformative political and social agency" (193). This premise is the production of a critical art object in relation to an effective public. Vidokle believes this public has been lost due to the rise of audiences as "groups of consumers of leisure and spectacle" (193). Hence, unitednationsplaza is conceived as a critical art project encouraging experimentation and with an emphasis on process rather than product, to take the place of the critical art object. The project takes as its departure point a historically valued function of art in its exploration of how to once more provide the conditions for perceiving art practice as having a political and social agency.

Devising a space for social interaction in the format of an artwork in order to create a space for and of engagement has many precedents in recent art history. Looking into one specific example will make it possible to discover whether, within the setting of an artwork, it might be possible to contest the relationship between art and society beyond the realm of speculation—and without being institutionalized in the process. This will provide for a more contextualized understanding of *Night School*, the last iteration of unitednationsplaza at New York's New Museum, which approached Vidokle and commissioned him to produce an artwork.

In 2006 Claire Bishop defined the "social turn" in art practice, referring to an enhanced "interest in collectivity, collaboration, and direct engagement with specific social constituencies" creating "intersubjective spaces" that become "the focus—and medium—of artistic investigation" (*The Social Turn* 179). Rirkrit Tiravanija's practice is a prominent example of this phenomenon. As a frequent collaborator with Vidokle, he also participated in unitednationsplaza. Möntmann examines Tiravanija's practice for deliberating on the specificities of the communicative spaces that the artist employs in order to explore a transgression of boundaries in the relationship between artist, work and viewer (*Kunst als Sozialer Raum* 106–32). Her analysis includes a discussion of the notion of authorship, the category of the aesthetic, and the understanding of the artwork as a dialogical entity.

The difference between Tiravanija's projects, which took place in the 1990s, and unitednationsplaza, which took place in the late 2000s, is that in the meantime many artistic and curatorial projects aiming at shifting the processes of production of communication and social interaction from the exhibition to the discursive sphere not only explored the ways in which this could potentially and speculatively provide for an alternative economy of knowledge that was not consumer-oriented, but also saw that potential fail in terms of a transferability from theory to practice, or from spectatorship to participation. An important question for this analysis is how discursive practices can be defined as art deliberating social space, and how they can be judged not only in aesthetic terms, but also in social or political terms.

For Möntmann, Tiravanija's practice found a way to produce social interaction by means of extending the notion of the exhibition space to become a situation and process (*Kunst als Sozialer Raum* 112), thereby challenging a traditional conception of the exhibition space, the authorship of the artist, the role of the curator, the function of the institution, and agency of spectatorship. While this had already been addressed in the 1970s when artists such as Daniel Buren challenged the communicative structures of the exhibition—incorporating a process of production into the terminology of the exhibition by working "in situ"—the position of the viewer as a perceiving consumer largely remained intact. With Tiravanija the configuration of the role of the viewer as a producer of knowledge changed, which in turn affected institutional hierarchies and the form taken by the governing processes of subjectivation. Tiravanija critiqued the demand for subordination of the viewer in the interest of the institution calling for participatory practices instead of cognitive perception, substituting the notion of "spectator" or "viewer" with "visitor" in order to describe the changing role and function with respect to modes of action. Tiravanija challenged the nature of the exhibition space by physically transforming it into an installation of a kitchen or an apartment. The higher the degree of transformation, the more these spaces could be freed from traditional behaviour patterns of spectatorship and used socially. For unitednationsplaza the degree of transformation was not very high, since the project was already taking place outside the institutional space, and using a preexisting office space, kitchen and bar. However, both Tiravanija and Vidokle set up functional realities that were formerly alien to the art space. As a kitchen, a bedroom, a seminar room or a bar they already constitute a social space. It is the context of art in which their nature as social spaces has a disturbing quality, which both Tiravanija and Vidokle aim to use in favour of more diversified action patterns on the part of the public. By offering a use of a different space (that of the kitchen or seminar) in the context of providing a different use of space (that of art), both Tiravanija and Vidokle functionalize space for the purpose of social interaction.

In contrast to Tiravanija, Vidokle's claim that art should resurrect the public as an agency reflects a political agenda. Tiravanija suspends the usual behaviour patterns of spectatorship and provides zones of social emergence. Compared to the case of unitednations-plaza, here the notion of art as a medium for sociality is less important. There is no self-reflexive ambition on the part of the artists or the participant, at least not one that is articulated as the work's intentionality. As MoMA curator Laura Hoptman said in relation to *Untitled 1992/1995 (free/still)*, an installation of a soup kitchen in the museum:

> What this work did was to invite people to interact with each other in a social way. ... People were not invited to participate in a performance that was to be documented in order to feature as art, but their being in the space was part of the art itself. (MoMA)

Defining precisely what happened in the space as part of an artwork, or even art itself, is irrelevant to the nature of these interactions. What does happen, however, is that emphasis is placed on what constitutes art when it is perceived as art. By introducing into the gallery space something that had not, up to that point, been perceived as an action attributed to artistic practice, the focus is turned onto the conditions under which art is perceived to be art. Vidokle's interest is in pushing this focus further into the direction of thinking what agency of spectatorship the awareness of the conditions for art perception entails. In relation to the demand for artistic practice to engage with society the project acts self-referentially in that it is an example for the demand it also aims to fulfil. However, in response to this demand the project fails on the relation between what it proposes and what it is seeking to change. The project brings people together in a noninstitutional space to talk about current concerns in artistic practice (one of them being the conditions of practice and their remaining social and political agency). In so doing, the project seeks to devise a space for social interaction in order to transform the audience from listening consumers into an "effective public." There is a mismatch however, in the relationship between what the project is supposed to do and what it actually does. The high level of speculation and experimentation that the medium of the discursive entails, including forms of collaboration, is framed within a restrictive contextualization of relationships between institution, public, and art. From Vidokle's viewpoint as initiator and organizer of the project, the platform for building relations that the project set up, is obviously linked to his position as an artist pursuing new forms of public engagement. But does the experience from the perspective of the participants link these two spaces of production together? This would mean presupposing a transformative function for the self-referentiality of the project's format in relation to the subject matters that emerge in the spaces of discussion. It is this transformative function that Vidokle perceives as a result of the project in its condition as an artwork when he says: "To me this means that the public can be resurrected and the modality of critical art practice can be preserved given some changes to how art experience is conceive and constructed" ("Opening Remarks").

In deliberating the function of unitednationsplaza in the context of artistic practices, the dissemination of artworks, and the role of institutions, Vidokle describes the project in retrospect "a form without content, a host without qualities" and as an "extended version of Slavoj Zizek's exam design ... where he makes the students come up with both the question and the answer" ("From Exhibition to School" 199). Vidokle uses this quote to underline the way in which unitednationsplaza worked as an "artwork in his own setting" (199).

Night School—a "game within the game"

The last iteration of the "exhibition-as-school" format took place under the title *Night School* in 2008 and 2009 at New York's New Museum.[39] After unitednationsplaza came to an end in Berlin, the New Museum's Head of Education, Eungie Joo, commissioned Vidokle to realize a series of monthly talks at the museum. This particular project presents an interesting example for continuing discussions around processes of institutionalization of critical art practices in relation to the project's claim for finding new forms of public engagement.

Much more precisely than unitednationsplaza, *Night School* was defined and conceptualized as an artwork. *Night School* was similar to unitednationsplaza in format and content, inviting almost the same series of speakers, but much more regulated. Its processes of institutionalization can be compared to how Beatrice von Bismarck ("Game within the Game") characterizes the experimental and speculative nature of discursive practices when implemented in major art institutions.

---

39 From the press release: "Night School is an artist commission in the form of a temporary school" ("Night School").

Night School corresponds perfectly with the characteristics Bismarck deliberates for the institution within the institution, the "game within the game." Its time span of just over a year was "temporalized in its make-up, self-reflexive and orientated towards different publics" ("Game within the Game" 128). The monthly events consisted of four days, including public discussions with invited speakers and regular meetings with a core group of around twenty participants preselected by Eungie Joo, Anton Vidokle and Liam Gillick. They met at the museum, a bar, or someone's house so that "the working context forms a space that is generated by its own use, through which one can 'do' something with the place and permeate it with discursive and social movements" (Bismarck, "Game within the Game" 128).

Bismarck outlines how the maintenance of this self-reflexive nature of the production of social space is very much in the interest of the hosting institution if it is to maintain its power position and control the kinds of engagement that take part in it. The institution achieves this by creating another institution internally that seemingly possesses a higher degree of manoeuvrability with its proposition to work against and in antithesis to its host. Concerned as she is with the role of academies and art schools today, Bismarck argues that evoking the model of the artist-run temporary institution is not a form of resistance against the divisions between public and private, or viewed and viewer, facilitating their transgression, but in fact functions solely to reinforce these divisions. The traditional role of the educational institution takes on a "gatekeeper" function in that it "creates a link between art production and the formation of its public(s), thus creating a continuous crossover between internal and external ruling and standards" (Bismarck, "Game within the Game" 127). The distinction between internal and external is becoming only more confused by the strategies of reoccupation when the space of the academy or school hosts within itself the formation of publics alongside art production.

> This conflict-charged, but dynamic and contingent handling of regulations and standards, carries a resistant potential that can be brought into play to preserve relative autonomy in the institution's room for manoeuvre. In this respect it makes sense to set up a working context within the institution that can in itself illustrate and perform the conditions and qualities of the institution, confront them with each other

and negotiate them, without itself becoming entirely subsumed within the institution. (Bismarck, "Game within the Game" 129)

What Liam Gillick claims is the potentiality of the discursive—confronting a socio-economic system by mimicking and paralleling its structure—is problematic for Bismarck in terms of the mediated parallel positioning that discursive practices choose to adopt in relation to the institution in order to live off it in a somewhat parasitical relationship.

However, from another perspective, it is precisely this strategy of building an institution within an institution that Maria Lind articulates as a form of institutional critique. Situating Vidokle in a so called "fifth phase of institutional critique," labelled as "institution building," it is "the whole 'institution of art,' the apparatus itself that is being scrutinized and challenged, not least its economic side, again from within the belly of the beast" (Lind, "Dilemmas" 28). Instead of addressing the institution directly, the critique operates by pointing to the functioning (or malfunctioning) of the institution as contextualizing artistic practices within larger cultural, social or political contexts. This is achieved by "instituent practices," a term Lind borrows from Gerald Raunig, representing an "active making of new modes of working and coming together in various ways, including transversal ones" while facing the dilemma of "whether and how critique can be performed" (Lind, "Dilemmas" 30). It is in response to this dilemma that the fact that "Vidokle's projects are generally not cloaked in 'critical' rhetoric" has to be perceived: "Instead, they simply offer structures and procedures that allow for something that differs from most of dominant discourses and mainstream activities" (Lind, "Dilemmas" 30–31). The lack of what Lind calls a "critical rhetoric" is also praised by Media Farzin in her account of unitednationsplaza as a deficiency that has an enabling function, presenting the project's potentiality:[40]

> In turning from an object-based production to a discourse-centred approach, the artist reserves the option to not do and not make. The audience, in their turn, is allowed the option to not engage, to not take part—or to envision a completely different way of engaging. (39)

---

40 Defining potentiality after Rogoff and Agamben as "to be in relation to one's own incapacity" (Agamben 177–85; Rogoff, "Academy as Potentiality" qtd. in Farzin 38).

In this context, one of the participants of the "core group" of *Night School*, offers a different reading of Vidokle's "institution-building" process. Taraneh Fazeli believes that although transferring a self-initiated group structure into a larger museum might raise questions about the status of the institution as such and could therefore be a form of institutional critique in which "expanded 'publics' would be addressed," the danger is "that dissent and contention will fall away in favour of unity-seeking discourse in a hermetic quasi multiplicity," enabling a process of self-determination that often results in an overt self-congratulation (129). Especially *Night School* demonstrated that the exhibition-as-school concept established those very divides that it set out to overcome in the name of public: The level of participation from the audiences that came to the monthly lectures was limited. In contrast to unitednationsplaza (referring to the Chris Evans performance), where "the blockading incident may suggest there was a porosity that allowed discourse and action, theory and praxis, to produce each other," active participation was absent and even though interruptions were welcomed by the presenters, "the audiences at most events remained cautiously mute" (Fazeli 130).

Gillick points to the notion of a physical displacement that concerns the role of the institution, the artist, as much as the viewer or participant in bringing us closer to a "functional reality" in which artistic practice can engage with society by means of developing relations: "Vidokle's project fought the notion that anyone who thinks about what to do and how things could be better operates within the realm of the utopian via the contingencies of every day" ("The Binary Stadium" 50). It is in between the spaces of utopian dismissal and continuous belief in a future that holds the potential that "you'll find components of cultural 'movement' that have little to do with classical ideas of representation or how you might be feeling or what's going on 'outside,' but without losing the precise connection to other people in other situations" ("The Binary Stadium" 52).

The lack of this functional displacement is the key to the failure of *Night School*. As an institution within an institution it entered into a dependent relationship that left little much room for manoeuvre. It seemed content with an ambition "to transform social and subjective realities into a format in which we can handle and conserve it, but not to interfere and take an active part in the production of social and political realities" (Möntmann, "Art and its Institutions" 8). The problem for Möntmann is that the historical backdrop to any institutional constitution is the way in which social principles and values are formed. In the ongoing phase of collapse in state funding these principles and values are shifting. Institutions are increasingly driven by the urge to establish and maintain those power structures that help sustain the legitimation of their role as providers of education and knowledge products, rather than engaging in its processes of production. In terms of public participation, or "public acting," as Andrea Phillips calls it, this is what unitednationsplaza (in contrast to *Night School*) might at times have been attempting to critique when it blurred traditional patterns of behaviour at a lecture or seminar. But *Night School* only reaffirmed the situation with its attempt to counter educational forms of knowledge production by producing other, albeit temporary, versions of it. It is in this sense that Vidokle's characterization of the educational distortion against which the project is pitted, unfortunately reads as just another description of *Night School*:

> The academic structure of educational institutions, with their insistence on the necessity to comply with previously established rules and standards, often guarantees that for all the promise of experimentation and innovation, each successive generation of students evolves into a replica of the preceding generation. (Rosler and Vidokle 75)

At best we have to understand *Night School* as continuing the exploration into the potentiality of the discursive that unitednationsplaza presented. At worst, it could be defined in terms of its role as part of the New Museum, an "enterprise art institution in late capitalism," within which "an educational commission is a consumer commission" (Möntmann, "Art and its Institutions" 9). In the case of *Night School*, proposing to provide for new forms of public engagement, adopting a semi-autonomous framework within the sphere of institutional cultural production did not precipitate the exploration of a critical and political potential of discursive practices. Instead, it threw the project back into setting off a crisis of legitimacy for its host, for which it adopted "corporatist logic, flexible working conditions, event-style programmes and a populist concept of the public sphere" (Möntmann, "Art and its Institutions" 9).

The Artwork as Dispositif

Möntmann explores the shifts in mind-set needed if one is to conceive of artistic practices that generate social space when talking about the discursive as a functional site for social interaction with reference to Foucault's notion of the "dispositif" (Foucault, *Power/Knowledge* 194–96 qtd. in Möntmann, *Kunst als Sozialer Raum* 110). This term specifies the topological and functional structures, and the mechanisms and strategies that manifest the exercise of power for generating social order. Foucault uses the notion to analyze the configuration of social relationships and the rules that they follow (whether implicit or explicit). These rules form the apparatus, itself a system of relations comprising discourses, laws, administrative means, architectural forms—in fact anything that structures life as we know it and exercises a guiding influence on our behavioural patterns. It is within the context of a dispositif, which a discursive practice partly constitutes, that "it can be said that the artist models the 'interface' of the public and the institution as a field of application available on both sides" (Möntmann, *Kunst als Sozialer Raum* 111). Vidokle defines the function of his project as an artwork in precisely this way. The previously mentioned relationship between sociality and publicness that Vidokle is interested in can now be more clearly defined from his perspective: The artwork, even if resulting from collaborative practice, negotiates notions of publicness within the production of sociality that occurs in the curated encounter as a platform, or interface, for a production of social space in which notions of public and institution can meet.

Recalling how Verwoert describes Vidokle as an authorial host who assumes the position of a guest to the curated encounter he produced ("Gathering People" 15), curator Monika Szewczyk compares Vidokle to Diego Velázquez portraying himself in *Las Meninas* (1656):

> One of the greatest paintings ever made shows the artist stepping away from his creation; and, crucially, this takes place at that moment when absolute sovereignty appears: the king and queen reflected in the mirror behind him are figureheads of the regime of his day. (Szewczyk, "Anton Vidokle" 56)

Szewczyk is discussing here how Vidokle defines his artistic practice in terms of collaboration, in his pursuit of an answer to the question of how art self-reflexively produces the conditions for its own production. She accuses Vidokle of having assumed the position of an artist without taking into account the context in which it is perceived as art, while also refusing to act solely as a curator, a role that Vidokle himself describes as entirely "predicated upon the existence of artistic production," having a "supporting role in its activity" ("Art Without Artists?"). The curatorial role of facilitating the space of production that Vidokle clearly fulfils in initiating and organizing projects such as unitednationsplaza and *Night School* is packaged as an artwork that appeals for judgement on aesthetic terms. But judging the projects purely on their formal appearance entails a great danger, one that is inherent to the doubling of presenting a moment of reflection on the conditions of production as a product of it—of making art the product of its contextual appearance. "The proliferation of discursive projects does carry the risk of what Simon Sheikh has called 'talk value'—that it can turn into discussion for the sake of discussion, like any other formalism" (Lind et al. 114). Fellow curator Dieter Roelstraete defends unitednationsplaza in that it has been "healthily aware of the dangers of calling any form of art-talk 'performative,' and therefore 'art,'" aware of the "all-too-self-conscious 'excesses' of discussion, where every utterance is too quickly and lazily fetishized into an art project" (Lind et al. 115).

Going back to Szewczyk's argument around what kind of judgement the constitution of *Night School* as an artwork involves, she asks: "What is the subject of aesthetics? And what is the universal truth governing this odd experience combining thought and feeling, perception and action?" ("Anton Vidokle" 64). To answer these questions would mean calling for an aesthetic judgement of all that constitutes the discursive as an artwork: the relations between the participants, the presenters and audiences, and the speakers and listeners. Continuing the Velázquez metaphor, this call for judgement is best described with the image of the painter withdrawing from the canvas in order to observe the capacity of art to bring people together. The subject of the artwork is art as a social medium. So we might say that Vidokle's interest in using art to deliberate social space has a calculated dimension. Vidokle seems not only to anticipate, but also to presume the sense of a regained speculation when it comes to defining the roles, functions and identities that form part of it or are a result of it. He presupposes that by bringing people together art can

have a transformative function, enabling artistic practice to comply
with the demand that it engage with society.

But should discursive practices be appropriated as a medium to
generate artworks? Should they not better function as an infrastructure, just like the exhibition space, in which the processes of production provide for a testing ground for relationships? Even though the
projects succeeded, at least on some occasions, in suspending role
divisions and hierarchies, did they really "provide the matrix for the
generation of social situations in the art world" (Möntmann, *Kunst als
Sozialer Raum* 111)? Or was the realm of production being confused
with what is, allegedly, produced in it? Is the artwork the gathering of
people, or a presupposed production of sociality that occurs in it?

Claire Bishop emphasizes what it means to describe a discursive
project as art: "the significance of dematerializing a project into social process" and "the possible achievement of making dialogue a
medium" ("The Social Turn" 180). She highlights the importance of
considering projects that aim to relate art to the realm of the social as
works of art, instead of merely "as collaborative projects in the most
general sense, because only if judging the work's conceptual significance as a social and aesthetic form" can criticism address the "dis-
ruptive specificity of a given work," and not base discussion solely on
a "*generalized* set of moral precepts" ("The Social Turn" 181). In this
context Bishop criticizes Grant Kester for confusing the criteria for
defining art when he suggests that the articulation of a relationship
to the social constitutes an artwork.

> He [Kester] challenges us to treat communication as an aesthetic
> form, but, ultimately, he fails to defend this, and seems perfectly con-
> tent to allow that a socially collaborative art project could be deemed
> a success if it works on the level of social intervention even though it
> founders on the level of art. ("The Social Turn" 181)

Bishop stresses the importance of maintaining a categorical distinction between judging a work on its aesthetic qualities and its socio-political relevance. Both criteria of judgement are valid and applicable, but the one should not be subsumed by the other, believes
Bishop, who is critical of Kester's attempt to "think the aesthetic and
the social/political *together*, rather than subsuming both within the
ethical" ("The Social Turn" 181).

Undoing the Social

Analyzing Vidokle's project focussed primarily on discussing its format, which comprised a discursive model of practice framed within claims pertaining to the production of art as a social space fostering public engagement. Vidokle's articulations on his role as author and artist have been reviewed in relation those of the project's participants and collaborators in order to render the project in the context of artistic and curatorial discourse on the function of art as social space and the attribution of collectivity to the processes of production of social space.

A conclusive analysis of these particular examples of discursive practices in relation to a demise of the exhibition space requires a disambiguation of terminologies around the social. This is necessary for an enquiry into how discursive practices provide a platform for the production of social space and the emergence of sociality as a condition for relational activity.

Looking again at Latour will help to complement the partial and constrictive articulations Vidokle uses to characterize unitednationsplaza as a project fostering a shift from viewers and consumers to producers. Largely unimaginative in his formulations of how exhibitions inhibit forms of emancipated spectatorship, Vidokle conflates collaborative practices in the medium of the discursive with the production of collectivity as a condition for social transformation, which he entirely attributes to the agency of art.

Examining Bruno Latour's notion of gathering and assembling the social provides an approach to unitednationsplaza from a perspective that can address the relationing between art, sociality and publicness through a curated encounter very different from Vidokle's, one that avoids the production of any hierarchy or cause-effect relationship between them. I shall draw a parallel between Vidokle and Latour that demonstrates the nonarbitrariness of discussing of unitednationsplaza and Vidokle's role within the project in relation to Bruno Latour in the context of actor-network theory (ANT). Drawing such a parallel is, however, an entirely artificial endeavour and used here solely for the purpose of furthering the argument around social dimensions of knowledge production emerging from, and generated by, the artistic and curatorial practices that this research aims to elaborate.

Both Vidokle and Latour intend to break with the presuppositions of practice in their respective fields. They both seek out forms of practice that are not only responsive, but also reflexive of its social, political, and cultural conditioning. There is an important difference between them, however. Latour is no social constructivist, and he does not search for a social dimension in scientific practice—that would mean elaborating on the construction of facts in an otherwise predetermined social setting. Vidokle, on the other hand, assumes the position of a social constructivist who looks for a specific social dimension of artistic practices. While Vidokle does make an effort to avoid certain predetermined social settings, such as the exhibition space, the discursive sphere of production is no less conflictive in terms of its predetermined space of action. This recalled the previous discussion of the notion of authorship in relation to patterns of hospitality. Vidokle even goes so far as to derive a renewed claim that artistic sovereignty from the particularities of discursive models of practices not only produce art but also produce the conditions for art to become art.

> One of the qualities that define our contemporary notion of art is a certain claim to artistic sovereignty that historically became possible with the emergence of a public and of institutions of art, around the time of the French Revolution. An artist today can aspire to such sovereignty, which implies that, in addition to producing art, one also has to produce the conditions that enable such production and its channels of circulation. The production of these conditions can become so critical to the production of work that it assumes the shape of the work itself—such is the case with unitednationsplaza. (Lind et al. 115)

The difference between Vidokle and Latour is that when Latour proposes an alternative social theory, he first of all breaks with all terminologies and conceptions of the social, society, and all those structures that determine it, such as the subject/object divide, or the nature/society dichotomy. Vidokle, on the other hand, uses unitednationsplaza to reinstitute the divides, dichotomies and premises that characterize the domain of art as one in which sovereignty is ceaselessly negotiated.

But despite Vidokle's claims, how could unitednationsplaza be materially registered and thereby defined in terms of the potentiality of discursive practices as producing a functional reality without falling back into the trap of rendering the project using dichotomies such as the discursive versus the medium of the exhibition, viewer versus participant, or art versus nonart? So, how can the unitednationsplaza experience (relational activities providing for a reflexive approach in terms of how social, political, and cultural issues condition knowledge production) be articulated in arguing for its materiality as a way that extends the artistic and curatorial as realms of contemporary practice towards the production of agency?

From Matters of Fact to Matters of Concern

Bruno Latour is predominantly concerned with methodologies for exploration, with a shift in perspective from the process of production to the conditions of how to produce. In *Laboratory Life* (Latour and Woolgar) Latour analyses the ways in which scientific practice is being practiced, attending to the fundamental question for every practice of how it is that facts become evident and knowledge is produced. Latour and Woolgar's account of the scientific work in the laboratory of the neuroendocrinologist Roger Guillemin meticulously not only describes what happens in the laboratory, but also presents the discussions between the people working in the laboratory and the ways in which they present their work to the scientific community. It questions how scientists constitute facts and what kind of role rhetoric strategies and experiments play within that process. His observations of participants led Latour to dispute the idea that scientific facts result from experiments. Rather, hypothesis, statements, opinions, and extant postulations go through a series of transformations in the form of tests and experiments, in which their materiality produces their cultural conditioning. The common thread throughout is the notion of scientific truth. "A fact only becomes such when it loses all temporal qualifications and becomes incorporated into a large body of knowledge drawn upon by others" (Latour and Woolgar 106). Here, Latour is contradicting the idea that scientific facts are either "found," or "discovered." Instead the laboratory is described as a space of production in which facts are manufactured and manifested by means of strategic debates between scientists. They ascertain their collective hypothesis to the extent that it later finds its way as a fact into books, where its history of emergence is no longer told. Latour rejects this generation of facts and goes on to develop the claim around a shift from matters of fact to matters of concern ("From Realpolitik to Dingpolitik"). On a methodological level, the shift from matters of fact to matters of concern signifies a shift from natural to social studies, obliterating the distinction between the natural and the social. Latour strongly opposes the way in which the so-called "second empiricism" of social studies represents a higher order of explanation in relation to the first empiricism, that of natural studies. Instead, Latour proposes that scientists "learn how to feed off uncertainties, instead of deciding in advance what the furniture of the world should look like" (*Reassembling the Social* 115).

In this context Latour's enquiry into the very premises of his own practice as a social scientist goes so far that he avoids using the expression the "social" altogether. In fact, the first edition of *Laboratory Life* still featured the subtitle "The social construction of scientific facts" (Latour and Woolgar). The authors later dropped the word "social," however, in order to characterize the laboratory not as a social construction, but as a socially solidified construction of facts: The materiality of things in the laboratory is transformed by various processes of experimentation in which natural products are ontologically disentangled for presentation as scientific facts perceived as cultural phenomena. The ways in which Latour describes scientific practices should not be misread as confirming that scientific knowledge comes about by means of social relations. On the contrary, he accounts for science as a place of instrumental fabrication of knowledge through strategic forms of action, which are necessarily social because every interaction is social (Latour and Woolgar 28).

The way in which Latour deals with the questions of how truths and certainties arise entails a break with sociology and its vocabulary around the notion of "the social" as some kind of fixed entity. The attempt to redefine the term "social" in *Reassembling the Social* as an actor-network account must be understood in the context of his preliminary works *We Have Never Been Modern* and *Pandora's Hope*. "Social" is not used here as a category. It no longer denotes a space of its own, an antagonism or an element in binary opposition to nature. The term has been opened up and blurred so radically that it is no longer meaningful for drawing any defining distinction whatsoever.

Actor-Network Theory

Actor-network theory (ANT) looks for the relational connections that form networks challenging knowledge production in dichotomous structures. It relies on what can be called a material culture of thinking that refuses to reduce to categorizations such as subject and object and instead spends time carefully elaborating on different stages of mediation between them.

> Truth and falsehood. Large and small. Agency and structure. Human and nonhuman. Before and after. Knowledge and power. Context and content. Materiality and sociality. Activity and passivity ... all of these divides have been rubbished in work undertaken in the name of actor-network theory. (Law and Hassard 3)

Developed in the late 1980s by Bruno Latour and Michel Callon, ANT is an approach to social theory that considers people and objects as equals in social networks. ANT's analysis of social formations begins at a point where "action should remain a surprise, a mediation, an event" (Latour, *Reassembling the Social* 25). Actions are not limited to those carried out by people; they include various phenomena including natural elements and technological artefacts. Latour uses the word "actant," a term borrowed from semiotics, to describe everything that causes, or has a stake in, a chain of operations. ANT proposes that our social connections need to be defined anew every time, taking into consideration how things have an important stake in the development and maintenance of social formations. Nature, culture, technology and society, the natural, the ideal and the material, thus no longer contradict one another. ANT does not differentiate between those who act, and that which behaves, eliminating any distinction between structure and system, process and action, or subject and object. Rather, the theory is based on an extended concept of the "thing." Here, a thing is much more than simply an object, and it can have its own agency as an issue and concern. Things such as computers, bacteria, machines and power stations are understood to be hybrids, or quasi-objects. They can no longer be unequivocally assigned to the realm of either nature or society. They represent a certain quality of in-betweenness and reproduce themselves exponentially by means of making associations and developing networks. The task of social scientists is to describe rather than explain, and they cannot allow themselves to fall into the trap of assigning a dual meaning to the social: "Behind the innocuous epistemological claim that social explanations have to be ferreted out lies the ontological claim that those causes have to mobilize forces made of social stuff" (Latour, *Reassembling the Social* 103). Instead of trying to explain the actions of actors, and by extension predicating a causal relationship, ANT avoids any form of explanation and instead describes "how things come together," producing a material register of that which is often being reduced to the appearances in our consciousness (Latour, *Reassembling the Social* 75).

ANT replaces the traditional concept of the social as some form of fixed bond and as an existing base upon which things can occur, and instead argues for methods of understanding social formation as an endless process of production. In so doing, the theory challenges traditional sociology in more than one way. The scientist is not superior to the actors he observes. There is nothing more visible from the outside that is not also visible from the inside. In other words, there is no blind spot to social action. Neither is there a hidden meaning to the relations that are revealed by the scientist. The scientist is no longer in a position to mediate between nature and society because that divide does not exist in reality, but only forms part of the "modernist settlement" that Latour and ANT so vehemently oppose (*Reassembling the Social* 73). Referring to the modernist settlement he describes as a production of certainties based on dialectical hierarchies in which epistemology, ontology, and psychology are forces that are supposed to provide explanations for the relations between mind and nature, nature and society, and society and mind, respectively.

Latour concludes his critique of dialectical thinking by describing how people are "locked not only into the prison of their own categories but into that of their social groups as well" (*Pandora's Hope* 7). According to Latour, the modernist settlement is not only a (somewhat abstract) theoretical construction, but also a pressing political problem, because objectivity, gained from the dialectical dispositions, is used to generate forms of social order. In contrast, the kind of alternative settlement that Latour starts to outline in *Pandora's Hope* and later articulates as a social theory using ANT as its theoretical foundation in *Reassembling the Social* is a process-oriented form that observes "science-in-the-making," in which, as Latour says, "we do not *lack* certainty, because we never dreamed of *dominating* the people" (*Pandora's Hope* 15).

Latour credits artistic practices with the potential to call the modernist settlement into question. He renders artistic practices as a construction site. He does not in this context, however, allude to a construction of facts as a fabrication of reality. Instead, he points to a string of associations for which "the whole idea of a building made of social stuff vanishes" (*Reassembling the Social* 92). The idea of the social as a fixed characteristic or form of explanation gives way to clusters of associations, spatial formations that do not produce matters of fact, but matters of concern. These even resist social explanations in that they are "uncertain, and loudly disputed, taken as gatherings," whose "traces" can be found everywhere (*Reassembling the Social* 114–15).

> It provides a rare glimpse of what it is for a thing to emerge out of inexistence by adding to any existing entity its time dimension. Even more important, when you are guided to any construction site you are experiencing the troubling and exhilarating feeling that things *could be different*, or at least that *they could still fail*—a feeling never so deep when faced with the final production, no matter how beautiful or impressive it may be. (*Reassembling the Social* 89)

Sociality by Association

Latour's critique of object-oriented sociology and the dominating position of the social researcher can be applied to artistic and curatorial practices within the medium of the discursive. With reference to Latour's articulation, and contrasting somewhat Vidokle's self-positioning, the artist or curator should not exhibit superiority towards the actors. The relations built in the space of associations do not retain any hidden meaning to be deciphered by the artist or curator, who is no longer in a position to mediate between art and society, because art—conceived of as a relational activity—always entails the production of sociality. Such understanding, as proposed earlier with the account of ANT, conceives of practices as relation-building activities operating within a hybridity in which it is impossible to dissaggregate that which is structure or process, being the result or the enabling factor in processes of knowledge production. This hybridity relies on taking the concept of agency and applying it not only to the human, but also to the nonhuman world. However, this does not mean that any matter or material entity has an agency autonomous from the human. Rather, it is the network of agents, *actants*, and the relations between them that are looked at for understanding practices within what can be called a material culture of knowledge production.

When talking about agency in relation to objects, things, and nonhuman entities in the context of art, the question what agency the artwork can assume in terms of having material power is obvious. In his book *Art and Agency* British anthropologist Alfred Gell looks at the relation between objects and humans and develops a theory of abduction for how objects contain embedded forms of human agency. The artwork or artifact builds a representational front for the people's intentionality. Daniel Miller describes Gell's account not as a mere theory of "casual inference," but as a theory of "inferred intentionality" based on a "refutation of an aesthetic theory of art" (33). He thereby also points to the limitations of this theory, which I would like to highlight here in the context of proposing a postrepresentational approach not only to the notion of art, but also to the context of materiality: The relationship Gell proposes between object and human agency is consistent of a circular process in which it is impossible to clearly differentiate between object and subject in terms of agency, however the dualism of the subject-object divide remains foundational for the theory. Latour, in contrast to Gell, is rather disregardful of the concept of intentionality precisely in order to surpass this dialectic and, instead, suggests thinking agency as a result of an engaged notion of practice that takes account of the different kind of effectivities that material objects and processes employ as an implication of the positions they hold within networks of relations such as artistic practices—whether exhibitionary, discursive, or performative—that always include human and nonhuman actors.

In this sense it proves worthwhile looking at how exactly the account of unitednationsplaza could benefit from being read as ANT-based. Latour's description of how "groups are not silent things, but rather the provisional product of a constant uproar made by the millions of contradictory voices about what is a group and who pertains to what" (*Reassembling the Social* 31) is echoed in Verwoert's description of people getting together during unitednationsplaza as a form of gathering driven by the speculative character of the discursive, which provides for all the different voices housed under one roof ("Gathering People" 17). More directly, he also refers to the experience of the process of forming a group as an "'imprint of the momentum,' which is a collective effort, not a private property" ("Gathering People" 19). This refers to a revised concept of actors' identification with their action and the forms of agency expressed through it. For Latour, the relation between actor, action, and agency is not causal, but can only be revealed in describing a process of links, traces, associations, and translations, and the description of the group is never independent from its materialization in actions. Similarly, Verwoert describes the constitution of the group as the collective effort that results from experiencing the form of gathering while participating in it.

Katharina Schlieben describes how this form of culture of practice replaces the study of social order by tracing associations and gathering fragmented accounts in order to assemble a contact zone as a productive opportunity, rather than instrumentalizing artistic practice for the dissemination of already validated forms of knowledge.

> Latour's inquiry on the gathering as "thing" and its representation is consistent with the question of the performance of collective practices and their actors, and their respective mechanisms of representation. It also addresses the implicit moment of the social per se, which we may regard as a network in which elements correlate, complement each other and offer new scopes for action. (Schlieben 20)

In Latour's vocabulary "social does not designate a thing among other things, like a black sheep among other white sheep, but a type of connection between things that are not themselves social" (*Reassembling the Social* 5). This connection is a network connection, although here the term "network" should be understood not as a series of inter-connected points, but as what designates "the ability of each actor to make other actors do unexpected things" (*Reassembling the Social* 129). The "implicit moment of the social" that Schlieben describes can therefore not be defined as a result of an action. Instead, it is its beginning.

> The question of the social emerges when the ties in which one is entangled begin to unravel; the social is further detected through the surprising movement from one association to the next; those movements can either be suspended or resumed. (Latour, *Reassembling the Social* 247)

In relation to unitednationsplaza, the Chris Evans performance could be regarded as the event through which the notion of a material register of the production of sociality emerged, the reason being that the performance explicitly unravelled the ties—the conception of interaction as a form of participation between speaker and guests—which had previously been set up. The performance dealt with the restrictions of its own condition in such a way that it made the uncertainties deriving from this condition the subject matter of its exploration. Or, in other words, the scenario that Evans devised can be described as especially "anti-social" in order to shed light on the processes of relation-building and translation that the quasi-academic setting of unitednationsplaza obstructed, rather than provided for. The artist showed how collaborative processes can generate spaces of communication that based on their material register offer new scopes for action. This particular example can be described as an ANT experiment that requires the rendering of the assemblage as encompassing much more than solely people, and include such elements as the failed audiovisual transmission, the projectors, the door, the hand that knocked, the sound of the knocking, etc. When defined as the forming of associations within relation-building processes, the social can be traced through the many material entities that participate in such processes. However, this definition of a transformative function ascribed to forming relations, bringing people together and using the element of uncertainty as a condition for practices does not provide for an implication of a social function for art or artistic practices.

The fundamental difference between Vidokle and Latour lies in the attention and determination with which Vidokle critically addresses the conditions of art production as deficient in not responding to the "need to engage with society in order to create certain freedoms, to produce the conditions necessary for creative activity to take place at all" ("Exhibition as School" 8). It is, however, paradoxical that at the same time as attempting to critique the conditions for art production the project itself rests upon a notion of art production. To clarify the nature of the paradox, one should look at the relation between ANT as a proposition for a social theory and its contextual critique of theories of the social. Latour gives an account of ANT as providing for an alternative social theory for which he debunks each and every premise upon which theories of the social have been founded. This is very different from Vidokle, whose theoretical conceptions and practical implications are founded upon a number of conjectures around art as a social medium that presuppose that the social is an attribute linking art with public engagement. This might actually prohibit forms of active engagement, rather than engender it.

Vidokle's interest in using art to deliberate social space is far from unconditional; it assumes that by bringing people together art can function to transform a curated encounter into a space of real social action, where collaborative discursive practices produce sociality. But Latour proposes that there is no society, no setting, and no framework that predetermines sociality, which can only be traced by observing how actors materialize their own existence in the group as it forms through their actions. The social is not some positive concept that can be instituted or manufactured in the sense of transforming how and by what it is governed. Rather, the question addressed at the curated encounter must be how processes of subjectivation and imagination can be instituted in a different way, for example by providing a space in which there is the possibility to track those associations and connections that "might end up in a shared definition of a common world" (Latour, *Reassembling the Social* 247). This is what Brno Latour frequently calls "collective," although this is certainly not a reference to the construction of the collective in the discursive as it appears in unitednationsplaza. Here, we saw a set of practices that produced the collective as a specific form of subjectivity organized in a space devised by the host, who, as its author, acted as a parasite to the collective condition that he created for his own positioning as an artist in the context of social and political practices.

The deployment of Latour's observations on the production of sociality in group formation to enhance my analysis of unitednationsplaza is pursuant to the idea of using Latour's articulations to facilitate the development of a vocabulary pertaining to a material register of the curated encounter in discursive practices, with specific regard to arguments bearing on socially transformative functions of artistic and curatorial practices. The aim is to uncover the figurative representations we often apply in terminologies relating to the social. I propose that any transformative function of artistic and curatorial practices lies in developing an exceptionally powerful and resilient attitude towards any argument that employs art as a social medium from an idealistic point of view. Arguments such as these often go in hand with a sense of instrumentalization, and use art as an explanatory force intended to arrive at an objectification or commodification of sociality that could further a production of certainties or implication of domination. The question, then, is not whether art is a social medium, but whether art functions as a space in which to account for the associations and connections that might be tracked producing a material register of practices.

This chapter further developed the analysis of exhibitions as communicative spaces, by addressing the question of whether discursive practices also function as spaces in which the process of emerging dialogues and collaborations translates laterally the matters proposed by artists—and other cultural producers from different backgrounds and contexts—into a materiality that can perpetuate its own currency as a matter of content beyond the structure that nurtured it. Again, this has nothing to do with the concept of an art object or artefact having or assuming agency for, or instead of people. Rather, by building a "functional reality" (Gillick, "The Binary Stadium" 52) the discursive gains relevance as a communicative space whose ontological and epistemological status are dependent on the relations that emerge from negotiating different material registers of subject and object, and which can only be defined by their observation, description, and discussion.

Action is Overtaken

In an essay published in 2012, well after unitednationsplaza and *Night School* came to an end, Vidokle continues to develop his thoughts on art's potentially transformative function. Instead of outlining a project aimed at achieving a transformative function, he articulates and explores the paradox that locks artistic practices into a situation of no escape from the "supra-institution of Contemporary Art," which hinder any such transformations. Vidokle describes how "recent biennials and Documentas have evaded thematisation specifically under the banner of a vague and relativistic, open-ended idea of heterogeneous plurality." He claims that these are only proof of how "the classification of art as 'contemporary' emerged as a convenient means of playing two sides of a paradigmatic shift simultaneously." (Vidokle and Kuan Wood 4–7)

> Contemporary art has a very peculiar way of distancing itself from
> the universalizing impulses of modernity by replacing these impulses
> with a much more concrete, actual universal format for drawing art
> from all corners of the globe together into a single, massive container.
> (Vidokle and Kuan Wood 4)

The situation that art production faces when not being content with
"using the currency of the regime that governs it," as Vidokle describes it, requires not a search for an alternative model of production for artistic practice, but the realization that the change in perspective has to occur on another level, one that engages in a conflict
with the ways in which art has been used "to promote liberal and
democratic values" in the history of art in the Western hemisphere
(Vidokle and Kuan Wood 6). He might have added that artistic practices are too easily defined as an intrinsically democratic relational
activity. This recalls Claire Bishop's criticism of Bourriaud's concept
of relational aesthetics as resting "too comfortably within an ideal of
subjectivity as whole and of community as immanent togetherness"
("Antagonism and Relational Aesthetics" 67). Vidokle refers back to
Marcel Duchamp to argue against the commodification of discursive practices and to search for a renewed sovereign position for art
production. Vidokle credits him with "breaking the contract" between the exhibition and the work of art based on Duchamp's symbolic and representative value, which enabled artists to use the exhibition as a site to reconsider the conditions for art production
(Vidokle and Kuan Wood 1). But the enclosure of this revision reducing the politics of any given artwork to having its diplomatic capacity confined to the contemporary art system prevents the artist from
acting from a sovereign position. This was Vidokle's central motivation for initiating unitednationsplaza devalorizing the communicative potential of the exhibition space. In the face of another phase of
recuperation of artistic sovereignty for processes of production in
the knowledge economy, Vidokle looks to the curatorial as potentially providing a framework that can put into practice the demand
for a sovereign position of art deliberating a communicative space
for negotiating its own transformative function:

> Could it be, then, that if we are to take the lessons of institutional
> critique to heart, that a Duchampian break today would necessarily
> have to take into consideration not only the aesthetic field and its
> logics of museological enclosure, but would also have to identify the

weak points and systematic inconsistencies of the meta-museum of global liberal democratic capitalism that has absorbed it? ... Today, when artists seeking the freedom to work as they please do so by employing curatorial methodologies in their work, and when curators themselves seem to be the proven beneficiaries of Duchamp's contextual break, should it not be the task of the curator to pose these questions concerning sovereignty and contextual freedom? (Vidokle and Kuan Wood 6)

Vidokle would not go so far as to suggest that the curator would not have been any less engaged in maintaining and expanding the enclosure of contemporary art, and also does not explain what form the curator's Duchampian contextual break might take. Again, here Latour serves to map out a possible answer, claiming to break free of any attempts to relate art and life, art and reality, and art and the social as a form of classifying reality.

Reality is an object of belief only for those who have started down this impossible cascade of settlements, always tumbling into a worse and more radical solution. Let them clean up their own mess and accept the responsibility for their own sins. (Latour, *Pandora's Hope* 14)

In *Reassembling the Social* Latour states that there is no social. It has long evaporated, or was never even there "in reality" (42). This is because reality is a category that cannot be observed without an act of definition. But the social can, if it is taken away from being a definition of a group, an intentional action and a classification of behaviour. All these explanations only serve to bridge the gap between the "out there" and the "in us." Instead of groups, there is group formation; instead of societies, there are collectives; instead of actors, there are the many things that make actors act, such as actants, hybrids and quasi-objects. According to ANT, action is overtaken, which simply means that it should remain "a surprise, a mediation, an event," which, when wanting to follow the string of actions, poses the challenge of not conflating all the agencies into some kind of meta-agency of "society" or "culture." Instead, analysis should begin from the "under-determination of action, from the uncertainties and controversies about who and what is acting when 'we' act" (Latour, *Reassembling the Social* 45). It is only in those short moments when associations between things and humans are built that the social can be gazed upon in its process of emergence, not as "social stuff"—some kind of product—but as associations, describable only in following the many transformations and translations that took place.

My analysis of unitednationsplaza sought to accomplish exactly that, by describing the transformations and translations of relations with the help of Vidokle's own articulations and those of his collaborators and participants to the projects. Its intention was to reflect the complex recursive structures and processes between art production and its social, political, and cultural conditioning in the same way that Vidokle articulates that "the production of these conditions can become so critical to the production of work that it assumes the shape of the work itself" (Lind et al. 114). However, subsuming relation building processes in a curated encounter entirely under the notion of the artwork is wrong, because the artwork cannot simultaneously be both the material that produces relations and the structure that provides its processes of interaction. My analysis shows that unitednationsplaza can be perceived in terms of an experiment that made working on the conditions of art production its product. This brought an understanding of how the notion of art contemporaneously resides in its exhibition making, communication, distribution, and circulation. Furthermore, the analysis demonstrated just how quickly those processes could be turned around to attain the status of product.

The fact that Vidokle never describes the project in terms of curating, and frequently even insists that the facilitating role of the curatorial is secondary to a sovereign positioning of the artist ("Art Without Artists?") signals a central denial of the possibility of comprehending art at a systemic level. He also fails to see that curatorial practices can "assume more of art than the primacy of its production" (Malik). Arguing for abandoning the hierarchization in notions of curating facilitating art production, Suhail Malik calls for an understanding of how "curating can organize art's present and future as a demand and not just a fact." Malik does not specify how art's present future can be organized as a demand in difference to a fact. But from the context of his essay, which focuses on criticizing the educational turn, the notion of demand can be understood as a form of enquiry that insists on the necessity for its relevance to be addressed with respect to how its production is conditioned socially, politically, and culturally. In analogy, we could recall Latour's proposition for a shift from matters of fact to matters of concern ("From Realpolitik to Dingpolitik"), which requires a change in perspective from the process of production itself to the conditions of how to produce, that is to track the associations produced materially that define a relational understanding or practice in terms of producing sociality.

Malik does not talk about unitednationsplaza specifically, but he critically addresses the "assumption that better politics—and something like better art—will happen through the formation of spontaneous communities, of common interests coherently realized, of self-authorized informal educational-artistic endeavors." In this context the notion of art's present and future to be organized as a demand can further be understood referring to the way art implies a negotiation of issues and concerns that extend well beyond its immediate context of experience. Such negotiation processes aim to establish the universality of art's manifestations. As an example of such a demand, we could bring into the picture Vidokle's demand for art to be able to produce an effective public.

While Vidokle does not attest any role to curating in relation to such demand other than facilitating its production and articulation, in fact not accrediting any power to curators, Malik suggests a relation between curating and art in which "curating must assume its power to comprehend art at a systemic level as its own condition," enabling curating to "take art out of its sclerotic indifference to itself." This argument rests on a series of presuppositions. On the one hand, for Malik to request for curating to assume power refers to how curating, and particularly exhibition making, has been perceived to have a primarily facilitating function for the presentation of art. On the other hand, Malik claims that art is unable to address a relationship between its strategies and conditions of production. Therefore, to put Malik's request for curating in other words, curating must assume a position of organizing the ways in which art's presentation and experience produces a reflexive understanding on its conditions of production. Crediting curating with such an important capacity of signification, consequently the practice has to be understood as grounded in, on the one hand, a notion of conflict with regard to claims around art's production of autonomy and sovereignty, and, on the other, institutional forms of governmentality.

.

The Performative Quality of the Curatorial

What agency does the curatorial assume with regard to the production of sociality and knowledge? Having previously explored different formations of individual and collective agency with regard to situations of hospitality in the curated encounter, the time has come to outline the question of what political, social or cultural function this agency can assume. This chapter therefore articulates a relation between curatorial strategies and the realm of cultural production, further exploring questions around institutional politics and the role of artists and curators in addressing concerns around the ongoing economization of the cultural sphere. This elaboration on the notion of a "curatorial complex" will serve to both describe how contemporary curatorial practices working across different formats and seeking to escape the logic of representation, are situated in knowledge-power relations and contribute to their formation. Ultimately, this chapter will outline the idea of a material turn in curatorial practices as a form of counterhegemonic commitment in the curatorial complex.

Adressing the proliferation of the curatorial in an expanded field of exhibitionary, discursive, and performative practices involves reviewing projects that posit discursive forms of practices alongside more conventional forms of exhibition making. This will advance the discussion around the discursive in relation to claims for social engagement in artistic and curatorial practices. At the same time, the notion of the communicative exhibition space fostering forms of emancipated spectatorship will be reviewed in this context.

As a starting point for this exploration, this chapter discusses the *Former West* project in order to exemplarily enquire into the dispositives, institutions, and economic and social parameters in which contemporary curatorial projects are embedded. *Former West* is a long-term international research, exhibition, publishing, and education project, a speculative platform considering the cultural, social, economic, and political consequences of the changes that the year 1989 brought to the West.[41] It was initiated in 2009 by Maria Hlavjova,

---

41 The term "Former East" is used as a catch-all for the former communist states of Central and Eastern Europe, including the Soviet Union and the countries of

artistic director of Basis voor actuele kunst (BAK) in Utrecht, and Charles Esche, director of the Van Abbemuseum in Eindhoven, and Katrin Rhomberg, at the time curator of the 6th Berlin Bienniale. The curators of the project are joined by a number of research advisors who take part in programming the events and exhibitions of *Former West* ("Former West: Team"). In addition, many artists, curators, and thinkers around the world regularly contribute to the programme, which makes *Former West* both a platform and a resource for thinking about and through contemporary art.

The analysis of the project emphasizes the specific cultural technologies involved in producing and organizing "imaginaries" as a political component in the generation of sociality. This term was introduced by curator Simon Sheikh into the *Former West* context, in reference to the Greek philosopher Cornelius Castoriadis, who defines imagination as an indispensable concept for describing the formation of social structures: Societies form through institutionalizing imaginaries by means of subjectivity, meaning, the formation of social relationships, etc. (Castoriadis 71–74 qtd. in Sheikh, "Vectors" 64). Jacques Lacan refers to the imaginary as one of three interdependent elements of order for human existence and the constitution of psyche, alongside the symbolic and the real. He firstly introduces the concept of "imaginary order" pointing out how the toddler is captivated and excited by his reflected image in the mirror. This marks an inherent duality in the process of self-identification. Hence, imaginary order is organized by the production of images (Lacan 60–71).

Central to this chapter is the notion of producing imaginaries pertaining to both the individual and a collective body of people, because the curators of *Former West* repeatedly refer to it as a political quality of a society dealing with the entirety of its constitution (Hlavajova et al., *On Horizons* 8–9; Sheikh, "Vectors" 160–66). The analysis of *Former West* focuses on the implications for processes of knowledge production in curatorial practices of the proposition of the production of imaginaries by means of artistic practices and in the curated encounter. Using several examples from this long-term project, priority is given to contrasting the medium of the exhibition with the discursive, with an emphasis on the various curatorial strat-

---

the Warsaw Pact: Albania, Bulgaria, Czechoslovakia, GDR, Hungary, Poland, and Romania.

egies and on the potential of communicability that lies in the diverse mediums of practice. This serves to evaluate the political quality associated with each format for the production of imaginaries.
The analysis focuses on notions of sociality and communality as
both a requirement for and a product of the curated encounter, as-
sessing what function such conceptions assume in the development
of curatorial practices into modes of practice towards the formation
of the social sphere.

Beyond the confines of the *Former West* project, this chapter enquires into notion of producing imaginaries against the backdrop of
artistic and curatorial practices expressing an interest in finding new
relations in art and society, articulating horizons of social, cultural,
and political expectation in the curated encounter as a space of experience (Bishop, "The Social Turn"; Wappler).

From the Exhibitionary to the Curatorial Complex

In his seminal text *The Exhibitionary Complex,* first published in
1988, Tony Bennett looks at the function of the exhibition in modern
societies and shows how the exhibition came to present an alternative mode of production of knowledge and power, ultimately seeking to empower its public through education. Rather than addressing one particular exhibition Bennett describes the typology of the
exhibition in the context of the formation of societies, defining the
exhibitionary complex as a set of institutions and their accompanying knowledge-power relations. Locating its formation towards the
mid-1800s with the advent of The Great Exhibitions—the anteced-
ents of World Expos, national exhibitions and biennials—the museums opened their doors for the first time to a more general public,
transforming themselves from private domains to public arenas.
They became "vehicles for inscribing and broadcasting the messages
of power ... throughout society" (Bennett, "The Exhibitionary Complex" [1996] 82). Bennett identifies a relation between the formation
of the exhibitionary complex and the development of the bourgeois
democratic polity, in that it presents a "set of cultural technologies
concerned to organize a voluntarily self-regulating citizenry" (84).
The exhibitionary complex also always provides moments of spectacle and forms of symbolic representations of the self, for which it
acts not solely in a disciplining fashion, but also as a space of pro-

duction of affect. In this regard the modern museum, identified as a complex of knowledge-power relations,[42] governs through various forms of affective empowerment.

Curatorial discourse is very much aware of Bennett's observations and the interpretations and further developments emanating from the field of sociology and from visual cultures (Rose 240–43). In fact, curatorial discourse itself could be viewed as the contemporary arena of debate around the political function of the space in which art is installed (in an exhibition or in more discursively configured spaces) as a form of cultural production. The discourse around the notion of the "curatorial" deals in particular with how such knowledge-power relations are formed in and by curatorial practices. Like Bennett, Nora Sternfeld focuses strongly on the knowledge-power complex, not with a view to locating the curatorial as caught in a web of institutional disciplinary mechanisms, but in order to understand curatorial agency as a form of actualizing notions of "power" and "knowledge," in line with postcolonial theorist Gayatri Spivak's verbs that indicate forms of "how to do something" (*savoir*) and "being able to do it" (*pouvoir*) (Spivak 25–27 qtd. in Sternfeld, "Being Able" 151–56).

> If we think curating beyond representation as "being able to do something," then it involves processes that produce themselves—so it is no longer about exhibitions as sites for setting up valuable objects and representing objective values, but rather about spaces for curatorial action in which unexpected encounters and discourses become possible. (Sternfeld, "Being Able" 152)

In light of the ways the exhibitionary complex has contributed to forming discourse around curating practices, I propose a consideration of the notion of a "curatorial complex." The function of this term is to describe not particular curatorial projects but the typology of large-scale curatorial projects such as biennials, Documentas, or large-scale projects such as *Former West*. In order to outline what the notion of a curatorial complex could specifically refer to, I will look into how spaces for action, as Sternfeld calls them, are built and what function they can assume in the context of contemporary forms of

---

42 The term "knowledge-power relations" originates in Michel Foucault's discussions of how mechanisms of power produce various kinds of knowledge used to reinforce exercise of power (Focault, *Power/Knowledge*).

cultural production. Introducing the notion of the curatorial complex, which entails a discussion of curatorial discourse, focuses the analysis of *Former West* less on the history of the activity of curating in institutional or independent contexts—as exercised by curators or artists—and more on approaching the curatorial as a methodology of practice that has a distinct political quality. Sternfeld considers this political quality to be particularly empowering for producing sociality that can alter the knowledge-power relations. But Bennett's remarks on the exhibitionary complex suggest that the curatorial complex must first of all be conceived as dependent upon these relations determined by the economic, political, social, and cultural conditions that define the times in which they operate.

In order to develop the notion of the curatorial complex I will continue from the previous chapter to describe and analyse how the relationship between art and the social—particularly the part curatorial practices play in establishing this relationship—has been a focus of curatorial discourse since the 1990s, particularly with regard to art's capacity to act politically. The following articulation is by no means representative of the growing interdisciplinary field of curatorial discourse and should not be mistaken for any kind of historical account or conceptual overview. Two recent examples of curatorial discourse have already taken on this task. Paul O'Neill has given a detailed historical account of the emergence of curatorial discourse since the late 1960s and he locates the "consolidation of a curator-centered discourse in the 1990s, when a history of curatorial practice began" (*The Culture of Curating* 9). Terry Smith has discussed many prominent curatorial projects of the recent decades in great detail, providing a historical account of artistic and curatorial projects and their relation with the emergence of intellectual discourse (57–100).

The Field of the Curatorial

Over the course of the 1990s a series of symposiums and seminars were organized in response to a growing frustration with how curating was increasingly becoming a practice of exhibition making that fed rather than challenged the apparatus of cultural production, not providing a critical dimension to the contextualization of artworks but merely situating the production of exhibitions in the midst of an increasingly consumer-led entertainment industry. Some events debated the roles and responsibilities of curators in this context, including the 1992 symposium *A New Spirit in Curating*,[43] organized by Ute Meta Bauer at Künstlerhaus Stuttgart, *Stopping the Process* a symposium organized by the Nordic Institute for Contemporary Art, Helsinki (Hannula), and *Curating Degree Zero,* the touring archive and publication of the same name (Drabble and Richter), to name but a few. Also in the mid-1990s, publications such as the aforementioned *Thinking About Exhibitions* (Greenberg et al.) and *Curating: The Contemporary Art Museum And Beyond* (Harding) offered a selection of essays from curators, critics, critical theorists, sociologists, and art historians that discussed the role of the curator, communication, display, narrative, and spectatorship from the perspective of the realm of cultural production. In response to the growing visibility of the figure of the curator, not least embodied in the prolific practice of figures such as Harald Szeemann or Pontus Hultén, awareness increased with respect to how much the role of the curator as a cultural agent was entangled in systems productive of value, power, and reputation. This led, on the one hand, to a discursive turn in curatorial practices, foregrounding the format of the symposium, seminar, interview, etc., and, on the other, the development of theoretical approaches. The attendant critical discussion of the authorial position of the curator, the objectivity of the space of the exhibition, the neutrality of the museum and the economic and political entanglement of institutional practices produced what Nora Sternfeld calls a "reflexive turn" in curatorial discourse, leading to the evolution of a plethora of transdisciplinary and transnational curatorial practices that reinstitute curating as a cultural practice in new, different and more experimental ways ("Kuratorische Ansätze" 75).

The format that came to dominate the realm of curating practices in the 1990s was the discursive. In part this was a response to the crisis of representation in the exhibition space, and in part it was inspired by artists foregrounding the discursive as a material for their practice. To define the curatorial as a discursive space of production is linked to claims for the potential of curatorial practice to act as a medium not only of enquiry but also of critique towards the

---

43 Participants included Bart Cassiman, Eric Colliard, Colin De Land, Corinne Diserens, Helmut Draxler, John Miller, Hans-Ulrich Obrist, and Philippe Thomas.

social, cultural, and political conditions of the cultural practices. It is in this sense that Mick Wilson positions the value of the discursive against that of commerce, with its critical communicative experience, making the public sphere "the promise of multiple sociable *fora* of reasoned discussion which are unconstrained by the imperative of the state and un-tethered from the transactional logic of the market space" (204). Both Wilson and Paul O'Neill describe how the gesture of generating discussion, conversations, and debate by means of curating is linked to an "evacuated role of the critic in parallel cultural discourse" (O'Neill, "The Curatorial Turn" 242), making the space of curating a space of issuing critique. In pointing out the dangers of the curator orchestrating the production of critique Wilson refers to Liam Gillick, who, in an exchange with Saskia Bos, describes the conflation of the curatorial with the critical space as affecting criticism in the sense of that it "has become either a thing of record, or a thing of speculation whereas curatorial voice has become a parallel critical voice to the artist that contributes a parallel discourse" (Wilson 205; Bos and Gillick 74). Wilson therefore concludes that, "this pattern of development presents itself as the displacement of an exhausted critical discourse—and the partially evacuated role of the critic—by a dialogical process variously facilitated, co-ordinated or enacted by the curator role in conjunction with the role of the artists" (Wilson 205).

One of the first large-scale events that purposely used the realm of the discursive in this sense was Documenta X (1997), curated by Cathcrine David—not to replace the exhibition space, however, but to complement it. The *100 Days—100 Guests* programme invited artists, architects, philosophers, urbanists, economists, and other cultural figures from all over the world (particularly Arab and African countries), to debate what David called "the great ethical and aesthetic questions of the century's close: the urban realm, territory, identity, new forms of citizenship, the national social state and its disappearance, racism and the state, the globalization of markets and national policy, universalism and culturalism, poetics and politics" (David and Sztulman 17). David articulates her curatorial methodology as "retroperspective." The event programme therefore needed to be considered together with the Documenta publication *Politics-Poetics* (David and Chevrier) that covered the entire postwar period in 800-plus pages of montaged texts, images and interviews. While the book was conceived as a backdrop to an interpretation of artistic activity from 1945 until the end of the twentieth century in the context of shifting political, cultural and social relationships in times of globalization, David stated firmly that her agenda for the discursive programme was more pragmatic than programmatic:

> It makes no claim to anticipate the course of developments in the future or the possible evolution that can already be glimpsed in the works and attitudes of younger generations, but it does lay the accent on certain strong alterities of contemporary culture, etc. (David and Szutlman 12)

The unprecedented *100 Days—100 Guests* programme configured a relation not only between art and theory, but also between the critical and the curatorial. By offering a space for reflection, the discursive allowed for curating to affirm its status as a cultural practice producing a critical debate on the conditions of its own practice, its temporal and spatial context, and, more precisely, its contemporary and geo-political context.

Many scholars have praised David's Documenta X for introducing a decisive change in the history of curatorial as cultural practices. Irit Rogoff refers to Documenta X as "the most visible moment of shift in a somewhat uneasy relation between curating, artistic practices and knowledge production, and political imperatives" (Bismarck and Rogoff 26), as it did not intend to resolve this relation but to produce a friction between the hegemonic discourse in which an institution such as Documenta is firmly situated and the counterhegemonic aspirations Documenta X pursued. Oliver Marchart analyzed and identified those shifts that Documenta X (and later 2002's Documenta 11 directed by Okwui Enwezor) introduced to the field of curatorial practices, particularly with regard to large-scale exhibitions and biennials, as processes of politicization, attempts to "decentre" the West, forms of theorization, and strategies of mediation. But while praising the progressive effects that particularly Documenta X and Documenta 11 achieved, Marchart points to the inevitable tendency of large-scale exhibitions to *produce* hegemony. Marchart describes this phenomenon as the "irony of the political":

> The counterhegemonic effects that these shifts produce have to be read in relation to the history of large-scale exhibitions as formerly national and now global hegemony-producing machines. Hence, while attempting to critique dominant culture such large-scale events also always produce it. (*Hegemonie im Kunstfeld* 7-10)

The social, cultural, and political function of the mega exhibition was a specific subject of interest in curatorial discourse at the turn of the millenium, largely in response "biennialization," the exponential growth in temporary exhibitions and art events on a global scale that can be criticized for its fostering of a form of cultural consumerism for a distinguished and well-educated middle class. Publications such as *The Manifesta Decade* (Vanderlinden and Filipovic, 2005) reflected critically on the shifting conditions of exhibition making and the ways in which cultural policymaking influences curatorial practices, with particular reference to *Manifesta, European Biennial of Contemporary Art*. In their introduction to this compilation of essays and texts by curators, artists, theorists, and art historians, Vanderlinden and Filipovic characterize the period from 1989 to 2005 as a "long decade" full of shifting paradigms and practices of large-scale exhibitions that are in need of analysis, particular because the cultural repercussions of the political events—from the geographical and political remapping of Europe and its neighbouring terrains in 1989 to the rejection of a European constitution in 2005—had not been identified and reflected upon. "The impetus to frame this study from a European perspective was a strategic one, especially at a moment when the question of what Europe is or hopes to be is altogether uncertain" (Vanderlinden and Filipovic 13).

It has become a curatorial strategy to contextualize the production of a discourse on curatorial practices—and exhibition-making in particular—by reflecting on social, political, and cultural conditions, predominantly in order to differentiate between these practices and market-oriented productions and displays of contemporary art. For example, for their 2010 Taipei Biennial at the Taipei Fine Arts Museum curators Hongjohn Lin and Tirdad Zolghadr proposed "an exhibition on the politics of art" that could reflect on "how art is being produced, circulated, and consumed."

> An exhibition, therefore, is never an innocent collection of artwork, but rather a set of social relations upon which the production of art is constructed. To invoke the politics of art is simply to make these social relations visible, so that the division between the social and the aesthetic is no longer distinguishable and thus, rendered obsolete. (*Taipei Biennial*)

This form of self-reflexive strategy in curatorial practice is, in part, a reaction to how art history traditionally canonized the reception of contemporary art focusing on aesthetic qualities of particular works within individual art practices, often without any consideration of the social, political, or cultural context of their emergence. A critical reaction to this process has been established for equally long by artists, curators, and art theorists, both in practice and in theory.

Lin and Zolghadr's proposition is a personal response to the biennial phenomenon[44] from a centre position. Their interest in eradicating any division between the social and the aesthetic is a response to how biennials—even though they have made a significant contribution to discussions on the dialectics of margin and centre and disintegrated the predominant presence of Western artists in large-scale exhibitions—maintain comparable dialectics for their own field of production. For artists and curators alike, participating in biennials comprises a form of validation of their work on an international scale, leading to increased public visibility and market figures. From their own position as biennial curators, and rejecting the idea that artistic and curatorial practices should be a product of the biennial culture, Lin and Zolghadr devise a self-reflexive curatorial strategy that uses the exhibition as a research device on the matter of art and its production.[45]

Curating vs. Curatorial

The desire for expressing self-reflexivity has long characterized much of intellectual curatorial discourse, particularly since the mid-2000s, with the introduction of the distinction between "curating" and "the curatorial," and the subsequent development of the curatorial as a mode for "getting away from representation to a very large extent, and trying to see within this activity a set of possibilities for much larger agendas in the art world" (Bismarck and Rogoff 22). Particularly around the beginning of the new millennium the methods and strategies for learning how to curate and come to define the practice of curating were subject to continuous examination. The loss of the

---

44 There is wide discussion of the biennial as a contemporary cultural phenomenon, see in particular *The Biennial Reader* (Filipovic et al.), an anthology on the global biennial phenomenon.

45 For a critical discussion of the Taipei Biennial see Milena Hoegsberg's "Notes on Self-Reflexive Curatorial Strategies" on the 2010 Taipei Biennial and Shanghai Biennial.

figure of the curator as the mere exhibition organizer and the blurring of disciplinary boundaries with regard to the role of art blending into the social led to a discourse on the function, role, and responsibility of curating practice. Partially in response to the proliferation of institutions providing training in the area of curating in the last two decades, a distinction was drawn between the applied and the academic model: The practice of curating was being contrasted with the notion of the curatorial, a distinction prevalent in Goldsmiths' Curatorial/Knowledge PhD program led by Irit Rogoff and Jean-Paul Martinon.

> If "curating" is a gamut of professional practices that had to do with setting up exhibitions and other modes of display, then "the curatorial" operates at a very different level: it explores all that takes place on the stage set-up, both intentionally and unintentionally, by the curator and view it as an event of knowledge. So to drive home a distinction between "curating" and "the curatorial" means to emphasize a shift from the staging of the event to the actual event itself: its enactment, dramatization, and performance. (Martinon 4)

This distinction serves to focus on the processes of communication and production of narratives that take place in an exhibition or event, thereby disregarding those that lead to the production of this event in the first place, its planning, and organization. Martinon and Rogoff speak of curating as producing "a moment of promise, of redemption to come," whereas the curatorial is what "disturbs this process," engaging works of art in a process by which they are "precipitating our reflection ... encouraging another way of thinking and sensing the world" (Martinon 4).

The research on the curatorial was undertaken in response to the growing diversification of curating practices not only in the realm of visual art, but also throughout cultural production in general. In the attempt to move away from discussing the technical modalities of curating practices (the ways in which works are put together), the term "curatorial" sheds light on what is being produced, not only from the perspective of the curator, but also from that of the viewer, artist, institution, or any other stakeholder. Whereas the initial distinction was drawn for the spatial realm of the exhibition and the dialogue created between artworks, space and viewer, the curatorial has increasingly come to define its own discursive field of production, where it is considered as a form of knowledge production that results from discursive practices in cultural, social, and political contexts. As a discursive field it appears to not be defined in terms of centre or periphery. Rather, it gives and takes from various disciplines. According to the proponents of the term, the curatorial cannot be constricted, which provokes endless attempts to define it. It can therefore be regarded as a multifaceted practice that takes from, and merges, into many different fields of knowledge, practice, and discipline.

> The curatorial is a jailbreak from preexisting frames, a gift enabling one to see the world differently, a strategy for inventing new points of departure, a practice of creating allegiances against social ills, a way of caring for humanity, a process of renewing one's own subjectivity, a tactical move for reinventing life, a sensual practice of creating signification, a political tool outside of politics, a procedure to maintain a community together, a conspiracy against policies, the act of keeping a question alive, the energy of retaining a sense of fun, the device that helps to revisit history, the measures to create affects, the work of revealing ghosts, a plan to remain out-of-joint with time, an evolving method of keeping bodies and objects together, a sharing of understanding, an invitation for reflexivity, a choreographic mode of operation, a way of fighting against corporate culture, etc. (Martinon 19)

The above quote is one of the very recent examples that come to define what is meant by the "expanded field" of the curatorial. From the perspective of the original distinction, the focus of what the curatorial is or does is shifting ever further away from a contention with art. It is in this sense that Paul O'Neill speaks of the "curatorial turn" that has affected the practice of curating, a turn away from practice to discourse, where "curating is 'becoming discourse' in which curators are willing themselves to be the key subject and producer of this discourse" (O'Neill and Wilson, *Curating and the Educational Turn* 257).

For others, such as Maria Lind, however, the centrality of the artworks remains important. She credits the curatorial with the capacity "to do something other than 'business as usual' within and beyond contemporary art" with its "viral presence consisting of signification processes and relationships between objects, people, places, ideas, and so forth, that strives to create friction and push new ideas" (*Performing the Curatorial* 19–20).

Curatorial practice's reference to its own discursive positioning in the field of knowledge production is often paired with the articula-

tion of a political quality in the curatorial. A plethora of recent publications are testimony to this tendency, including *Curating Critique*
(Eigenheer et al.), *Cautionary Tales: Critical Curating* (Rand and
Kouris), *Curating Subjects* (O'Neill and Andreasen), *Cultures of the
Curatorial* (Bismarck et al.), *The Culture of Curating and the Curating
of Culture(s)* (O'Neill), and *The Curatorial: A Philosophy of Curating*
(Martinon), all of which devise an intellectual curatorial discourse
by exploring the history of curatorial practices, particularly exhibition-making, in light of current and divergent fields of practice that
reflect on exhibitions and events in their social, cultural, and political context.

All this discourse leads to questions of how curatorial practices
can function as critical cultural practices and what methodologies
and strategies of production exist to analyse curatorial work in this
capacity. The self-reflexivity of this discourse is furthermore enhanced by the ways in which curators themselves constantly refer to
their own practice or the practice of their colleagues. This results in
a cycle of reflexivity as both condition and product of curatorial
practice. Self-motivated critical thinking about their own practice in
the context of socio-political and cultural particularities produces
reflexivity as a strategic starting point for the work of curators who,
in so doing, locate their work in the midst of the discursive field of
the curatorial. Drawing on Luhmann and Bourdieu's analysis in the
first chapter ("The Communicative Space of the Exhibition"), we can
speak of a habitus of self-referential communication that characterizes contemporary curatorial discourse.

One important question, however, remains unanswered in large
part of curatorial discourse: Does self-reflexivity as a curatorial
methodology assume a specific function in the context of the exhibition, the symposium, the interview or the performance in relation
to the viewer, visitor or participant? Or does it merely serve to locate
and position one's own practice in the field of curatorial discourse?

This question arises with regard to the previous analyses of Fullerton's exhibition *Columbia* and unitednationsplaza, where the element of self-reflexivity was not articulated by the artists or curators,
but emerged from the analysis of each project itself. The first chapter
("The Communicative Space of the Exhibition") characterized the
moment that kicked off a process of communication in and around
the works in Fullerton's exhibition as an event of suspicion. In the
case of unitednationsplaza it was the lack of any objects and the

subsequent positioning of the element of the discursive as a form of art production that led to the question about the function of art for the production of sociality. The following analysis of *Former West* will exemplarily elaborate on the matter of how self-reflexive strategies of curatorial practice operate via the production of communication and sociality. The knowledge-power relations at stake are a central concern, here, as they imply a perspective on the curatorial as a technology as well as a "dispositif" (Foucault, *Power/Knowledge* 194–228). It is in this context that we might speak of a "curatorial complex," a set of methodologies and strategies of production that present the "curatorial" both as a typology and a way of thinking.

Former West

The analysis of *Former West* as a multidimensional curatorial project explores the circularity of curatorial discourse on its specific "curatorialness," focusing more on the strategies and methodologies of its players and less on the material—artworks, objects, people, communications, things—that it organizes and produces. *Former West* is rooted in the intellectual curatorial discourse of recent years, as briefly and selectively introduced on their website:

> Former West is a long-term international research, education, publishing, and exhibition project (2008–16), which from within the field of contemporary art and theory: (1) reflects upon the changes introduced to the world (and thus to the so-called West) by the political, cultural, artistic, and economic events of 1989; (2) engages in rethinking the global histories of the last two decades in dialogue with post-communist and postcolonial thought; and (3) speculates about a "post-bloc" future that recognizes differences yet evolves through the political imperative of equality and the notion of "one world." ("Former West: About")

Directed by Maria Hlavajova, artistic director of Basis voor Actuele Kunst (BAK) in Utrecht, the Netherlands, *Former West* has shifted in direction and focus several times between its founding in 2008 and 2016, but the format in which it operated has remained constant. *Former West* set up discursive relations that acted as a framework for different formats of curatorial, artistic, and academic research practices in order to find a space and place so they can manifest themselves and develop, through congresses, seminars, exhibitions, or

publications, for example. This loose series of temporal manifestations ranged from large-scale public events such as international
congresses (Utrecht in 2009, Istanbul in 2010, Vienna and Utrecht in
2012) to the 2013 Berlin summit, and artists' solo exhibitions, or thematic group shows at several institutions across Europe. In 2014 the
project embarked on its "culminating phase," during which various
Public Editorial Meetings were being organized, leading to a *Former
West* publication (Hlavajova and Sheikh). Many more intimate research interviews, seminars and summits took place in between the
congresses, and all events were streamed live and are well docu-
mented on a website, the virtual home of *Former West*, which serves
as an online platform, a chronology, and an archive, hosting a vast
amount of material produced in congresses, seminars, exhibitions,
and publications. So if any event is missed, it can be accessed in the
form of documents, recordings, images, etc.[46]

My interest in this project primarily emerges from the difficulty
in attributing the various formats that *Former West* used (exhibitions, seminars, research interviews, publications, etc.) to specific
technologies or strategies of practice. In addition to the blurring of
boundaries between different forms of practice—artistic, curatorial, academic—the project situated art as a medium for exploring
the precarious socio-political conditions of cultural practices in
contemporary times. As will be described in the following analysis,
the curators of *Former West* see it as a proposition for using art as an
exploratory device to engage in research around the question of
how the world we live in could be imagined otherwise—more specifically, as a "former West."

The formal and conceptual ambitions of the project respond to
the legacy of many other projects that pursued the idea of freeing
the exhibitionary complex from its representational character in
order to disrupt the established order of knowledge and power. This
meant accompanying, if not replacing, the medium of the exhibition with educational, performative, and discursive spaces of production. The discursive space allowed for the negotiation of much

---

46 The website also hosts a library specific to the research interests of the project.
    It more or less mirrors its physical presence at BAK, which contains over 600
    publications comprising exhibition catalogues, monographs and books on
    postcolonial studies, cultural studies, art theory, political history, geopolitics,
    and social sciences.

more theoretical and scientific content, and this has led to a popu-
larization of scientific knowledge, resulting in an intellectualization
of the art field, particularly of how relations of power and knowledge materialize in exhibitionary and performative strategies of display and enactment.

In order to contextualize the mutual dependency of form and
content it is necessary here to mention a number of primarily discursive projects that seek to construct an anti-hegemonic, discursive
space of production. Examples range from Joseph Beuys' *Bureau for
the Organization for Direct Democracy by Referendum* at Documenta
5 (1972), the aforementioned *100 Days—100 Guests* programme at
Documenta X, and the Documenta 11 platforms in 2002. More recently, at the 2005 *Cork Caucus*, a three-week international cultural
gathering in Cork, Ireland, transdisciplinary meetings with artists,
cultural practitioners, and political activists enquired into relations
between art and democracy (Steiner and Joyce 2006). *A.C.A.D.E.M.Y.*
(2006) was a series of exhibitions, workshops, seminars, and performances—initiated by Angelika Nollert together with Yilmaz Dziew-
ior, Charles Esche, Bart de Baere and Irit Rogoff—investigating the
political quality and critical capacity of the specific space of the art
academy given the changes that the Bologna declaration would
bring to the educational realm.

Writing as one of the curatorial realm's chief protagonists, Irit Rogoff questions the function of the various discursive and educational
turns that have been claimed for artistic and curatorial practices
(Rogoff, "Turning"). She points out two characteristics of contemporary cultural practices particularly curatorial ones, that shed a first
light of the intricacy of the "curatorial complex": the issue that curatorial practices face with respect to how much they contribute to the
construction of hegemonic knowledge-power relations even when
they attempt to resist, avoid, or defer them by searching for a political quality in artistic and curatorial practices.

The start of Rogoff's analysis below is a good description of the
situation that *Former West* faces as a long-term, independent, publicly funded collaborative research and exhibition project. Rogoff
describes the process of discursive and educational turning following Documenta X and Documenta 11.

> There already exists a certain amount of infrastructure within the art
> world, where there are available spaces, small budgets, existing pub-

licity machines, recognizable formats such as exhibitions, gatherings, lecture series, interviews, as well as a constant interested audience made up of art students, cultural activists, etc. As a result, a new set of conversations between artists, scientists, philosophers, critics, economists, architects, planners, and so on, came into being and engaged the issues of the day through a set of highly attenuated prisms. By not being subject to the twin authorities of governing institutions or authoritative academic knowledge, these conversations could in effect be opened up to a speculative mode, and to the invention of subjects as they emerged and were recognized. (Rogoff, "Turning")

Examining whether it is particularly useful to use the term "turn" to label the urgency to rethink either formats and strategies of cultural practices, Rogoff refers to the circularity of enquiry and designation that emerges given that those formulating the enquiry are also the ones creating the playing field.

> Delving into these questions is made more difficult by the degree of slippage that currently takes place between notions of "knowledge production," "research," "education," "open-ended production," and "self-organized pedagogies," when all these approaches seem to have converged into a set of parameters for some renewed facet of production. Although quite different in their genesis, methodology, and protocols, it appears that some perceived proximity to "knowledge economies" has rendered all of these terms part and parcel of a certain liberalizing shift within the world of contemporary art practices. (Rogoff, "Turning")

The logic of production that characterizes cultural practices that add to or entirely forego the medium of the exhibition is rendered here as one that operates on the basis of infrastructure production, means of distribution and dissemination of information, meaning, and knowledge. The methods of research are understood to be provisional and the knowledge economies characterized by their structures, categories, and criteria are still in the making. This elusiveness is consistent with the formal openness of such projects, including all kinds of activities and mediums of practice. The methodology of the curatorial focuses on the curated encounter as an infrastructure that in the first place provides a structure—form—for any production of content to take place in, as a possibility of speculation. Here, the curatorial methodology is akin to the discursive model of practice as described earlier for unitednationsplaza. In this case, however, the production of speculation is not rendered in the context of an artwork, but rather posited as a means to align art with the political. Wilson and Gillick propose that in the curated encounter devised by means of discursive strategies of production, it is not art that is produced, but something else: a discourse parallel to that of art production, in which art becomes enlisted in the greater scheme of repositioning the relationship between what is produced in the curatorial—meaning, knowledge, engagement, sociality—and those for whom it is produced—viewers, audiences, publics (Wilson 205; Bos and Gillick 74).

Former West—Conceptual and Formal Foundations

The following analysis of *Former West* does not seek to be an account of the entire of the project, which ran for eight years. After briefly introducing the methodological and thematic scopes of the project I will focus my discussion on a selection of events contrasting the format of the exhibition with discursive events, enquiring into their different function for setting up a communicative space generating dialogical forms of engagement between participants, audiences, and publics. The examples on which I will focus my analysis are the 2nd Former West Research Congress *On Horizons: Art and Political Imagination*, which took place at Istanbul's Technical University from 4 to 6 November 2010; the exhibition *Vectors of the Possible* (2010), curated by Simon Sheikh at BAK, Utrecht; and *Documents, Constellations, Prospects* (2013), a weeklong event including exhibitions, performances, discussions, seminars, and lectures at Haus der Kulturen der Welt, Berlin. These parts of the overall project were selected to engage with the question of whether the collapse of various spatial, temporal, and topical formats might offer a way for curating to further establish itself as a signifying practice seeking to produce a powerful shift from an emphasis of representation to cultural production as an emancipatory practice. A particular subject for enquiry is the relationship between the medium of the exhibition and more conversational models such as the seminar and the workshop, as well as in relation to performative strategies. With regard to the focus of this analysis on curatorial agency and its forms of production, the Berlin summit *Documents, Constellations, Prospects* is interesting as it conglomerated exhibitionary, discursive, and performative formats for opening up a space of speculation producing a relation between art and the political. This produces the research question of whether—

and, if so, how—by means of curatorial practice different categories of spectatorship and participation can merge towards the production of a different kind of public, one that assumes agency towards the production of sociality and knowledge.

Methodologically, *Former West* emerges from a series of contentions reflecting the conditions of cultural practices today. In the project's first years, up until 2012, most of the exhibitions, events, and seminars that *Former West* organized dealt directly with the sociocultural ramifications that 1989 introduced to the world and how these ramifications are addressed in artistic and curatorial practices. It is always from a position of embeddedness that the project's initiators, curators and advisors address the complexity of articulating the possibility of a "former West" from within a predominantly West-centric art world, pursuing the idea of, "uncovering the breaches in which we can make out the West's formerness and harness the emancipatory promise of the imaginary 'former West' in both art and society within the landscape of rapidly changing global relations" (Hlavajova et al., *Former West* 8–9).

In more recent years the project has moved from being concerned with the past to speculating about the future. This is most evident in the 2013 Berlin summit *Documents, Constellations, Prospects* (2013) and the *Public Editorial Meetings*.[47] The final publication was conceived in these meetings to renegotiate the knowledge accumulated and assembled over the course of the project along thematic trajectories concerned with the current conditions and future prospects of art and cultural practices, in relation to their institutionalization, the way they address and constitute publics, and their overall mode of existence within the current economic and environmental perspectives.

Former West—Initial Research Phase

Former West started in 2008 and 2009 with a series of lectures, seminars and research interviews on the question of what the term "former West" could describe. This produced a first map of discursive

---

47 Five Public Editorial Meetings took place between 2013 and 2015. A complete list with contributors is available in the final publication (Hlavajova and Sheikh 721).

relations between the people involved (including Paul Gilroy, Etienne Balibar, David Held, Mark Duffield, Boris Groys, Helmut Draxler, and Heimo Zobernig), their work, and the ideas they developed in the process. For example, in their interviews with Boris Groys[48] and with Etienne Balibar,[49] respectively, Hlavajova and Esche seem to question whether the notion of a "former West" and the year 1989 are relevant starting points[50] to frame their research. Interested in the personal experiences and views on the historical and present condition of East and West, these conversations map out the broad field of discussion that *Former West*, as a project, later touches upon, located roughly within the dialectics of East and West, 1989 and 2009, modernity and contemporaneity, communism and neoliberalism, nationalism and socialism, the global and the local, and the universal and the particular. The conversations are of a generic nature and give the impression of wanting to piece together the puzzle of what the notion of "former West" could entail when it is taken to determine the intellectual framework of the series of installations of the project that are to come. Notably, art itself is less of a topic of conversation. However, on a formal level the interview is a prominent medium of curatorial practice[51] and therefore important to consider for talking about curatorial methodology underpinning *Former West*. It can be assumed that the style of these conversations is a conscious choice as it provides for the networking research trajectory through which the foundations of the ideas put forward by the project are continuously debated by the project curators, artists, researchers, and a most likely specialized public in various geographical, political, and cultural contexts.

In this initial research phase the process of knowledge production on the possibility of constituting the notion of a "former West" for the project was at the same time already the first product of the project. From the very beginning there was an equation of research process and product that constituted and continues to constitute the project's self-reflexive approach. From the outset, *Former West*

---

48 Held on 18 January 2009 in Cologne.
49 Held on 7 September 2009 in Utrecht.
50 In addition to 1989, Hlavajova refers to the credit crisis of 2008 as another significant point in time relevant to the project's articulation of the perspective of a former West (Groys, Interview by Charles Esche, and Maria Hlavajova).
51 The most prominent example is Hans Ulrich Obrist's series of interviews (Obrist, *Interviews Vol. 1* and *Interviews Vol. 2*).

disclosed its organizing principle: to gather ideas (whether in the form of works of art, theories or the mere articulation of ideas) from many different sources (cultural theory, art practice, philosophy, social sciences, political activism, etc.), giving them time and space to articulate and develop. The first public announcement of the project on e-flux in January 2009 further emphasized the project's analytical, exploratory, and reflective interest:

> Former West—a term never fully articulated as a counterpart to the widely used "former East"—considers the question: What impact did the events of 1989 have on the art of the "West"? The project examines significant artistic and cultural developments from 9 November 1989 to the present, speculating on whether 11 September 2001 (destruction of the World Trade Center, New York) and 15 September 2008 (breakdown of the international financial system) might represent new milestones in our artistic, cultural and political histories. More than two decades after one of the greatest political changes in the last 150 years, the project reflects on the cultural output of the 'new world order', and embarks on a process of coming to terms, if provisionally, with our recent past. Former West aims to address this history through researching and charting art and culture from 1989 until the present to explore how significant changes in society are reflected and understood in all their complexity in new artistic productions.

The conception of the 1st Former West Research Congress, held on the eve of the twentieth anniversary of the fall of the Berlin Wall at the Ottone, Utrecht, should be viewed in the light of the preceding extract. The event focused on a discussion of the terms "1989," "West," "Former," and "Art." The curators let these terms sit next to each other in their introductory talk, which provided the speakers and participants with several different forms of engaging with what serves as a mental map by which the project can belong to the idea of a "former West" that it itself creates, while at the same time critically framing this proposition with regards to still extant social, political, and economic divisions between West and non-West.

1989

While *Former West* is searching for the "meaning of 1989," it is careful not to reduce the events of 1989 to the evening of 9 November when, as a result of miscommunications and unclear wordings, the East

German regime granted free travel to East Berliners, who then marched to the inner Berlin checkpoints and had them opened— and later that night climbed the Berlin Wall at the Brandenburg Gate. While these are the historic images that mostly define the moment of change that 1989 introduced in our collective memory, there is a string of events to be examined as part of the notion of "1989."[52]

> 1989 represents the case of the unglamorous fight for everyday democracy and consumerism, which, although already available in the West, resulted in the end of a perverse Cold War stability and unleashed an avalanche of critical shifts on a planetary scale. ("Introductory Notes")

Revisiting the changes that 1989 brought provides impetus to the construction of a notion of the "former West" as a category "in order to help us to rethink the West away from its own hegemonic self-narrative, to which it tirelessly clings despite the breaking point two decades ago that introduced to the world a radically new condition." This is not a historical project, and the curators of the first congress Charles Esche and Maria Hlavajova are not interested in recounting events in a historical fashion. They instead focus on the impact that 1989 as a historic landmark represents in our collective cultural memory and, from there, reexamine what they call "a cascade effect of new, transnational processes, the consequences of which we still struggle to come to terms with" ("Introductory Notes").

American Historian Mary Elise Sarotte locates such a struggle in the discrepancy between the possibilities of change in world politics introduced by the events of 1989, especially in the night of 9 November, and their subsequent ceasing to exist in the process of stabilizing the balance of power of the Cold War Era that came into being post-1989. Sarotte uses architectural terms to describe the transformation that the events of 1989 initiated: the construction process is like a prefabricated house in which all details, right down to the position of each light switch, are predetermined. Literally breaking through a wall in the attempt to destroy an architecture that had stabilized post-1945 Europe for forty years did not manage to destroy the foundation of the present order, but merely replaced the old

---

52 Such as the protests on Tiananmen Square, Beijing, the beginning of the end of Apartheid in South Africa, the death of Ayatollah Khomeini in Iran, the end of a number of South American dictatorships, and the withdrawal of Soviet troops from Afghanistan.

structures with a newer, stronger, and more resistant version, that is nevertheless made of the same material. In this same sense Hlavajova and Esche are interested in examining 1989 not "as a time of ending, but of beginning" (Sarotte 3). *Former West* seeks to explain not the end of the Cold War, but the creation of a post-Cold War order in global terms. The events of 1989 only help the *Former West* research to "recognize this larger picture of how the world had changed dramatically in that year" and "see how 1989 was a decisive moment in the history of the twentieth century, and one with planetary consequences" ("Introductory Notes"). However, *Former West's* concern with and relation to history is a starting point for understanding the present not in an effort to prepare or predict the future, but in an attempt to speculate a formation of a world order that, although different from the existing one, could nevertheless result from the same historical incidents and take into account the complexity of global relationships that they produced.

West

While the curators recognize that there is no single notion of "West," the most obvious notion of "West" to which the project wants to associate the quality of "formerness" is that of the Imperial West, "the West of imperial dominion, one that is associated irretrievably for the rest of the world with conquest and plunder" ("Introductory Notes"). However, the more complex notion of the West addressed in the context of 1989 is the notion reconfigured in 1945 that classified world membership as first, second, and third grade depending on its economic power.

The ambiguity that this definition of "West" entails at the outset of the project is that it presents at once its starting point for critique as well as its immediate environment and space of action. As a manifestation of cultural practices today, the project realizes and recognizes that its realm of production, that of contemporary art, was highly affected by the ideological political antagonisms that were played out by a conceptualization of East against West in the Cold War.

> The latest, post-1945 West was bound in particular forms of political antagonism with its rivals. Officially it maintained a static balance of terror through the doctrine of mutually assured destruction while fighting proxy wars of influence far from home soil. This military logic was accompanied by active competition in terms of social pol-

icy and artistic creation. Defenders of western art, when discussing contemporary practices, praised the radical innovation of the artist's choices and sought out forms of so-called autonomous production that demonstrated the extent to which aberrant forms were possible in democratic governmental regimes. In return, the post-1945 "East," built on very similar imperial western foundations but with a different critique, also defined its distinction in aesthetic terms. Officially it controlled its art to ensure proletarian understanding and rejected formalist experimentation as bourgeois affectation, while still sharing most of the historic European narrative. This meant than when this new East became the former East, most of the shared cultural concepts on both sides of the European divide were awkwardly reunited in ways that are still not fully acknowledged. ("Introductory Notes")

The problematic from which the ambition to define a former West emerges is the fact that post-1989 the West of imperial dominion found ways to still maintain an ideological space, namely in the increasing commercialization of art and other cultural practices, the so-called realm of creative industries. This realm of production has, however, been largely acknowledged in critical discourse and debated since the 1960s through, for example, Adorno and Horkheimer's critique of industrial cultural production. Today there is a large realm of critical art practices that curators argue is a parallel universe to the commercialization of art. *Former West* was interested not in reconciling the realm of critical and commercial art practices but in working with the dialectics between them. Several exhibitions and events in the context of *Former West* worked with this dialectic directly, such as the exhibition *Surplus Value* (2009) by Romanian artists Mona Vătămanu and Florin Tudor or the *3rd Former West Research Congress* (Vienna/Utrecht, 2012). The congress focused on the role of contemporary art, arguing that it might have reached a dead-end with regards to its ambition to critically deal with the economic, political, and social problematics to which it responds.

Former

The term *Former West* offers a spatio-temporal constellation of the past in the present. It defines a position and a perspective, both in time and (ideological) space. An abstract concept—in the sense that it is neither material nor tangible—is thus reified into a space and scope of action. It defines a discursive realm that is conveyed in the connections, associations, attributions and correlations that the people make between the term itself and the ideas and thoughts produced and debated in the congresses, exhibitions, seminars, and interviews that took place within the framework of the project. *Former West* does not imagine a past West, "suggesting the decay of a more glorious version in an imagined past," but is "informed by a desire for a more useful and accurate understanding of Western Europe's place in the entangled global culture that has emerged post-1989" ("Introductory Notes"). The curators suggest perceiving the changes wrought by the events of 1989 as an ambivalent victory for the West, one that was by no means as triumphant as the West itself later portrayed it to be. Instead, the West stepped into a vacuum unprepared for the world leadership role apparently expected of it.

> This unconsciousness proved very significant in subsequent years because, rather than the West as a value system, it was economic globalization, world-integrated free trade, or simply profiteering that were the de facto winners of the Cold War. Thus, the rapid growth of globalization, following reforms in China as well as in the post-Soviet sphere, radically changed the map and identity of the West without the latter having a clear sense of how and why it had come about—or indeed even that the transition to "formerness" was taking place. ("Introductory Notes")

In this sense the "former" is understood to have the capacity to establish a time span in the contemporary moment that incorporates the past not as something that has passed but as something that can be reconfigured in its meaning according to its contemporary context.

Art

When I participated in the first congress of this conceptual framework of the project, in their opening remarks Maria Hlavajova and Charles Esche invoked in me a sense of belonging as much as alienation. I felt sympathetic to the proposed notion of a "former West" as it suggested a rethinking of one's own position in the contemporary global context that is characterized by "the inextricably intertwined global histories of colonialism, communism, capitalism, imperialism, and nationalism (among other isms), and open up a space for thinking the world otherwise." On the other hand there is the question of how such a rethink might be accomplished from the domain of contemporary art, which the curators addressed from the beginning of the project as a contested realm in a period of absolute capitalist hegemony. But especially because it is becoming more complex to find a critical position for artistic and curatorial practices, *Former West* was designed to serve as a space in which the field of contemporary artistic production might be able to find a critical position.

> By producing trenchant critique of the contemporary moment, that is at once disclosing the status quo and proposing how our political and social futures can be reimagined, art actualizes a crucial part of its potential. It is precisely this—setting up a horizon in a horizonless world, if you will, replacing the aimless wandering with a sense of a possibility of a new direction—that *Former West* wants to establish with and from the field of art, both poetically and politically. ("Introductory Notes")

Former West thus self-reflexively situated its ambition in a nexus of affirmation and critique. On the one hand it understood the impossibility of simply articulating a prospect of a better world, realizing that this is a gesture that has been "written off overnight as an outmoded, laughable claim and replaced readily with the endgame of liberal democracy and practices of administration with the goal not to change the world but make it work pragmatically for one's immediate needs" ("Introductory Notes"). But on the other hand, it proposed the development of alternative models for the future that take into account the specific contemporary condition by having enquired into its past. For the curators, pursuing the argument concerning what I call a "conundrum of practice" is the very function that contemporary art assumes in today's society.

> Contemporary art is able to work in ways that we might term extra-disciplinary, in the sense that, over the last 20 years, it has successfully sloughed off at least a part of its own disciplinary burden and can encounter other fields with less need for self-justification than is the case for other divisions of knowledge. This advantage, though small, is significant when it comes to a study such as Former West, in which the general self-understanding of a specific society and its formation is at stake. An extra-disciplinary dimension in the form of art that speculates on the uncertainties generated by political and economic change allows for a space of thinking that might be up to the challenges of this task—or at least provide the means to represent what is at stake. ("Introductory Notes")

The curators understand art to be functioning as a strategy of investigation, in that they describe it as "a useful device to measure a more general consciousness of the state of global relationships and help us to collectively think beyond them," making art "a systemic form of imagining from the conditions at hand towards something that is not yet formed." Art, as an "extra-disciplinary dimension," produces knowledge in its capacity of having a documentary function "about how and in what ways the formerness of the West came to be manifested in art and its presentation" ("Introductory Notes").

In this sense art is not only what engages in a process of production that *Former West* enables, but also a device through which *Former West* pursued its interest in the political, social and cultural constellations of the recent past and imminent future. The relationship between art and *Former West* was a reciprocal one—at least, that is how the organizers would like it to be understood. If *Former West* produced a contention with art by means of its presentation and generation, can it in turn be stated that it is from and within the realm of art that a "former" West was being produced? If so, how can art function as a research device?

Art as a Research Device

Bringing into focus the relationship artistic practices build as forms of cultural production within the political environment and economy in which they are situated enables *Former West* to acknowledge the possibility of the agency of the curatorial. Therefore the curators explore the idea of using art as a device for researching into the social, political, and cultural conditions of artistic practices. The self-reflexive curatorial methodology of using art as a research device—from the perspective of practice and within the realm of art—is described by Claire Bishop as particularly relevant to the moment of 1989 and its place in the context of other attempts "to rethink the role of the artist and the work of art in relationship to society," such as "1917 (in which artistic production was brought into line with Bolshevik collectivism), and 1968 (in which artistic production lent its weight to a critique of authority, oppression and alienation)" (*Artificial Hells* 193). Bishop points to the loss of a collective political horizon after the fall of socialism due to "collapse of *grand narrative* politics in 1989" that resulted in a "certain impulse of leftist thinking [that] visibly migrated into Western European artistic production," which gave rise to the notion of the "project" as an umbrella term for different types of art production: "collective practice, self-organized activist groups, trans-disciplinary research, participatory and socially engaged art, and experimental curating" (*Artificial Hells* 195).

Former West subscribed to many of those categorizations of practices and continued to explore them in seminars and symposia. In March 2010 the research seminar *Russian Avant-Garde Revisited* at the Van Abbemuseum in Eindhoven explored the influence of the utopian projects of the Russian avant-garde on contemporary cultural production. Only a few days later, another seminar titled *Where the West Ends?* followed at the Museum of Modern Art in Warsaw discussing art in the former Soviet Union prior to and immediately after 1989. In April 2010 the London symposium *Art and the Social: Exhibitions of Contemporary Art in the 1990s* at Tate Britain looked at the landscape of exhibition-making in the early years of the former West (Europe and North America). By discussing the broad landscape of projects in art and curating in the 1990s and directly involving those who launched them or participated in them, such as Maria Lind, Marion von Osten, and Stephan Schmidt-Wulffen, to name but a few, *Former West* was quick to establish its function as a site of production and resource for contemporary discourse in the expanded field of artistic and curatorial practices.

The self-reflexive approach of *Former West*—in congruence with the way self-reflexivity emerged as a curatorial strategy post-1989—made the project a playground for the notion of the expanded field. The project's curatorial methodology was produced from a set of self-reflexive strategies of production from the field of intellectual curatorial discourse, some of which are described at the start of this chapter. In this sense *Former West* might be deemed simply one more example of contemporary projects that assume a critical position towards the political, economic, and social conditions of the realm of cultural practices of which they form part. However, such an analysis would not make clear why *Former West* in particular should be the subject of enquiry. Other similar multifaceted and large-scale projects would then be equally interesting subjects for study, such as *GAM—Global Art and the Museum,* initiated by Peter Weibel and Hans Belting in 2006 at ZKM, Karlsruhe, whose "aim is to spark a debate on how the globalization process changes the art scene and to undertake a critical review of the development twenty years after its onset" ("Global Art Museum"). *Former West,* on the other hand, was interested in further pushing the set of boundaries from which it emerged, both in regard to the ways in which large-scale projects collapsing exhibitionary, discursive, and performative strategies of production can be described in the language of curatorial discourse, and in relation to the question of what cultural, political and social function such projects can assume beyond the field of art.

Hence, the project itself was a research device into the "curatorial complex." Many of the events placed emphasis on describing the knowledge-power relations in which artistic and curatorial practices operate. But how precisely is the curatorial methodology of enquiry into a relation between art and the political collectively produced and put forward by the participants of *Former West*? Outlining the curatorial methodology is, therefore, not simply an argument to be analyzed, because it can also be used to think through the complex roles and sociopolitical responsibilities curatorial practices assume in the field of cultural production against the backdrop of their self-reflexive curatorial discourse. This gives reason to closely examine the claims of the curators, which for large part of the project, particularly in 2009 and 2010 around the twentieth anniversary of the fall of the Berlin Wall, wrestled with the idea that looking into the constitution of the past can produce political imaginaries—not only with regard to world-changing events such as those in 1989, but also and particularly in relation to curatorial discourse itself.

The Curatorial as a Fabrication of History

The analytical approach to curatorial discourse during the initial research phase of *Former West* engendered an interest in conceptually historicizing parts of curatorial discourse in order to situate the project in it as an example of curatorial practice. For example, Esche articulated the importance of addressing the exhibitions from the 1990s as historical phenomena—even if many of them date back only 20 years at the most. This enabled the project to appreciate the exploration of experimental forms of practice championed by projects such as *Sonsbeek '93* (1993), *Culture in Action* (1993), and *Chambres d'Amis* (1991–93) and thereby understand that in today's social, cultural, political, and economic context of exhibition-making the expansion into different forms of production, such as participation and collaboration, has become a norm. For Esche, examining this change by looking at exhibition history held the promise of providing for a critical analysis of the differences while also articulating expectations regarding contemporary practices. Simon Sheikh took this interest further in order to develop a curatorial methodology based on a self-reflexive approach that looks into the power of imagination as a political tool.

In his presentation at the 2nd Former West Research Congress, titled *On Horizons: Art and Political Imagination*, as co-curator of the congress, Sheikh proposed pursuing exhibition history as a form of historiography in relation to an understanding of the function of the notion of "horizon" as an instrument for delineating a political function in artistic and curatorial practices. As the title of the congress suggests, the research perspective was overall directed less at the past as a temporal space, and more to the idea of horizontality as a form of spatial definition of the relation between past, present, and future. Through the notion of the horizon the curators expressed their interest in the ways art can be understood to function as a research device in the sense of a political imaginary. In this way, art's potential "to set up a horizon in a horizonless world" was being explored, as curators Esche and Hlavajova had previously argued for as the imaginative potential of *Former West*.

Sheikh proposes looking at conceptual history as a form through which contemporary history can be approached, especially for curating, and later articulates the idea of political imaginaries as how art's political function of its poetical imagining can be explored. This is particularly interesting in relation to the exhibition *Vectors of the Possible* that Sheikh curated during the same period at BAK, Utrecht. Here he seems to have applied some of the arguments developed at a discursive level in his presentation. The question that arises here is: What is the relation between theory and practice in Sheikh's curatorial methodology?

2nd Former West Research Congress—On Horizons:
Art and Political Imagination

In his presentation at the Istanbul congress Sheikh first introduced the notion of "conceptual history," a term and concept originated by the German historian Reinhart Koselleck, who defined the terms social history and conceptual history as practices of historiography that account not only for the facts and dates of history, but also for the ideas from which the terms emerge, that they present, and that contextualizes them in retrospect. The relationship between social and conceptual history, a form of research into the history of history, is reciprocally affective. They are related to each other without either being reduced to the other or derived from the other. The difference between them is that social history accounts for the becoming of history while conceptual history accounts for its facilitation in and through language and discourse. Social change leads to conceptual reflection, which in turn brings about social change.

Sheikh is interested in Koselleck's work for its exploration of the relation between history and art through exhibition history, as distinct from art history as the historical study of art. Proposing that curatorial practice can serve to study history, rather than history serving to study art, Sheikh points to the usefulness of researching the history of exhibition making in order to reassess the post-Cold War world with the aim of addressing and exploring the notion of a former West.

He refers to a "conceptual history of exhibition making," which would necessitate positing the ontology of an exhibition as discursive, partaking in the formation of a general social history and not solely the history of art. In his argument he therefore establishes a direct relationship between exhibitions and their cultural and social context, making the history of art as a discipline somewhat redundant for contextualizing the works in the exhibition. This would allow curatorial practice to contribute directly to a formation of social history, which would require broadening the notion of the exhibition in the same way that conceptual art widened the scope of the aesthetic of the artwork based on "the idea that conceptual art proposed, namely that art is based on ideas, that art are indeed a series of propositions, whether object-based or not" (Sheikh, *Exhibition Making 19*). Accordingly, in the same way that conceptual art addressed the politics of aesthetics in art practice, exhibition history would be concerned with the politics of historiography for its practice. In order to get exhibition history to orientate its approach to history on conceptual history, Sheikh adopts Koselleck's idea of exploring how historiography can be the study of ideas, rather than the study of facts, subjecting the ideas produced to discourses of power rather than chronology:

A word can be unambiguous in use due to its ambiguity. The concept, on the other hand, must retain multiple meaning in order to be a concept. The concept is tied to a word, but it is at the same time more than the word. According to our method, a word becomes a concept, when the full richness of social and political context of meaning, in which, and for which, a word is used, is taken up by the word. Concepts are thus concentrations of multiple meanings. (Brunner et al. XXII)

While Koselleck proposes to periodize history not according to time, but with the help of theoretical concepts such as "democracy," "freedom," or "state" (5), Sheikh suggests that terms and concepts such as "formerness," "postcolonialism," and "postcommunism" should be imposed on exhibition-making, and that they should be used as "prisms through which one can address and analyse them and their articulation" (*Exhibition Making* 20–21). This would then produce a typology of exhibition-making that offers different contextualizations from those encountered in predominantly object-based art history. A conceptual exhibition history could instead account for the history of the curatorial concept and the articulations it produces, such as the relationship between work and viewer, the constitution of publics, modes of public address, and representation. Consideration of a conceptual exhibition history as a historiographical practice would entail accounting for the tension of the social transformation and linguistic articulation in which curatorial practice is situated. In the early 1990s, Benjamin Buchloh voiced criticism of conceptual art's tendency to change the criteria used when judging art, such that the definition of the aesthetic becomes "a matter of linguistic convention," entailing the danger of the aesthetic also becoming "the function of both a legal contract and an institutional discourse (a discourse of power rather than taste)" (140). This criticism could also be applied to Sheikh's proposition of making a conceptual exhibition history the discursive convention for evaluating exhibitions and their historical context. The form of evaluation is then particular to the discourses, with their ideologies based on how the curatorial reflects and produces social, political, and cultural constellations.

Sheikh and Hlavajova cast this element of production in the notion of "horizon" that serves as a concept to articulate and establish a convergent relationship between social history and curatorial practice. This proposition follows the "loss of horizon" that the curators observe as having taken place for cultural practices post-1989:

> With the (default) victory of capitalist democracy over the competing system of communism in 1989 (and with it the removal of the opposition which, while central to both blocs' ideological premises, ironically kept alive a certain hope for change), the striving for a better world driven by the horizon of overarching social progress seems to have been reduced to a commitment to the production of wealth for its own sake ... and for the benefit of a very select few. (Hlavajova et al., *On Horizons* 8)

The political horizon Hlavajova and their colleagues refer to as having been lost is the extinction of an opposition. They aim to "recharge" the notion of horizon with new meanings in order to think of it "as a critical instrument for emancipatory, experimental artistic, and intellectual work" (*On Horizons* 8). In a both spatial and temporal dimension the notion of horizon should serve as a "line 'demarcating' that which is not yet within our grasp" (8). In this context they enlist contemporary art "with its faculty of imagination and of the imaginary" to "play a crucial role in the construction (and deconstruction) of political imaginaries," based on the belief that "there is a space within the field of contemporary art where art works and art exhibitions do set up a horizon penetrating the space of the (otherwise) impossible, or even pointing to what is (said to be) unimaginable" (9).

In this context Sheikh explores the space of the exhibition as "a passage to a new space of experience, where a new horizon becomes visible," which serves the idea of radical imagination ("Vectors" 164). Sheikh casts today's problematic of "the marriage of liberal democracy and free market capitalism [being] instituted as a fundamental and historically inevitable category," as a "society-defining authority" ("Vectors" 155), which acts as a horizon for present actions in that it seems overwhelming and inescapable. In the same way, Ernesto Laclau renders the horizon as a "structure of signification" that constitutes experience and can be experienced as a form of expectation (102). According to Laclau horizontality is a liminal experience that has a figurative "grounding function" because "it only shows itself through the impossibility of its adequate representation" (110). This institutionalizes the idea of a horizon as a signification that organizes society, to the extent that, "there cannot be a society, an orga-

nization of social and political, without the positing of a horizon"
(Sheikh, "Vectors" 159).

Art can define a horizon as "a floating signifier that unifies experience, that creates a worldview," not only as a metaphor, but as an
image (Sheikh, "Vectors" 160). The shift from metaphor to image is
important to Sheikh, who articulates it as a shift from the aesthetics
of politics to the politics of aesthetics. To understand horizon as an
image, as one moment in the process of imagining, makes it possible
to conceive of art as a device for situating a horizon. Sheikh claims
that assembling objects and generating spatial and discursive relations provides a horizontal line "that makes viewing possible" ("Vectors" 161).

Sheikh's intersection of the claim for a conceptual exhibition history as establishing the curatorial as a signifying practice in response
to the loss of a political horizon post-1989 sees—at least theoretically—the practice of exhibition-making contribute directly to the
formation of social history. This provides a route to thinking of curatorial practice as a form of historiography with an understanding of
horizon as a device to think through art in political terms. Sheikh
puts this idea into practice in his exhibition *Vectors of the Possible*, to
which the curator refers as a research exhibition presenting artworks
that examine the notion of horizon for the relation between art and
politics, thereby presenting ways to imagine the world.

Vectors of the Possible

This exhibition showed works by Freee, Sharon Hayes, Mathew
Buckingham, Chto Delat?/What is to be done?, Runo Lagomarsino
& Johan Tirén, Elske Rosenfeld, Hito Steyerl, and Ultra-red. In a short
text at the entrance to the exhibition as well as in the exhibition leaflet, the curator identified the relation between the works. Sheikh
introduced the works as "vectors of the possible," leaving the viewer
intrigued to find out what the possible would be and in what way an
artwork can indicate a possibility ("Vectors of the Possible" 7). By
providing one? Or by merely illustrating one? The argument around
the figure of the horizon functioning to make a particular worldview
apprehensible and contestable is applied to the notion of an artwork
that is understood to trigger an image of a horizon. The horizon provides a demarcation to which one can relate in both a spatial and a
temporal dimension. It is the relationship with that demarcation

point—produced by establishing a horizon—that sets up a scope of action articulated as a "vector of the possible," which therefore refers to what is realizable within that scope of action. Hence, Sheikh describes the artworks in the exhibition as, "proposals of what can be imagined and what cannot ... reckoning possibility and impossibility in un(equal) measures, always detecting and indicating ways of seeing, and thus of being, in the world, in this world" (*Exhibition Making* 224).

Sheikh differentiates into various categories the ways in which the works in the exhibition "fulfil" their function as vectors of the possible. Several works in the exhibition deal with the idea of Utopia as a form of political imaginary. For example, Elske Rosenfeld's installation *Our Brief Autumn of Utopia* (2010; fig. 27–28) presents a documentation of the roundtable Zentraler Runder Tisch, a committee comprising various members of East German parties and experts from West Germany that between November 1989 and March 1990 developed a new constitution for a reunited Germany. The artist displays two video documentations, of the first and last session of the roundtable, one example of the printed constitution and a slideshow in which a hand is projected "reading the constitution," showing each page. The viewer is invited to experience the meetings by watching a recording of the first and last session, witnessing the ambitions in the first and the admission of the failure of the project in the last section of the film. The title *Our Brief Autumn of Utopia* hints to the fact that the constitution was never actually enacted. In the context of the curatorial framework it is the reference to "utopia" in the work's title that should identify it as a form of political imaginary. The round table's goal of realizing the potential of an alternative democracy supports the reading of the work as positing an imaginary. The element of imagination is key to the viewing of this project, if only because the documentation is incomplete, with only two sessions featured. The artist's work recreates in the present a political imaginary from the past. The question that this work raises in the context of the exhibition is whether timeliness is a condition for political imaginaries? Does the documentation regenerate the imaginary that was created, and for what purpose? According to Sheikh, the utopian character of the work raises to question of what future the implementation of the alternative constitution would have brought about that would have been different to the integration of the former East Germany into its Western capitalist counterpart ("Vectors of the Possible" 17). Sheikh

Fig. 27-28: Elske Rosenfeld, *Our Brief Autumn of Utopia*. 2010, text and
video material, dimensions variable. Installation view, second floor,
Vectors of the Possible, 2010, Basis voor actuele kunst, Utrecht. Photo:
Victor Nieuwenhuis. Courtesy BAK, Utrecht.

Fig. 29: Hito Steyerl, *Universal Embassy*. 2004, mini-DV, sound, 4 min.
Photo: Victor Nieuwenhuis. Copyright VG Bild-Kunst, Bonn 2017.
Installation view, second floor, *Vectors of the Possible*, 2010.

interprets Rosenfeld's work as a research project looking "at this lost history not in order to resurrect or rewrite the past, but in order to imagine another, alternative future." It fulfils a role in this regard by being an example of "how a work of art produces other imaginaries of the world and its institutions, rather than merely reiterating already existing ones" ("Vectors of the Possible" 17), an approach that the curator applied to other works in the show, such as Hito Steyerl's *Universal Embassy* (2004; fig. 29).

The single screen video projection of a four-minute film recounts the activist project *Universal Embassy* that was established in 2001 by the artist Tristan Wibault in the former headquarters of the Somali diplomatic mission in Brussels, which sought to host and help individuals without papers fighting for official recognition. Sheikh asks: "Can we imagine a world without borders, with the state and its monopoly on granting rights? Can we imagine universality as equality?" ("Vectors of the Possible" 19–20) Viewing this work in the context of the idea of artworks functioning as vectors of the possible, it seems that this idea could better be applied to Wilbaut's Universal Embassy project than to the ways in which Steyerl choses to recount it. I would argue that Steyerl uses the documentary style in her work to critically address the idea of positing a political imaginary using art projects in order to question the way Wilbaut tries to represent the nonrepresented. At the same time, Steyerl's documentation of this attempt adds another layer of representation to the issue, producing a series of contradictions that point to the Janus-faced nature of the documentary form: "documentary forms do not depict reality as much as first producing it" (Steyerl, "Documentarism").

Hence, thinking about both Steyerl's and Rosenfeld's works of a documentary nature in the context of Sheikh's notion of political imaginaries leads to the question of whether these works can and want to fulfil any function as vectors of the possible if the visibility that they raise for the respective issues they deal with is framed by a strong set of power relations set up by the curatorial context. This question is one of those addressed to Sheikh's interpretative context, as it seems geared more to the subject matter of the works than to how the work deals with the subject matter (formally, aesthetically, etc). The works as such can be misread or read in a reductive fashion.

This also applies to other works in the show, such as Sharon Hayes' *In the Near Future* (2009; fig. 30–31), a series of 35mm colour slides projected in various rooms of the exhibition. The images show the artist holding up protest banners and signs in urban public spaces. However, none of the people surrounding Hayes seem particularly engaged in the protest. The slogans on the signs such as "organize or starve," "actions speak louder than words," "never forgetting" do not relate to a particular contemporary event that sparked the protest, but are taken from historical protests. In his reading Sheikh emphasizes the lone figure of the artist: "How are such statements readable now, and what do they mean when they are no longer the expression of the people, as signified not by the crowd of demonstrators, but by a lone figure holding a sign, putting her body on the line?" ("Vectors of the Possible" 17–18). The curator understands Hayes work as an image of a sign of protest and not the protest itself, which for him questions protest as a format of demonstration. The works therefore articulate their presence in the space in a relation between memory, history, and public space. According to the curator, they can be read as a vector of the possible in the sense that the distance and form of removal from the performance of the protest that Hayes projects creates an image of protest that resonates with the viewer as a potentiality. That same idea can be derived from another work in the

Fig. 30-31: Sharon Hayes, *In the Near Future*. 2009, multiple slide projection, 35mm colour slides, dimensions variable. Installation view, second floor, *Vectors of the Possible*, 2010, Basis voor actuele kunst, Utrecht. Photo: Victor Nieuwenhuis. Courtesy BAK, Utrecht.

Fig. 32: Foreground: Hito Steyerl, *Universal Embassy*. 2004, Mini-DV, sound,
4 min. Background: Freee, *Protest Drives History*. 2008, billboard poster,
colour, 4 x 12 m. Installation view, ground floor, *Vectors of the Possible*,
2010, Basis voor actuele kunst, Utrecht. Photo:
Victor Nieuwenhuis. Courtesy BAK, Utrecht.

show, Freee's *Protest Drives History* (2008; fig. 32), a large billboard
poster showing the three members of the Freee collective holding a
large banner saying "Protest Drives History" against the backdrop of
a barren landscape. Displayed on a semicircular wall at the back of
the ground floor room, the poster literally creates a horizon in the
same way that Hayes' images were projected in a horizontal line next
to each other onto the wall low above the floor. This format of installation is a particular curator's choice: "By positioning the horizon as
an image and not just a metaphor, it implies a specific aesthetics—
not only an aesthetics of politics and political movements, but also a
politics of aesthetics" ("Vectors of the Possible" 19–20).

The relation between the artworks and the curator's definition
of their role within the exhibition is quite pragmatic. Given the
ways in which these works have been displayed in other exhibitions, the shortcomings of the narrow interpretative context that
Sheikh provides become apparent. For example, Sharon Hayes
showed the same work in a solo exhibition at Contemporary Art
Gallery, Vancouver, in 2011. The formal aspects of the presentation
were much the same. Again, a row of projectors displayed the 35mm

slides in rotation, showing more than 200 images that Hayes collected from the audience—she invited audience members to take photographs of her during the performances in six cities between 2005 and 2009. The meaning of this work becomes apparent through the viewer giving it time and space to unfold without any specific context in mind. In fact, I would go as far as to argue that the work aims to eschew a specific contextual reading. The slogans on the protest signs have been taken out of their context, even though they clearly read as protest slogans. Furthermore, the excess of images—their repetition in terms of motif or location—is key to understanding the work as a relation between the body, the words on the sign, and the time and place of public action. Due to the disconnect between the words and the time and place of public action, the work escapes a specific contextual reading and draws attention to speech itself as an act of protest. However, like Sheikh, curator Jennifer Papararo of the Vancouver exhibit analyses a similar capacity in the work in order to relate past and future: "Hayes binds the 'now' of her performances to the documentation of past events, blending past and present in anticipation of a future of actions, establishing the triangular 'speech act' of public protest with its potential use in mind" ("Sharon Hayes"). But, in contrast to Papararo, Sheikh derives his reading of the work as a vector of the possible in relation to the notion of horizontality, not from the performance itself—referring to the relation between text, body and place—but from the image created by the presentation of the work through projection.

Sheikh's understanding of the works in relation to the horizon notion is directly geared towards assuming a specific role and function for the dialogue between works and viewer. The horizon is articulated as functioning like a device for "interpreting" and "illuminating" the works (Exhibition Making 224). This disables the idea of horizontality being something that the works can suggest and trigger outside of a framework that presupposes it. Hence, the idea of exhibition-making facilitating a setting for the reception of artworks in which art can act as a device to situate a horizon seems to be either fulfilled on a very literal level (in the sense of work installed as projecting horizons), or does not come to fruition at all as the notion of horizontality is not something the works can suggest or trigger if the framework already constitutes this idea. Rather, the individuality with which the works could be understood to be presenting an image of a horizon as a figure is taken to constitute a universal theory of horizontality as a condition for "understanding exhibitions as political imaginaries in the ways in which they present a worldview" (*Exhibition Making* 222).

Sheikh defines both exhibition and artwork as "elements of signification, but the exhibition has the dual function of also being the signifying element that makes possible the field of meaning for the works, and that sets up a limit for them" (*Exhibition Making* 233). The limit is twofold, at once describing the horizon as a limit of perception as well as the concrete limit of the space. Within this liminal space, artworks are supposed to function in the sense that they can puncture the horizon provided by the context. In this sense the exhibition *Vectors of the Possible* attempted to make use of the artworks' individual understanding of horizons in that it presented them as potentialities for a transformation of "critique into a discussion of political, ontological possibility in the form of the horizon, and art's capacity for positing and suspending it" (Sheikh, *Exhibition Making* 222). That capacity can only be explored by the curatorial facilitating a temporal-spatial relation for artworks that opens up for possibilities of interpretation on the conditions of the works themselves and not on the conditions of the interpretative framework that is preconditioned for them, in which they function as supplementary arguments. From the curatorial perspective of articulation, it seems that the works in the exhibition are no more than accumulated horizons to whom a political function is being attributed. Paradoxically the restrictive interpretative context of the exhibition should provide for the reading of the works as potentialities and images of possibilities. But how can a political imaginary emerge from a narrative that is restricted by such a narrow framework? As a viewer myself, I felt that I was not given the space to determine a horizon for myself in order to then situate the works within it. Even constituting a horizon with help of the works felt difficult as their interpretation was narrowly cast in the rhetoric of the interpretative framework.

Vectors of the Possible was an unfortunate attempt to implement discursive relations built elsewhere in an exhibition, using artworks as a system of referencing that is then denied the possibility of producing connections that cannot be planned or foreseen in the curatorial framework. Some works were read, as described earlier, quite literally as an image of a horizon, which actually defies their possibility to be read as producing any form of radical imagination. The exhibition as a "collection of horizons" is in that sense the very opposite of an imaginary.

Part of the problem lies in the notion of the horizon itself, which is used as a linguistic device to confuse politics with aesthetics. From the perspective of the curator, the works in the exhibition function as a device for trying to convey a transformation from an aesthetics of politicization to a general claim of politicization of aesthetics, framed as a curatorial responsibility.

Sheikh derives the notion of the horizon from the political context and directly refers it to the aesthetic, putting both politics and aesthetics as forms of enquiry in the same position of finding ways in which they can relate expectation and experience—referring to what is imagined and how what is imagined is being instituted. To affirm this shift Sheikh returns to Koselleck who claims that every encounter with a horizon creates a new space of experience and thereby establishes a new horizon of expectation. The liminal is a shifting experience in its own right. Consequently, Sheikh arrives at the question of whether "aesthetic [experiences], like political events, create rupture?" ("Vectors" 164). Sheikh enlists art for making visible what was previously beyond the horizon, shifting the experience of the horizon. This he calls radical imagination, where art can make possible what has previously been thought of as impossible in the sense of producing a difference. A moment at which art can register "vectors of the possible" can only be arrived at through a rupture, a break with the present—one that might by definition be unforeseeable.

> Here we must return to the idea ... of radical imagination, which is where art has a crucial role to play in providing vectors of the possible, posing questions of possibility and vicinity, as well as making invisible limits visible within the ontology of the horizon. Art works and exhibitions can suggest and assess how a horizon must be placed in relation to both experience and expectation in order to be effectual: how far and how close. And like a political project, an aesthetic project can be a kind of praxis, and can go beyond an assessment of this world and how we must critique it, but also in fact posit other worlds as possible. (Sheikh, "Vectors" 164).

Sheikh proposes a process of politicization of exhibition making in which the exhibition as a product of curatorial practice functions solely as a device in the quest for the production of something else. Both Sheikh and Hlavajova repeatedly frame what is supposed to be imagined as an "other world possible" (Sheikh, "Vectors" 164), or as "one world" (Hlavajova et al., *Former West* 8). While this notion can be unpacked in greater detail at seminars and symposiums when speakers propose different notions of terms such as "the horizon," "the common," and "the public," the exhibition as a medium of production assumes a problematic position within the broader research conducted by *Former West*. It is proposed to be a form of articulation of the imaginary, however what it seems to be producing is always only an image of the imaginary, an illustration of the ideas and expectations of *Former West* that are discussed elsewhere in the project.

The most difficult role within the positioning of the exhibition as a medium of articulation in the context of a preliminarily discursive project is that of the artworks, which seem to only be provided a space of articulation on the conditions of their potentiality to function as an imaginary, as an illustration and exemplification of such potential. Sheikh groups the artists' work together for the topics and issues with which they are concerned. Often, this can be an interesting strategy and is a widely practiced form of curating. It is not, however, a strategy that calls for particularly active viewer engagement when it comes to contributing to processes of knowledge production taking place in the communicative space of the exhibition. The visitor remains a viewer who merely takes on board the curator's narratives of interpretation. My criticism of such an accumulation is that even though thematically the images deal with similar issues, there is no communicative room facilitated for the artworks to develop their formal and aesthetic qualities towards an articulation of their politics. Ultimately, the question arises: Is it productive to accumulate a number of ideas (imaginaries) in order to speak about the power of imagination? Is it not the exact opposite that is being achieved when trying to convey the imaginary? In that case, imaginaries become mere images. The close-knit interpretive context superimposes the exhibited works over one another, which reduces the communicative space of the exhibition from a space of action to a space of reaction conditioned upon a predefined discursive context. Instead of being developed as an explorative medium, the exhibition functions as a liminal space of action. It can therefore not to be understood as a research exhibition in the sense of a communicative space able to provide its own politics of communication.

However, my criticism of Sheikh's exhibition knowingly using the artworks as references in a particular narrative around the political function of the aesthetic is not intended for praising the autonomy of the artworks and advocacy of the curator's responsibility for safeguarding that autonomy. Instead, I aim to show that, in this case, the discursive encapsulates the format of the exhibition to the extent that it actually restricts its potentiality to function as a communicative space from which a process of production of experience, sociality, or knowledge, can emerge.[53] Returning here to the notion of exploring a material register of the curated encounter the relationship between the discursive sphere of knowledge production and the format of the exhibition could have been rendered differently. For example, by articulating the precise choice to situate Sharon Hayes' projections only slightly above the ground or to deliberately display Freee's poster on the curved wall in the lower floor room. This would recurrently invoke a material dimension of the curated encounter, which could function to point to the dominant narrative of dematerialization of artistic practices in the attempt to produce forms of imagination.

The Political Function of the Curatorial

However, it seems questionable whether an articulation of aesthetics on the level of artistic practice can really be transformed into a political articulation on the level of the curatorial. This question is one addressed to the relation between art and politics that curatorial methodologies seek to foster and strengthen through their practice. One issue at stake in this context with regards to *Former West* is how art can function as a research device for thinking about "reality," a term that is often used for describing the social, economic, and political conditions in which cultural practices are embedded and from which they emerge. In this context *Former West* develops its ambition to "infuse the contemporary with the sense of possibility" in an attempt to "point us in the direction of how we can reshape the debates about the things to come" (Hlavajova et al., *Former West* 9)

What Boris Groys described as "the desire to transform society through the power of art" is the reality *Former West* desires and strives for, but not in a naive way (Hlavajova et al., *Former West* 14). To under-

---

53 In the same way that the first chapter "The Communicative Space of the Exhibition" described for Michael Fullerton's exhibition *Columbia* and *The Potosí Principle*.

stand the reality of cultural practices through art's capacity to reflect and to produce was one of the central research questions from the beginning. At the level of curatorial practice this interest translates in the project into many attempts to create a space of action that can serve as a platform for analysis while pointing to the necessity of politicizing practices creating communicative spaces as spaces of action—an intrinsic condition for considering the relationship between art and reality as one that is in flux. It is through this development of spaces of action that the question emerges in what ways cultural practices are political.

No work and no action is political in and of itself. Carl Schmitt defined the political not as a subject area or field, but only the degree of intensity of association and dissociation of people. Hannah Arendt described the freedom to discuss and thereby explore the discursive not as the medium of the political but as the form and content of the political in itself (*Was ist Politik?*). While from these positions the concept of the political can still be understood as fostering democratic decision-making processes that Habermas described as consensual (*Between Facts and Norms*), in the context of curatorial practice as an activity of generating spaces of action, the political might rather be conceived of as a conflict carried out in the space of action—an allusion to Chantal Mouffe's description of the political as "unavoidably antagonistic" (10).

To speak of a politicization of curatorial practice means to produce a space of action that fuels the potential for conflict. Here, Oliver Marchart, however, differentiates between curatorial practice producing a space of action that allows for the emergence of a conflict, and curatorial practice producing a conflict with regard to what constitutes the public sphere ("The Curatorial Function" 164). According to Marchart, the latter is a logical impossibility, an antagonism, because what is produced in the event of conflict cannot be intentionally organized, since, according to Laclau and Mouffe, it defies any form of organization and, therefore, domination (Mouffe 15). For this reason, it is wrong to describe the curatorial function in terms of an organization of antagonism and to deem this form of organization as making the curatorial function political. Nevertheless, so as not to attribute a political incompetence to the curatorial, Marchart demands a shift of perspective away from perceiving curatorial practice as producing the political in the field of art, in order to understand the curatorial function as constituting a political sphere that is no longer confined to the art world: "A conflict that breaks out in the art world alone will revolve exclusively around artistic questions ... which would not even satisfy the minimal criterion of universal accessibility, which knows no boundaries between fields" (Marchart, "The Curatorial Function" 164). It is precisely the recognition of the impossibility to organize the emergence of conflict that allows the curatorial to enable the political:

> Politics, in the sense of a genuine realization of the political, is always a praxis that aims at the impossible; namely, at whatever the hegemonic discourse defines in a given situation is impossible ... In the construction of a *counter*hegemony, lies the true potential for antagonism. (Marchart, "The Curatorial Function" 164)

The idea of conceiving the very notion of a "former West" in the context of capitalist cultural production can be understood as counterhegemonic and is what the project proposes to articulate. However, while a mere articulation of the idea by means of outlining the formal and conceptual context in the initial research phase of the project, as described earlier, served to set the scene, the idea of deriving forms of imagination through forms of organizing art failed, specifically because the production of a counterposition would have meant to employ the artwork in such a way that it provoked a counterposition to them in providing an imaginary, rather than reducing them to functioning as images of a preconceived imagination. Recalling Marchart, the exhibition *Vectors of the Possible* was an attempt to organize imagination as the impossible, something it inevitably failed to do.

Marchart casts the responsibility of the curator by producing a collapse between different fields of practices, much like Gramsci's organic intellectual with its function of "maintenance of the *hegemonic* bloc but also a *counter*hegemonic effort." This is not a singular activity but a collective effort to the extent that "the subject of the curatorial function is not an individual, but rather a *collective*" (Marchart, "The Curatorial Function" 167).

Former West: Documents, Constellations, Prospects

Documents, Constellations, Prospects (2013) was a weeklong series of exhibitions and events. The project took place at the Haus der Kulturen der Welt, Berlin, a congress hall erected in 1957 near the Reich-

stag and the then-border between West and East Berlin. The building was a gift from the US government to the City of (West) Berlin
at the height of the Cold War. Hosting a series of events under the
title of *Former West*, the project can be described as an attempt to
fulfil the curatorial function of disrupting the hegemonic discourse
of an institution to the extent that it produces an opening of the
institution as a form of positioning of a political praxis: "The curatorial function, understood as the organization of a public sphere,
thus consists not least in the political opening of the institution
of which it appears to be part" (Marchart, "The Curatorial Function" 170).

The seven-day summit was conceived to allow the collapse of different mediums of articulation of artistic, theoretical and educational practices. Curator Maria Hlavajova defined the proposition of
the summit as "uncovering—through various constellations of artistic and theoretical *documents*—the breaches in which we can make
out the West's formerness and harness the emancipatory promise of
the imaginary of "former West" in both art and society within the
landscape of rapidly changing global relations" (Hlavajova et al. *Former West* 8–9). The curators chose to even out any hierarchy between
formats or media by focusing on the term documents as being
brought together for a "composition of another kind":

> If artworks, lectures, workshops, and more are put together in a pro-
> visory manner, it is because their meaning must necessarily be made
> available for continuous rereading, shifting, reassembling, decon-
> structing, and recomposition. Such constellations necessarily privi-
> lege the processes of collective effort to produce knowledge, and fa-
> vour provisional structures that allow for conversation, incongruity
> and agreement, emergency and emergence, and—indeed—a sense
> of emancipatory prospects. (Hlavajova et al., *Former West* 8–9)

In the same way that Sheikh elaborated on the practice of articulation in the context of exhibition-making as a form of combination of
various elements (*Exhibition Making* 135–86), Hlavajova uses the
term "constellation" to describe a methodology of organization that
aims specifically to avoid elaboration of a particular order, manifestation of hegemony or production of linearity. Instead, the curatorial
methodology is geared towards a collective production of knowledge that has the potential to organize a different form of being together. Hlavajova denies the attribution of any form of singular au-

thority to the curator as a position from which to articulate curatorial practice as a mode of organization. The Berlin summit is,

> not confined to one domain or specific practice, it is neither a show nor a congress nor a series of presentations, but rather a platform collapsing the exhibitionary, the performative, and the discursive through the diversity of rehearsals, dialogues, impromptu performances and talks, lectures, screenings, workshops, and mutual learning. (Hlavajova et al., *Former West* 10)

In order to unpack the notion of constellation and the idea of emerging "emancipatory prospects" that emerge from it, it is necessary to look closer at the way in which the curatorial methodology of the project not only articulates a collapse of the different strategies of knowledge production—the discursive, the exhibitionary and the educational—but produces a constellation that urges its participants to take a position as part of the proposed constellation.

Dissident Knowledges

As part of the Berlin summit Maria Hlavajova and Kathrin Rhomberg curated *Dissident Knowledges*, for which they assembled a selection that included artworks, performances, lectures, readings, and conversations in an attempt to rethink the contemporary condition of the West and allude to its formerness:

> Taking crisis and instability as knowledge, this ideational landscape not only challenges the way things are, but actively thinks through how they could be otherwise, proposing in tandem the shape of things to come. The artworks at the core of these constellations, following much the same protocol, are bodies of knowledge: both the documents uncovering the cracks through which we might see the "formerness" of the West, and the resources for how to think differently. (Hlavajova et al., *Former West* 60)

In the overall context of the week's events, *Dissident Knowledges* was presented as one of five "currents" around which the summit was organized. But in contrast to the other currents (*Art Production, Infrastructure, Insurgent Cosmopolitanism, and Learning Place*) which presented a series of speakers and performances invited by Boris Groys, Irit Rogoff and Ranjit Hoskote, *Dissident Knowledges* was not a programmed day of discussions and performances, but an exhibition. It used the entire Haus der Kulturen der Welt building as its gallery space. In the main foyer, works were displayed on construction site fences. Marlene Dumas' drawings *Young Men* (*Man Kind*) (2002–7) were shown alongside video works by James Benning (*Twenty Cigarettes*, 2011) and installations by Marcus Geiger (*Untitled*, 2013) and Thomas Locher (*Reading Of,* 2013). *Dissident Knowledges* was not labelled as an exhibition, but combined exhibitionary, discursive, and performative strategies of production (fig. 33–35). Aernout Mik's performance *Untitled* (2013) took place at the end of a lecture in the main auditorium. Suddenly half of the people in the auditorium who were all dressed in business attire got up and started shouting, mumbling, talking or singing in various languages, constructing a cacophony of different voices.

The curators disregarded any difference in medium or format, considering all artworks equally in the context of *Former West's* research endeavour:

> Distributed as nomadic bodies of knowledge through both the time and space of HKW during this assembly, *Dissident Knowledges* ... proposes both temporary and spatial dynamic interventions in a gathering of artworks, performances, film screenings and brief improvised statements ... that not only defy conventional fictions about our contemporary history, but arrange for other formulations than those we have grown accustomed to over some quarter of a century into the making of the "new world order." (Hlavajova et al., *Former West* 60)

Whatever is conceived as "dissident knowledges" is intended to punctuate the viewer's or participant's thinking towards the ideas *Former West* proposes. Experiencing this array of "temporary and spatial dynamic interventions" is embedded in the pursuit of a construction of a particular narrative, that of articulating the "formerness" of the West. From the viewer's perspective, this is the only way to make sense of the works that otherwise seem to bear little formal or topical relation to one another. Furthermore, in the context of the dense, weeklong programme, paying particular attention to the sometimes hour-long video works is difficult. The curators must acknowledge the fact that the works operate in this context as interludes for passing time between lectures and seminars. It is intentional that the viewer should experience the works in passing, or so it appears given their placement in the space. The artworks are by

Fig. 33: [l-r] James Benning, *Twenty Cigarettes* (2011) and Chto Delat?/ What is to be done?, *Perestroika Timeline* (2009/2013). Shown in Dissident Knowledges as part of Former West: *Documents, Constellations, Prospects,* 18–24 Mar. 2013, Haus der Kulturen der Welt, Berlin. Photo: Marcus Lieberenz/bildbuehne.de. Courtesy BAK, Utrecht.

Fig. 34: Installation view of Christoph Schlingensief, *Ausländer raus— Bitte liebt Österreich [Foreigner out—Please love Austria].* 2013, installation by Nina Wetzel in cooperation with Matthias Lilienthal and with films by Paul Poet. Shown in *Dissident Knowledges* as part of *Former West: Documents, Constellations, Prospects,* 18–24 Mar. 2013, Haus der Kulturen der Welt, Berlin. Photo: Marcus Lieberenz/bildbuehne.de. Courtesy BAK, Utrecht.

Fig. 35: Installation view of Li Ran, *Beyond Geography*. 2012, video.
Shown in *Dissident Knowledges* as part of *Former West: Documents,
Constellations, Prospects,* 18–24 Mar. 2013, Haus der Kulturen der Welt, Berlin.
Photo: Marcus Lieberenz/bildbuehne.de. Courtesy BAK, Utrecht.

no means at the core of the building, never allocated the role of centre of attention, but are placed at the edges of the foyer, above the stairs in the mid-level and towards the very end of the basement.

Dissident Knowledges fulfils a particular criterion that Mick Wilson describes for the discursive turn in curating. It becomes a "framework of enquiry—in a way that builds upon conceptualism's romance with the exhibition as system—and a metaphor of public education is thus activated" (208).

Another testimony to this is *Learning Place* (fig. 36), a specially curated series of workshops and events for various groups of students of Curating and of Contemporary Art and Theory from international universities and academies. Boris Buden conceived the programme as a "weeklong educational performance modelled on an application for an academic job"—for which students were grouped together, each developing a curriculum vitae—which Buden characterizes as "the fiction of linear progression presented in the form of a gradual acquisition of knowledge, skills, and recognitions, a progression imaginable

Fig. 36: Participants of Learning Place, 18. Mar. 2013, at *Former West: Documents, Constellations, Prospects*, 18–24 Mar. 2013, Haus der Kulturen der Welt, Berlin. Photo: Marcus Lieberenz/bildbuehne.de. Courtesy BAK, Utrecht.

only in a life that unfolds through a homogenous, empty time with no meaning outside the CV" ("Learning Place"). Furthermore, Buden outlined his intention that his proposition should performatively engage in seminars and workshops while producing a CV that aimed for a Brechtian estrangement effect that "should strip the dominant educational practice of its self-evident educational normality and so foster its critique and necessary transformation" ("Learning Place").

Many students opposed this proposition, as they did not perceive the production of a CV as a form of critique towards the ideology of a linearity of continuous achievement as a measurement of success as suggested in the format of a CV. They also refused to be disciplined into groups of production within the confines of what Buden terms a performative engagement. At this point I will neither go into any detail of this debate, nor discuss the educational aspects of this gathering. What is of interest to me is the way in which Buden proposes to conceptualize a constellation of different people (students) into certain hierarchical settings (workshops, seminars) with a clear outcome and product in mind, particularly while positing this outcome as the source of critique by means of an estrangement effect. He

probably intends, or at least anticipates, that the students will counterposition themselves to the task the project involves. In this sense
the curatorial methodology that Buden follows is one that is similar
to Hlavajova's and Rhomberg's *Dissident Knowledges* exhibition with
regard to a particular disposition that Maria Lind describes as having
a "clear performative side," including "elements of choreography, or-
chestration, and administrative logics" (*Performing the Curatorial* 12).
The fact that Buden is not orchestrating objects but people and the
result is not a display but a performance does not change the curatorial methodology as a performative disposition. The curatorial is
conceptualized as a performative form of production generating
and constituting sociality, discourse, and critique over the conditions of knowledge production in contemporary times, particularly
within the context of cognitive capitalism.

The Performative Quality of the Curatorial

Maria Lind defines the performative aspect of the curatorial as "akin
to the methodology used by artists focusing on the postproduction
approach—that is, the principles of montage, employing disparate
images, objects, and other material and immaterial phenomena
within a particular time and space-related framework" (*Performing
the Curatorial* 12). Lind's research project *Performing the Curatorial*[54]
explores the curatorial as a methodology of organization and production "beyond the field of art" (12). In particular it explores the
nature of the "project exhibition, a collective research-based endeavour which sits at the center of transdisciplinary cultural and
political practices" as a site for the curatorial to be performed, taking
into account what Lind calls "unorthodox forms of mediation" (*Performing the Curatorial* 12).[55]

Lind and Hlavajova share an ambition to see the curatorial assuming the function of a "signifying practice." The process of mediation that such practice employs is, however, called into question by

---

54 Lind organized *Performing the Curatorial* at the University of Gothenburg in
    2010/2011. This series of seminars and symposiums was followed by a publica-
    tion that documents the proceedings.

55 Lind is not the first to outline the problematics of this terminology, but articu-
    lates it very well in terms of the complicity between the curatorial as a strategy
    of knowledge production and the project exhibition as a format.

Buden with regard to the perspective from which the curatorial can be said to assume a performative quality. Buden points to a series of historical transformations that affect the nature of curatorial practices as much as they affect the task of translation. It is in this engagement with the past, "symbolically condensed in the concept (and practice of production) of cultural heritage" (Buden, "Towards" 26), that the role of the curator presumes a constitutive effect with respect to the cultural and social value generated in the process of communication between art, on the one hand, and the public, on the other (Sheih, "Constitutive Effects" 149). The authorial position of the curator, one that implies a quest for originality, is to be found in the ways in which curatorial practice rearranges cultural heritage and filters what is communicated.

> Does the common ground on which the curator meets cultural heritage have anything in common with the grounds they each allegedly originate from? Is it a ground at all? Or is it precisely the disappearance of any pregiven ground, a sort of historically generated groundlessness, that has come to constitute their commonality, making it possible for them to face each other as though they have never met before? (Buden, "Towards" 26)

The curatorial can be defined as a signifying practice with regard to the processes of mediation it generates. Buden locates the performative quality of the curatorial in the vast dispersion that cultural heritage has experienced in the past decades in the social and cultural sphere. The curatorial is no longer a privileged site for accessing cultural heritage, and this also affects its constitutive effect towards a public, a concept that is equally difficult to grasp. The performative quality of the curatorial lies in the fact that it structures the situation in which it is performed through the mode of its addressing. Its associated constitutive effect extends well beyond the sphere of communication. According to Buden, the curator is not mediating between a sphere of art and a sphere of knowledge—generating a relation between the two—but "what he or she does address is neither art nor knowledge (as coherently unified prior to his or her address), but rather the moment of their incompleteness, a lack in each of them that urges art and knowledge to reach out to each other" (Buden, "Towards" 37–39).

Moreover, this performative quality is specifiable with Buden as the desire for the building of a relation between art and knowledge. In the curatorial, however, this intentionally never comes to fruition, according to Buden, because the curatorial performs a form of sociality that manifests itself as a desire to relate, which is constitutive of its own nature as producing the conditions for knowledge production, a transformational action in which Buden locates the voice of the curator in a way that recalls Hlavajova's and Sheikh's arguments around the production of imaginaries. All these conceptions rely on a notion of openness, or rather incompleteness, and even failure to produce—theoretically, at least. Within this conception the works supposedly act as resources within what can be termed a postproductionist curatorial methodology, a form of assemblage that approaches what is shown as documents, in an attempt to construct a particular narrative from their correlation, albeit a necessarily inconclusive one. The constitutive effect of the performative quality of the curatorial is that it creates a new and different interpretative context that partly disposes of the original constitutional context of what it displays and presents.

However, the examples of exhibitions discussed here as part of *Former West* seem to further extend the performative quality of the curatorial to produce a tight narrative in which the works act as mere carriers of information rather than resources of interpretation.

Given the knowledge-power relations that are put forward as part of *Former West*, the "curatorial complex" appears far less invigorating and emancipatory than might be wished for, in contrast to the "exhibitionary complex." It appears that the idea of affective empowerment has not been replaced; the narrative has merely been altered. Even though the function of art institutions might not be rendered as akin to the disciplinary mechanisms of the prison, as was at the core of Bennett's analysis, the ways in which the *Former West* artworks are gathered to construct and present knowledge in direct relation to the formation of power is no less romantic, as Wilson noted (208).

The Discursive Surplus

Curatorial methodologies have undergone major turns since the days when the museum was a site of public education, and in many ways *Former West* is emblematic of these turns—particularly the turn from practice to discourse (O'Neill, "The Curatorial Turn") discussed at the beginning of this chapter. In this context it is surprising how repressive the context of *Former West* is on the relation between works (or, rather, ideas) and viewer/participant with regard to knowledge production as a political function of cultural practices.

Part of the problem is the imperative to differentiate between what is shown or installed and the categories from which it aims to be distinguished. Artworks are presented as "vectors" or "documents," thematic sections are called "currents," and exhibitions are conceived as "interventions." The discursive appropriation takes place in response to the long-established categories of art production and mediation. In the attempt to avoid, dismiss, and forego these categories, new formats and their correspondent terminologies are articulated to the extent that they disguise the innovative quality of the more dialogical approaches to exhibition-making that lead to long-term collaborative productions between curators, artists, theorists, critics, etc., which are the merits of the changes that curatorial practices have introduced to the landscape of cultural production since the 1990s. As Paul O'Neill writes, the "triangular network of artist, curator, and audience is replaced by a spectrum of potential interrelationships" (*The Culture of Curating* 129).

While from the perspective of the position of the curators *Former West* very much exemplifies this shift, the way in which those potential interrelationships come to fruition from the perspective of the viewer and/or participant are less successful in many ways. This is what the previous analysis of the relationship between the medium of the exhibitionary and the discursive sought to discover. The gap between conceptual assumptions and perceptual expectations is one that no middle ground seems to cover; less so any form of mediation.

The question that the following conclusive analysis of *Former West* addresses is this: Why, despite the many efforts to conceive alternative forms of knowledge production that try to operate beyond the dogma of representation, does the project, particularly its discursive and performative elements, seem to fail to produce "emancipatory prospects" in terms of their function for the production of knowledge?

Earlier on I pointed to the confusion between imagination and image on the part of the curator with regard to the selection and display of the artworks. In my understanding Sheikh chose certain artworks quite pragmatically to demonstrate forms of potentiality: the image of a protester in Sharon Hayes' work (fig. 30–31), the image of a horizon in Freee's work (fig. 32) and the image of communality and debate derived from Elske Rosenfeld's work (fig. 27–28). The question asked in order to critically dismantle the curatorial methodology was whether the discursive rendering of an artwork as an image of a horizon could produce an imaginary. However, any such curatorial-symbolic image to which a material object gives rise is an ideological product. The meaning associated with the material object beyond its given particularity operates primarily in the realm of the symbolic. To conceive from there a turn back into reality, especially a political reality generated through imaginary positions, seems problematic. A constant shift between a material and a symbolic realm of production cannot be accomplished, because the categories of production in which art can be used as a research device cannot be altered, it would appear, taking into account the difficulties encountered in aligning one's expectations with experiences of the different instances of *Former West*. Instead of trying to transform the symbolic into the material, or aesthetics into politics, can a curatorial methodology be found that operates primarily in a material realm of production by producing and therefore highlighting a material dimension of the curated encounter?

The Dilemma of the Political

Answering such question involves the hitherto only rarely acknowledged and therefore also undertheorized material dimension of the kind of performativity at work in the curated encounter that Lind talks about when referring to curatorial methodologies as "signifying practices" in terms of mediation (*Performing the Curatorial* 12). In this context, Maria Hlavajova strongly aligns her interest in collapsing particular methodologies and strategies of curatorial practices such as the exhibitionary, the discursive, and the performative with Bruno Latour's notion of "compositionism," an attempt to perceive of a common world as "built from utterly heterogeneous parts that will never make a whole, but at best a fragile, revisable, and diverse composite material" (Hlavajova et al., *Former West* 60; Latour, "An Attempt" 474). In his *Attempt at a "Compositionist Manifesto"* Bruno Latour envisions an answer to the task of how to shed a new perspective on the search for the common, an idea that he sees his Compositionist Manifesto as sharing with the Communist Manifesto—in fact the only thing they share.

The notion of "compositionism" brings together a number of ideas and concepts that Latour developed such as the abolition of the Modernist dichotomy of nature/culture, and arguing for a hybrid relation between them (*We Have Never Been Modern*; *Politics of Nature*) and the preeminence of "matters of concern" over "matters of fact" ("From Realpolitik to Dingpolitik"). Latour attempts to combine the democratic ontology he fosters—which emerges from treating human and nonhuman entities as actors of equivalent standing—with a proposition for a form of democratic politics in a pragmatic sense. In the pursuit of compositionism as a "political platform" Latour contrasts this notion with that of critique, or rather the power of critique as what once determined modernity, and explores it in relation to the modern concept of nature as "a way of organizing the division (what Alfred North Whitehead has called *bifurcation*) between appearances and reality, subjectivity and objectivity, history and immutability" (Latour, "An Attempt" 476). Compositionism rejects the gesture of critique as a negotiation of what can be imagined with what there really is and as such negates any belief in transcendence.

> For a compositionist, nothing is beyond dispute. And yet, closure has to be achieved. But it is achieved only by the slow process of composition and compromise, not by the revelation of the world of beyond. (Latour, "An Attempt" 478)

As much as Latour denies a belief in transcendence, compositionism is also not a purely materialist proposition. He critiques the disappearance of agency in the cause-and-effect logic of materialism precisely because "consequences overwhelm their causes, and this overflow has to be respected everywhere, in every domain, in every discipline, and every type of entity" ("An Attempt" 485). The task of compositionism is to ensure the continuity of agents in space and time slowly and progressively by composing it from discontinuous pieces, increasing the level of disputability as "the best path to finally taking seriously the political task of establishing the continuity of all entities that make up the common world" ("An Attempt" 485).

Compositionism is, for Latour, a hybrid discursive practice that involves assembly and creation in a way that challenges the conceptual boundaries of material and nonmaterial, literary and nonliterary, natural and cultural things. It also challenges the notion of the author: When it comes to the task of composing, no authorship or scholarship is involved in putting together things while retaining their heterogeneity. Also, whatever is composed can at any time be decomposed.

In this sense it is easy to understand why Hlavajova would reference Latour's notion of compositionism in the context of her own curatorial practice, which, through the *Former West* project, explores a spatial and temporal unfolding of collective dialogue from within the space of art fostering openness, heterogeneity, and incompleteness in "processes of thinking through public negotiations" that produce "a crucial resource of what might become 'former West' knowledges" (Hlavajova et al., *Former West* 12–13). Here, Hlavajova might be referring to the series of *Public Editorial Meetings*, which took place from 2013–15. Developed by Hlavajova together with Boris Buden and Simon Sheikh, these meetings brought together contributors to and participants in the project over the years, in what are described as "gatherings [that] take the editorial meeting as their model for informal (re)negotiations of the living knowledge brought together through the course of the project" ("Public Editorial Meetings"). At the first editorial meeting on the last day of the Berlin summit, Hlavajova gave an account of the impossibility of any form of meaningful organization of knowledge over the project's ambition to speak of a former West, a proposition that at the beginning had appeared to be much simpler. Hlavajova credited the impossibility and growing complexity to the accumulation of information attributed to the notion of "former West" over the years. At the same time it is also in spite of this impossibility that the curators proceeded towards an understanding of their practice as gathering, assembling, registering, and chronicling the process from within the realm of art, through which a former West could come into being or be made meaningful.

The notion of meaningfulness can be dissected in various directions. It concerns not as much the quality of knowledge that is produced, but the very ability of producing knowledge within and from the realm of art—a kind of knowledge that produces a reflection, that makes it possible to "rethink the frame in which we think and work, but also the ways how we work, how we practice in the field of art" ("Public Editorial Meetings"). Hlavajova was describing a demand that *Former West* continuously articulates as being part of its curatorial methodology. The openness and publicness of the editorial meetings is a conscious choice to respond to the observed impossibility of meaningfulness with a gesture of deprivatization and transparency. In *Former West* notions of openness and indefinability, and the potentialities of knowledge production emerging from them, are defined as mere transitory constellations awaiting their awakening as dissidents, imaginaries, etc. Once again, by finding new forms of classification that avoid the known categories of art production, the potential meaningfulness of the project designated a political quality. But can a political quality be located in a project's infrastructure?

It is a difficult task to elaborate on the proximity of art and the political in the context of *Former West*, but nonetheless necessary if one is seeking to question the project's functioning, not only in terms of how it reflects on its social, cultural, and political conditions, but also in terms of how it produces these conditions through its own practice. Recalling Marchart, this would mean trying to posit and realize a potential for antagonism in artistic or curatorial practice. We have seen how exhibitions in the context of *Former West* failed to organize a counterhegemonic potential, specifically in the way that it situated artworks as fulfilling that potential. In the context of the more recent projects taking place as part of *Former West*, the question arises of whether the move towards eschewing any categorizations of the format of the curatorial or the role of the artworks within it—other than as "bodies of knowledge," and with regards to the idea of compositionism as a methodology—would allow for the proximity of art and the political without either being superimposed on the other, or being equated with the other. Referring to artworks as documents does not necessarily change their perception of them as artworks in an exhibition. Even though Hlavajova cannot be criticized for her intention to pretermit an ordinary perception of the relationship between artist, work, viewer and world, and instead call for a different more heterogeneous and flexible understanding, the way in which Halvajova applies the Latourian terminology to her cause results in a prefabricated notion that is similar to Sheikh's use of the imaginary for his exhibition *Vectors of the Possible*. All these conceptions of the curatorial seem to be intrinsically linked to the previously discussed belief of art's capacity to be political and to produce emancipatory prospects, implying a transformational quality in art that can be evoked by means of the curatorial. However persuasive this argument might initially appear to be, it would be positivist to identify the curatorial as a compositionist methodology whose performative quality has a constitutive effect on the material, to the extent that it could transform—or even produce—

the social, cultural, and political conditions of practice. Paradoxically, this would entirely defy the notion of impossibility that defines as essential if the curatorial is to articulate the political as the emergence of a conflict Marchart ("The Curatorial Function" 177).

The underlying desire for artistic and cultural practices to partake in "reality" in a "meaningful" way was discussed at a series of conversations that art historian Helmut Draxler and Christoph Gurk organized at the Berlin theatre Hebbel am Ufer.[56] It enquired into the personal and professional needs to which this desire responds, and debated the institutional claims at stake when art addresses the sphere of the political. In their opening statement Draxler and Gurk defined the political within the sphere of cultural production as "the ultimate promise of meaning, which not only seeks to abrogate the deep ambivalences of artistic productivity, but fundamentally promises to elude their own conditions and privileges," with the associated danger of generating a sphere of self-centred communications whose blind spot is the doubts and contradictions that would emerge from analysis and naming, and that makes one's own entanglement in power and capital productive as a cultural producer.

The situation that Draxler and Gurk describe is useful for rendering the paradox of the curatorial methodology used in *Former West*: The performative quality of the curatorial makes it possible for cultural producers to think of themselves as generating a political quality with their work, but it simultaneously renders it absolutely impossible. Draxler and Gurk mention the widespread assumption that an increased need for action by cultural producers in institutional contexts leads to the preservation of the capitalist status quo despite cultural producers having the ambition to destabilize existing power-knowledge relations. This puts cultural producers in a tight spot and, increasingly, art is expected to be identifiable as a place and practice able to raise awareness of political and social crises. All cultural production is then measured by its proximity to these crises, according to Draxler and Gurk.

In the case of *Former West* it can certainly be said that the curators locate their relevance in this context by articulating an idea, that of a "former West," while also producing it as an alternative to the still-prevalent cultural dominance of the West. This alternative

---

56 *Phantasm and Politics—A series of events on real longings and the desire for relevance in theatre, art and music* took place in 2013 and 2014.

in the form of the project's programme is, however, rendered in terms that try transcend the classifications and categorizations of the field of art. Instead, what the curatorial here produces is presented as documents, constellations, prospects, imaginaries, etc.—discursive positionings that produce a symbolic capacity from their material originality. Draxler and Gurk's analysis of contemporary art as heading for its own abstract negation—and even being concretized in the form of a utopia of nonart—is more than applicable in this context. Even though *Former West* does not entirely dismiss the category of art in favour of a productivist or otherwise utilitarian practice (like the 7th Berlin Biennale in 2012, for example), in a perhaps subtle but nonetheless affective way, indulges in the idea of use art as a research device aimed at the production of imaginaries or prospects that locate art in the realm of production of the real. This, however, presupposes that those involved either share this interest or can deal with these increasing demands and challenges.

As an ongoing self-reflexive project, *Former West* is only beginning to embrace the impossibility of its self-defined task and is still in the process of figuring out how to productively use the paradoxes it produces when images are used to stand in for imaginaries, and artworks are reduced to their symbolic value as ideas when presented as dissident knowledges. In some instances these paradoxes of production and reception are foreseen by the curatorial methodology and put into interesting constellations, such as with Buden's *Learning Place,* where students were supposed to produce a CV in critique of the growing demand for conformity in the education system. Another example is the *Public Editorial Meetings,* which can be perceived as articulating the complex position from which to perform transparency for the process of knowledge production.

Towards a Material Dimension of Curatorial Practices

Former West cannot be judged unequivocally. It is a testing ground for producing proximity between art and the political using diverse curatorial strategies and cultural practices.

This analysis contextualized the project with regard to the ambitions and claims for it made by the curators, particularly with respect to the notion of a "former West," the expanded field of curatorial practices in which the project is located, and the various forms of address and modes of production employed by discursive, exhibitionary, and performative methodologies of the curatorial. The ways in which the emancipatory potential of art was rendered was a common reference amongst all of the curators involved, but a variety of means were used to realize this potential in the curated encounter. At times they successfully established a relation between people, ideas, and things in which such potential would be produced as imaginaries of a different, alternative, and predominantly common world to its current social, political, and cultural manifestation. In other instances, the imaginaries that were envisioned to be produced by means of an active engagement were contextualized and framed in such a way that they assumed a representational function, and merely produced images. With respect to the claims for an innovative curatorial methodology based on forms of experimentation with (and even dismissal of) known categorizations and classifications of creative practices and their perception, the extensive discursive positioning of a social, political, and cultural value of art had, at times, a depoliticizing effect on how the project induced the production of imaginaries, primarily relating to a "former West."

What might serve as a pivotal component in a new attempt to generate different ways of positioning art in the realm of the social, and to debate the curatorial function as a political one based on the above analysis of both the comprehensiveness and the shortcomings of the *Former West* project, is the one common denominator that has never been doubted by participants, advisors, curators, and artists: the need to produce a common. In contrast to the ways in which the curators communicated the experimental nature of *Former West: Documents, Constellations, Prospects* (2013) as diverse, complex and multitudinous, its innovative potential actually lies in the way the pronounced formal equality of all mediums reduced the complexity of relationships between things and people in various constellations (lectures, performances, screenings, exhibitions, etc.). All formats suddenly became comparable, because what they shared was not the kind of knowledge produced in them, or the hierarchies employed for that production process, but the fact that their materiality issued a set of relationships that negotiate the role and function they assume with respect to the idea of building a "common" world. The very fact that these relationships can be regarded as material components forms the common ground from which they aim to produce a "common" world. None of the *Former West* debates reflecting on the relationships being produced looked specifically at the materiality of the people and things presented. This is particularly unfortunate because Hlavajova referred to Latour for her conception of the exhibition *Dissident Knowledges,* pointing to the connotation of "diverse composite material" as a description for everything that can be produced as part of the exhibition eschewing any order, format, or hierarchy (Hlavajova et al., *Former West* 62). "We need to have a much more material, much more mundane, much more immanent, much more realistic, much more embodied definition of the material world if we wish to compose a common world" (Latour, "An Attempt" 484).

To speak of a "material" turn in curating would entail thinking about what it could mean to speak of that which is negotiated in the curatorial process as material. As argued for in the previous chapter with the example of unitednationsplaza, this is different from talking about the particular materiality of artworks, objects, people, etc. Invocating a material dimension of the curated encounter requires to look at the self-reflexive interest taken by curatorial practices such as that of the *Former West* project in the positioning of their discursive, exhibitionary, and performative practices in curatorial discourse with less focus on their discursive constitution, and more on their material constitution. This would also mean enquiring less into the forms of speculation these practices open up discursively, and rather emphasize on the ways their material condition performs the social. An alternative conception of a performative quality of the curatorial such as this would assume that neither the social nor the political lay outside actors and networks. Consequently, the political would not lie outside the realm of art. A relation between art and the political cannot be posited discursively other than by following the ways in which people, objects, things, and ideas relate to each other in the curated encounter.

It is in this sense that my observations on the *Former West* project conclude with the affirmation of a political function of the *Public Editorial Meetings,* which aimed to negotiate the knowledges gathered throughout the course of the project in close connection to the politico-cultural transformations unique to the places in which they were held. These meetings followed the processes of social ordering they already addressed and established through the different forms of practices throughout the project's history. This entailed implementing a self-reflexive approach for a curatorial methodology that ac-knowledged its own radical contingency. Therein lies the potential for a conception of agency that is neither autonomous not intentional, but embedded in, and dependent on, the distinctive kinds of effectiv-ity that material processes produce as a consequence of the positions actors occupy as agents within the networks that curated encounters configure.

The nature of materiality is, in this sense, changing as a result of the new infrastructures—of which the curated encounters of *Former West* are examples of—that question our usual concepts of media-tion because they are neither a priori nor a posteriori, neither inside nor or outside processes of communication. The kind of materiality emerging from a self-reflexive understanding of the curated encoun-ter as a communicative space is producing new levels of universal experience as forms of sensible realities that refute instrumentalities applied to the notion of experiencing art relying on dichotomies such as symbolic and material, aesthetic and political. Instead, these sensible realities create new means of imagining the world that are solely conditioned by the ways in which the curated encountered is registered—materially, politically, socially.

To argue for a material dimension of the curated encounter means to no longer divide our attention between things and ideas, or create any kind of hierarchy between them. What the example of *Former West* proves is that attention to ideas often seems to render material forms into little more than expressions of meaning. This has the cura-torial methodology of the project fall back into a representational thinking, which ultimately claims the production of sociality stressing the self-understanding, intentions, and agency of the subjects involved beyond the objects. But by arguing for the production of sociality from a point of view emphasizing the materiality of communicative spaces that foster the production of sociality, a postrepresentational logic emerges in which the things and ideas curated encounters negotiate as a result of selecting and positioning them—bearing in mind their con-tingent character—is neither subordinated to, nor isolated from, com-munication as a process of knowledge production. Its social dimen-sion is a result of thinking its material register.

The Curatorial Complex

This book offers the term "curatorial complex" as an overarching framework for describing a structure with the ordering of things and people. The term emerges from a critique of the disciplinary mechanisms that museums and institutions traditionally employ to govern relations between art and public, to the extent that these relations become instrumentalized within and for the production of cultural hegemony. This definition of the curatorial complex refers to how Tony Bennett defined the political-discursive space of the museum as constituting a "technology of behaviour management" (*Culture* 62). Bennett distinguished between two main approaches for establishing knowledge-power relations in the exhibitionary complex. One approach understands the institutional space of the museum as the holy grail of universalist knowledge, schooling the viewer on its ideological formation by means of systematically arranging works of art and artefacts. In contrast to this function of the museum as an instrument for education—which rests on mechanisms of cultural differentiation in terms of class, gender, ethnicity, etc.—the populist approach makes the museum part of a leisure industry attempting to democratize the disposition of the museum, transforming it from an institution of discipline to one of popular assembly (Bennett, *Culture* 102–05).

Given that the field of cultural production has been subject to an array of social, political, and economic changes in the thirty years since Bennett made these observations our view of the field of cultural production must be dramatically adjusted—along with the role of curatorial practices within that field. When Bennett's text was first published, the political and economic dispositions of the Cold War era were still intact, although their constitution had started to crumble. However, even though, from a superficial perspective, the Cold War era appeared to have had a stabilizing power that made the world describable (through contrasts such as East/West, Socialist/Capitalist and democratic/authoritarian), beneath the surface of these dialectical dispositions this era betrayed as many fractures and wounds, severe inequalities and insecurities as do contemporary times. Contemporary cultural practices often aim to articulate and address these differences and inequalities. Therefore curatorial practices and their

often self-reflexive articulation and negotiation in curatorial discourse are disposed to find forms of practice that aim both to counter
disciplinary mechanisms of behaviour management and to avoid
nurturing a formation of culture as an asset in the knowledge economy responding to a further diversification of consumer markets.

The examples discussed in this book can be taken as exemplary
attempts to achieve precisely these aims. Thereby they function to
address and manifest a social dimension to forms of knowledge production specific to curatorial practices. By reconfiguring the communicative space of the exhibition or the speculative sphere of the
discursive, the exhibitions and projects discussed in this book from
a perspective emphasizing the material dimension of the curated
encounters work towards negotiating notions of spectatorship, public address and constitution, mediation and meaning production in
a different way (sometimes successfully; sometimes unsuccessfully),
to conceive of new ways of knowledge production that are neither
imposed, nor hypocritical.

From Production to Practice

The Formation of Knowledge

The enquiry into the fundamental idea of knowledge production
undertaken by this research was initiated by engaging with Michael
Fullerton's exhibition *Columbia* (2010), which blurred the boundaries between fact and fiction, and between information and meaning,
making interpretation an endless negotiation of the social, cultural,
and political conditions that define the exhibition as a space of communication. *Columbia* engaged the viewer by engendering suspicion
about the value of information for the production of meaning—a
suspicion that emerged from a contention with the artworks and
their politics of installation. This process led to the exhibition space
becoming a realm for the practice of communication that defines
the production of knowledge as a network of relations continuously
built and negotiated there. On the assumption of a particular knowl-
edge-building function of the exhibition space, this research enquired into *The Potosí Principle* (2010) exhibition in order to explore
a curated encounter that critically addresses forms of knowledge
production as systems of maintenance of knowledge-power rela-

tions in contemporary cultural production. Framing historical works in the exhibition with a critical and suspicious attitude towards the cultural conditioning of knowledge production in systems of power (government, religion, etc.), which emerged by setting contemporary works in relation to historical ones, the viewer was invited to participate in critically addressing the production of meaning for constructing an alternative formation of knowledge on history that is responsive to cultural conditions—not only of the past, but also of the present.

The analyses of both exhibitions produced a perspective on knowledge production, not as a diffusion process, but as a continuous process of production and reflection that is shaped as much by dissemination as by appropriation. Echoing Michel Foucault's claim that "knowledge is defined by the possibilities of use and appropriation offered by discourse," knowledge is not an object, a thing or an entity, but a disposition in and of practice ("Of Other Spaces" 202).

To further enquire into this disposition, the previous chapters focused on elaborating a notion of practice that responds to the oscillation in the exhibition space between structures and actions, and between knowledge formation and negotiation. A comparative analysis of Luhmann and Bourdieu yields a notion of practice as intrinsically self-reflexive. It operates by means of a recursive negotiation of structures and actions, a process that is dialectical in its disposition, but does not have the goal of creating a synthesis or dissolution of structures into action, or vice versa. Rather, practice is conditioned by an endless feedback loop between forms of production and their reflection. This notion of practice has a transformative potential with regard to the kind of knowledge it produces, because rather than applying something within the exhibition space to something outside of it, the processes of production negotiate the materialities and contingencies involved in them.

The Generation of Sociality

This materiality was taken to be the very essence of sociality. Beyond any artworks and their contextualizations, sociality is the material with which curating as a practice of communication deals. The forms of sociality that it produces and administers are not bound to their place of origin but exist in the ways their communicability and

connectivity acquires structural value for a further building of relations that can—in other social contexts—reassume a generative
function towards social formations.

In this context, moving on from discussing knowledge formations
in the space of the exhibition to the discursive sphere pursued several interests: testing whether the discursive sphere is a different and
potentially better way of providing processes of knowledge production that avoid the fixation of knowledge and rather focus on its dissemination and appropriation; debating whether the nature of social gatherings that curatorial practices in the discursive sphere
assume actually provides sociality; and discussing the problems of
defining knowledge as discourse generated through forms of producing sociality in the context of a field of cultural production operating in the understanding of the free-market economy in which
dematerialized practices become subject to processes of commodification.

The analysis of unitednationsplaza focused on discussing sociality as a particular scope of relationality, with reference to the interplay of those participating in communication, and the ways people
tend to build structures as modes for anticipating and cultivate cultures as forms of evaluation of what is communicated. Drawing on
the work of Bruno Latour provided for an understanding of sociality
as a particular form of relation-building that connects people and
things with regard to the issues and concerns that propelled them to
assemble in the first place.[57] To conceive of sociality as a condition
for the formation of public engagement helped to critically address
terminologies of "socially-engaged practices" or "art as a social space"
(Möntmann, *Kunst als Sozialer Raum*; Bourriaud, *Relational Aesthetics*). Methodologically, the second chapter "The Discursive Model of
Practice" made an effort to undo "the social" as a fixed entity that
produces hierarchies or cause-effect relationships in relation-building processes. The virtue of discursive art practices was articulated
as fostering a social dimension of knowledge production, which can
be perceived as a demand that art produces and that has to be ac-
counted for in curatorial practices. However, the agency of art can-

---

57 Focussing on Latour does not mean to disregard the work of other writers in
    this line of thinking, such as i.e. Arjun Appadurai (*The Social Life of Things* and
    "The Thing Itself"), Marc Augé (*Non-Places*) or Michel de Certeu (*The Practice
    of Everyday Life*).

not be conceived as automatically extending towards the resolution of this demand in the production of sociality being a tool for transforming the social, political, and cultural conditions prevalent in the field of cultural production.

The third chapter "The Performative Quality of the Curatorial" addressed this particular conglomeration and the confusion of claims between the production of sociality as a context for knowledge formations, on the one hand, and the ways in which a political effectiveness is accredited to the production of sociality in the field of cultural production, on the other. In the discussion of *Former West*, particular attention was paid to the self-reflexive curatorial methodology that characterizes both this project in particular and curating's recent turn from practice to discourse in general (O'Neill, "The Curatorial Turn"). The curators of *Former West* claimed that the constant negotiation of structure and action intrinsic to the self-reflexive curatorial methodology with its concurrent forms of production and reflection was a form of using art as a device for researching the social, political, and cultural conditions that determine the practice. The critical potential of the project's ability to address art's epistemic quality, provided for in the project's nature of altering its course of action according to the issues and concerns that came up over the years, was not as narrowly placed within a narrative around art's critical potential to address the social, cultural, and political conditions of its own practice, as was the case with unitednationsplaza. There, the forms of individual and collective agency produced in the assemblages of people and things were led astray towards reinforcing a hierarchical relationship between curator/organizer and participants, even though its rejection was precisely one of the starting points Vidokle articulated for the project. *Former West* was in this sense more successful in that it did not posit the project in a transformative context other than instating curatorial agency as a form for addressing the epistemic quality of artistic and curatorial practices pursuing a transformative potential. However, the need to frame the different research questions that *Former West* generated and discussed with an overall narrative around the production of commonality as a form of public engagement did also not serve the innovative character of the project in its goal of founding knowledge formations alternative to the predominant knowledge-power relations within the field of contemporary cultural production. Quite the reverse, in fact, because it limited the innovative character, producing the danger of assigning a mere illustrative function to the exhibitions, seminars, lectures, performances, etc. in efforts to establish a narrative-centred discourse.

The Social Dimension of Knowledge Production

The social dimension of knowledge production is primarily to be found in the collaborative nature of contemporary practices accommodated in project structures that allow for and foster the creation of communicative spaces for a dialogical engagement between what is presented, who presents it and who receives it—to the extent that the positions of presenter and receiver become obliterated for the purpose of production of sociality as a principle of communication. In this sense, all of the projects, whether more or less successful, strived to accentuate this social dimension of knowledge production in contemporary artistic and curatorial practices.

It is, however, important to state that in arguing a claim for curatorial practices to articulate, produce and exemplify a social dimension to knowledge production by making the production of relations its core interest, this research does not intend to suggest that any production of relations in an exhibitionary, discursive, or performative format necessarily equates to a production of sociality. It would be naïve to rest claims for an intrinsic social dimension to the curatorial complex on the potentialities that take place and emerge from transitory gatherings. Rather, the task is to show how an intrinsic social dimension of curatorial practices materializes in ways that provokes more emergent forms of those reconfigured structures of public address that artistic practices and curatorial discourse have played a significant role in configuring in recent decades—and continue to do so.

In their latest joint publication *Curating Research* (2015) Paul O'Neill and Mick Wilson commissioned a series of texts that questioned the way in which curatorial practices address and develop their own epistemic quality, given the risk that the knowledge formations being produced will be commoditized. To this end the editors focus especially on discussions of artistic and curatorial practices exemplifying the so-called "educational turn"—in reference to their previous publication *Curating and the Educational Turn* (2010)—which they describe as having "precipitated a very lively debate around the commodifying impact that a discussion of counter-hegemonic educational projects might effect by imposing a unifying rubric or brand upon these different practices," especially those practices that demonstrate a critical engagement with knowledge production, interlinking themes such as cognitive capital, immaterial labour, and forms of exploitation of intellectual and creative work (O'Neill and Wilson, *Curating Research* 18). The editors express their belief that this discussion needs to be pursued further, particularly in a period when reputational economics, market forces, and institutional politics are continuously co-opting and narrowing critical practices.

In light of the argument for the notion of a curatorial complex and the function of curatorial practices within that complex in fostering knowledge formations, the matter of further valorizing cognitive labour in the art field arises anew. Unfortunately, the processes of dematerialization prevalent in curatorial practices that pretermit the space of the exhibition affect these practices in a complex way. Their "discoursification"—the self-reflexive ways in which curatorial practices address and develop their constitution through forms of speculation that the discursive as a medium of practice lends itself to—needs to be critically addressed, particularly with regard to the prolific interest of curatorial practices in addressing their own epistemology and evaluating and reforming their epistemic qualities, as evidenced by publications such as *Curating Research*. Referring to the educational turn in general Simon Sheikh sees a direct relation between the "molding of artistic work into the formats of learning and research" and the interest of capital in immaterial forms of production of post-Fordist capitalism.

> There is a direct corollary between the dematerialization of the art object, and thus its potential (if only partial) exodus from the commodity form and thus disappearance from the market system, and the institutional reinscription and validation of such practices as artistic research and thus knowledge economical commodity. ("Objects of Study")

Sheikh does not evolve this analysis further at this point in terms of acting on it for criticizing the discursive nature of curatorial practices. He merely calls for a shift in perspective.

> Rather, we should learn from those structures as spaces of experience, as discursive spaces, and simultaneously to the implementa-

tion of its productive features, maintain a notion of *un*productive time and space within exhibition venues. We have to move beyond knowledge production into what we can term *spaces for thinking*. ("Objects of Study")

From the Discursive to the Material Turn

In contrast to Sheikh, I suggest altering the perspective on the speculative function of discursive practices for addressing the ways in which they control and limit their potential providing "spaces for thinking." Therefore, an intellectual shift from production to practice needs to take place in terms of how artistic and curatorial practices address knowledge formations in the pursuit of their own epistemic quality. This shift takes place on different levels of affect, concerning the relationship between curators and artists, organizers and participants, and with regard to the categories of spectatorship and participation works of art require to be perceived in. Performing this shift results in a change of perspective on many of the claims around knowledge production the examples discussed in this book. Hence, public engagement cannot be produced, but a process of communication can be put in place in practice for creating dialogical relations. Furthermore, the social is not a result of these relations and cannot be produced as a fixed entity, but comes to the fore when acknowledging its material dimension beyond dichotomies of subject and object that hitherto frame the production of sociality as a form of knowledge production. Rather, the formation of sociality can be incited as a particular form of relation building that is put into practice in such a way that the building of relations is conditioned by the network of actors including people and things with no subordination between them, and contextualized by the question of what the building of relations serves. In this context, curatorial practices must concede the possibility that their forms of materialization run the risk of being commodified, despite their intention to counter processes of hegemony production and critically address the economization of knowledge formations. Although the generative function fostering the production of sociality that curatorial practices can assume due to its often self-reflexive nature has the potential to be transformative, this is not done with the intention of provoking any kind of social effectiveness or political change. Rather, the transformative function facilitates the formation of curatorial practice itself, provoking a turn away from producing discourse toward practice; from arguing about the transformative potential as an epistemic quality of the curatorial to addressing and establishing such epistemic quality by means of curatorial strategies and methodologies that accentuate their own material register and contribute to the formation of knowledge producing its social dimension.

What do curatorial practices produce when they accentuate the materiality of the social dimension of knowledge production? As Maria Lind points out, "the curatorial is neither confined to contemporary art nor a consensual notion" (*Performing the Curatorial* 18). She refers to Irit Rogoff's usage of the term as a "particular kind of knowledge, one produced through trespassing across various fields as well as through spatial arrangements that allow for diverse ways to participate in 'intentional spaces,'" but makes sure to point out that, "the curatorial tends towards the theoretical and philosophical rather than the practical and hands-on" (Lind, *Performing the Curatorial* 18). With regard to this distinction, the consideration of a material turn in curatorial practices would entail distinguishing forms of agency and effectivity associated with material forces and recognizang the ways in which they shape social relations in practice. The function of things—in the extended meaning of matters of concern, in the Latourian sense—is a case in point ("From Realpolitik to Dingpolitik"). Developments in material culture theory call for a reevaluation of the relationships between objects, curators, and audiences or participants with regard to "the distinctive kinds of effectivity that material objects and processes exert as a consequence of the positions they occupy within specifically configured networks of relations that always include human and nonhuman actors" (Bennett and Joyce 5).

Exhibition-making in particular can be conceived as producing knowledge beyond the dichotomies of theory and practice, and of form and material. These dichotomies generally hinder the perception of the epistemic quality of curatorial practices as critically addressing how the production of social formations is influenced and conditioned by the field of cultural production and its creative practices. The communicative space of the medium of the exhibition provides a nurturing ground for conceiving a notion of practice for curating that necessarily entails a negotiation of materiality, not only of the relations produced, but also of the knowledge enacted when relations form sociality. This is what Ines Moreira refers to as the "process of becoming art ... a notion that refers to the relations which are human, material and technical in exhibition-making, articulating art installation as a collective and heteroclite activity" (233).

A "material turn" in curating means nothing else than for curatorial practices to become aware of the structural dispositions and processual transformations they effect in building knowledge-power relations. Curatorial practices need to assume methodologies of practice that focus on materializing the relationships between information, meaning, and experience in such a way that such relationships generate sociality not as a mere outcome of practice, but as its core substance. A material turn in curatorial practices therefore addresses the transformative potential of art in the curated encounter in an original way that does not diminish this potential for remaining a utopian ideal, but is nonetheless cautious when addressing its capability to change reality. It will become possible for curatorial practice to perform the social through its quest to realize its epistemic quality and transformative potential. Ultimately, the purpose of a material perspective is precisely to recognize where the constitution of power takes place in knowledge formations, for which an understanding of the mechanisms of agency production in the curated encounter is essential. This conception rests on the assumption that neither the social, nor the political lie outside of the realm of art and, subsequently to such assumption, would need to be brought into the curated encounter. Instead, a relation between art and the political, or art and the social is always being posited in the ways in which people, objects, things, and ideas relate to each other in the curated encounter.

This is the material that is negotiated in the curatorial process of devising the curated encounter. Therein artistic and curatorial practices are first and foremost considered "materially heterogeneous" practices. This means to primarily look at the distinctive forms of agency on the part of that which is produced, encountered and mediated in the knowledge formations taking place in the curated encounter.

Exploring a material register of the curated encounter constitutes an original contribution to the current field of theory and practice around the social function of artistic and curatorial practices. This research primarily examined the ways in which knowledge and sociality are products of material processes and in what way those products affect the knowledge-power relations they create and by which they are affected. The consideration of materiality entails the possibility for curatorial practices conceiving of its power relations taking place within the realm of practice, rather than outside of it. The exploration of methodologies of practice necessitates placing emphasis on the ways in which knowledge formations emerge from the curated encounter—in particular on how processes of dialogue and engagement foster the production of imaginaries in and for the communicative space created.

Perspectives in and for Practice

The claims I made in this book for curatorial practices to address and foster social dimensions of knowledge production via registering the specific materiality of the curated encounter lend themselves to a contestation in the field of practice, from within the practice of a curator. In this sense the final proposition to understand curators as culture producers strengthens and expands what has been introduced as a call for a material turn in curating. Thereby an alternative conception of the performative quality of the curatorial with regard to art's transformative function is proposed that consists in curatorial practices issuing forms of speculation that enquire less into the discursive positioning of all stakeholders in the curated encounter, but rather focus on highlighting how their material condition generates sociality.

Curators as culture producers

> "Culture" is—like "economy," "society," "technology," and so on—one of those expansive words that designate apparently real structures of social life, but which on closer inspection tend to break down into myriad component parts without any necessary coherence. (Bennett and Frow 3)

Tony Bennett's writings on "culture" strive to first of all establish the term beyond tendencies in the fields of sociology and cultural studies, which fix the term as referring to a specific entity of values and knowledge.[58] In reality, however, culture is intangible and, like

---

58 Bennett, *Culture: A Reformer's Science*; Bennett, "Culture after Distinction"; Bennett, "Exhibition, Difference and the Logic of Culture"; Bennett, *Making Culture: Changing Society*; Bennett and Healy, *Assembling Culture*.

sociality, it exists only in its process of production. The term thus refers to a value related to structure rather than to content. Such definition of culture contrasts the idea of culture as some kind of hidden structure that can be referred to "in order to account for social actions in ways that social actors themselves are not consciously aware of" (Bennett, "Making Culture" 612; Latour, *Reassembling the Social* 175). Here, Bennett uses what is essentially a critique of sociology to explore a concept of culture that is as contingent upon its formation in practice as it is contingent upon the forms of governance derived from it. Bennett is greatly influenced by Michel Foucault's work, particularly his concept of governmentality (Burchell et al.), whom he credits with having developed a perspective on culture that defines it "as simultaneously an instrument of governance and its object" (Bennett, *Critical Trajectories* 9). Bennett takes this perspective and further develops it, firstly through a critique of the mutual permeability between the notion of the "social" and the "cultural" as proposed by the "cultural turn,"[59] and secondly through an examination of various institutions and practices that act on the social, such as museums and their exhibition practices. He establishes the need to differentiate between the notion of culture and the social, because "they are more usefully regarded as distinct if analysis is to engage adequately with the ways in which culture has been shaped into a historically distinctive means for acting on the social within the strat-

---

59 The term "cultural turn" signalled a shift in the social sciences when it was introduced through the writings of Clifford Geertz (*The Interpretation of Cultures*) and subsequently through the writings of a series of French philosophers, anthropologists, and sociologists such as Pierre Bourdieu, Jacques Derrida, Gilles Deleuze, Roland Barthes, and Michel Foucault. They, in turn were influenced by the Frankfurt School (Theodor Adorno, Max Horkheimer, Walter Benjamin, Jürgen Habermas, and Herbert Marcuse) and cultural theorists and historians such as Reinhard Koselleck, and Raymond Williams. While in previous times social, political, and economic structures were understood as institutions with a constitution that is derived from their embedding in "culture" (their way of life, patterns of interaction, and meaning production), they are now considered to be formative of the social institutions. "A stronger way of putting this would be to say that this shift in the social sciences has entailed a breaking-down of the dichotomy between institutional and symbolic structures and practices, a recognition that economic processes or technological systems or political frameworks or kinship structures are always made up, amongst other things, of discourse, of beliefs, of negotiations amongst social actors, of the indeterminacies of action occurring in time" (Bennett and Frow 7).

egies of liberal government" (Bennett, *Critical Trajectories* 10). In this context, culture assumes a "constitutive condition of existence of social life" and functions like a language in that meaning is not accommodated in the things themselves but is only to be found in their relations (Hall, "The Centrality of Culture" 222). This makes it impossible for Bennett to analyse the relation between culture and the social beyond how culture employs ways (for example through art) to act on the social, which is how traditional sociology determined a concept of culture. Instead, Bennett describes both the social and the cultural not as abstract entities or domains, but as historically specific accounts and constellations of people and things. Hence, the social is not a configuration of some "social stuff" that is different from "nonsocial phenomena" (Latour, *Reassembling the Social* 1–4), which could then "be invoked, in the form of an encompassing social context or social structure, as an explanatory ground in relation to the latter" (Bennett, *"Culture Studies"* 26). Accordingly, culture is not something made up of "cultural stuff" (representations, for example) but a "provisional assembly of all kinds of 'bits and pieces' that are fashioned into durable networks whose interactions produce culture as specific kinds of public organization of people and things" (Bennett, *"Culture Studies"* 26–27). From this analysis perspectives on the role of curatorial practices within the field of cultural production can be drawn.

It is what Bennett calls the "process of making" of the relationship between culture and the social that curatorial practices negotiate when addressed as forms of cultural production. Curatorial practices produce culture in that they point to the conditions of social formations, their epistemic quality and function, enquiring into the process of production of sociality for knowledge formations. Curators Jens Hoffmann, Nato Thompson and Michelle White understand the term "culture producer" as successfully contributing to a blurring of boundaries between the role of the artist and the curator with respect to activism and the attempt to produce forms of public engagement by means of the respective practices. For Hoffmann this is a result of the 1990s,

> expansion of the concept of art, and of the politicization of the art scene. ... This development stands in close connection with the lived reality of many of the persons concerned. They write texts, work at night as DJs, are active in political groups, and have a job in the

media. The title of culture producer can subsume all of these different areas of activity. (Hoffmann, "God is a Curator" 108).

Thompson and White describe this "world of cultural production as
an economy through which we all must navigate" in an activist
manner: "Ultimately, my hope is that we are attempting to make
meaning in the world that allows a critical perspective on power as
well as producing alternative, desirous forms of resistant subjectivity" (60). For curatorial practices Thompson and White recognize
the problematic of "producing culture" while "in an emerging neoliberal paradigm of social production," pointing to the need of revis-
ing "how we use the tools we have toward social change" (62). But
while Thompson and White identify the curator's activity "as one
that positions projects within a power-dominated discursive field,"
so that "every project is an effort to legitimate forms of cultural production" in the sense of playing into neoliberal policies of meaning
production, their claims do not extend beyond calling for an "awareness of how the dynamics of power within a discourse are dispro-
portionately shaping it" (63–64).

Artist Alberto Duman criticizes this "wake-up call" for only reset-
ting the alarm clock to a more pleasing tune (98). In a review of *Issues in Curating Contemporary Art and Performance* (Rugg and Sedgwick), a collection of essays examining the role and function of
curatorial practice, Duman perceives most of the contributions in
the book to be "in resemblance to the main problematic of its subject," namely "making self-reflexivity a creed and the dilemma of
how to articulate critical intervention within the institution a matter
of endless discursive folds" (99). The "institution" to which Duman
refers is not only the nonprofit institution of the museum, but also
the result of a process of institutionalization of a critical discourse
on curating becoming a form of culture production. Duman proposes that self-critical curatorial discourse defines the curator as a
"footloose agent of creation and dissemination of knowledge,
stretching across previously unestablished axes or exploiting existing ones in the name of a progressive redistribution of governance
and counterhegemonic positioning" (100). Consequently, this creates an institution of a pseudo-critical form of curating where "ambiguity is the norm and travesty becomes form," leaving "little room
for antagonism, or the concrete refashioning of relationships across
the systems in which we operate" (101).

Relating to this critique means to situate the arguments developed in this book at the problematic nexus of curatorial practice and its self-reflexive negotiation in curatorial discourse. Particularly, my claims on how curatorial practices refashion relationships between people and things producing a material register of the curated encounter in ways that critically address the cultural, social, and political systems to which its forms of practices are subjected need to be revisited in terms of what social, political and cultural function this gives to curatorial practices.

> Unless the next stage in the stretching of curatorial practice into other fields might also incorporate its own epistemology, [and] notwithstanding the undeniable importance and political agency of a critique of modes of presentation in cultural production, the ambitious program of "curating as a form of critical intervention in understanding contemporary culture" set at the outset of this publication is lacking in some essential elements. (Duman 100)[60]

The aim of this book can ultimately be understood in the context of how Duman articulates the condition under which curatorial practices should address their own constitution within the field of cultural production.

---

60 Here, Duman is still referring to the publication *Issues in Curating Contemporary Art and Performance* (Rugg and Sedgwick).

Works Cited

"1st Former West Research Congress." *Former West,* www.formerwest. org/ResearchCongresses/1stFormerWestCongress/Program. Accessed 12 Dec. 2014.

"2nd Former West Research Congress." *Former West,* www.formerwest.org/ResearchCongresses/2ndFormerWestResearchCongress/Program. Accessed 12 Dec. 2014.

"3rd Former West Research Congress, Part One: Beyond What Was Contemporary Art?" *Former West,* www.formerwest.org/ResearchCongresses/3rdFormerWestResearchCongressPartOne/Program. Accessed 12 Dec. 2014.

"3rd Former West Research Congress, Part Two." *Former West,* www.formerwest.org/ResearchCongresses/3rdFormerWestResearchCongressPartTwo/Program. Accessed 12 Dec. 2014.

3rd International Istanbul Biennial. Curated by Vasif Kortun, Istanbul, 17 Oct.–30 Nov. 1992.

6th Berlin Bienniale. Curated by Kathrin Rhomberg, KW Institute for Contemporary Art, Berlin, 11 June–8 Aug. 2012.

7th Berlin Bienniale. Curated by Artur Żmijewski, KW Institute for Contemporary Art, Berlin, 27 Apr.–1 July 2012.

"A New Spirit in Curating: Internationale Konferenz zur Aktuellen Kunst und Ihrer Vermittlung." *Künstlerhaus Stuttgart,* www.kuenstlerhaus.de/a-new-spirit-in-curating-internationale-konferenz-zur-aktuellen-kunst-und-ihrer-vermittlung/. Accessed 12 Mar. 2015.

Adorno, Theodor and Max Horkheimer. *Dialectic of Enlightment.* Translated by John Cumming. Verso, 1997.

Alberro, Alexander. "Alice Creischer, Andreas Siekmann, and Max Jorge Hinderer: The Potosí Principle (2010)." *Mousse: The Artist as Curator,* vol. 45, no. 4, 2014, pp. 21–33.

Alberro, Alexander. "The Silver Lining of Globalization." *Texte zur Kunst,* no. 79, Sep. 2010, pp. 167–72.

Anonymous. *Imposición de la Casulla a San Ildefonso.* Ca. 17th c., oil on canvas, 229.5 x 178.5 x 6 cm, Museo Casa Nacional de Moneda, Potosí.

Appadurai, Arjun. "The Thing Itself." *Public Culture,* vol. 18, no. 1, 2006, pp. 15–21.

Appadurai, Arjun. *The Social Life of Things: Commodities in Cultural Perspective.* Cambridge UP, 1986.

"Archive: Columbia." *Chisenhale Gallery,* www.chisenhale.org.uk/archive/exhibitions/index.php?id=109. Accessed 9 Dec. 2010.

Arendt, Hannah. *Das Urteilen.* Edited by Roland Beiner and Ursula Ludz, Piper, 2012.

Arendt, Hannah. *Between Past and Future: Eight Exercises in Political Thought.* Viking Press, 1968.

Arendt, Hannah. *Was ist Politik?: Fragmente aus dem Nachlaß.* Edited by Ursula Ludz, Piper, 2003.

ARGE schnittpunkt, editors. *Handbuch Ausstellungstheorie und -praxis.* UTB, 2013.

"Art and the Social: Exhibitions of Contemporary Art in the 1990s." *Former West,* www.formerwest.org/ResearchSeminars/ArtAndTheSocial/Program. Accessed 12 Dec. 2014.

"Art Now: Michael Fullerton." *Tate Britain,* www.tate.org.uk/britain/exhibitions/artnow/fullerton/video.htm. Accessed 9 Oct. 2010.

Artaud, Antonin. *The Theatre and Its Double.* Grove Press, 1994.

Augé, Marc. *Non-Places: An Introduction to Supermodernity.* Translated by John Howe, Verso, 1995.

Baecker, Dirk. "Die Adresse der Kunst." *Systemtheorie der Literatur,* edited by Jürgen Fohrmann and Harro Müller, Fink, 1996, pp. 82–105.

Baecker, Dirk. "Systemic Theories of Communication." *Theories and Models of Communication,* edited by in Paul Cobley and Peter J. Schulz, Walter de Gruyter, 2013, pp. 85–100.

Baecker, Dirk. S*tudien zur Nächsten Gesellschaft.* Suhrkamp, 1997.

Balibar, Etienne. Interview by Charles Esche and Maria Hlavajova. *Former West,* 7 Sep. 2009, www.formerwest.org/ResearchInterviews/Etienne-Balibar. Accessed 7 Jan. 2013.

Bang Larsen, Lars. "The Long Nineties," *Frieze,* no. 144, Jan./Feb. 2012, pp. 92–95.

Baumann, Leonie et al. editors. *Crosskick: European Art Academies Hosted by German Kunstvereine. A Format Linking Art Education and Curatorial Practice.* Walther König, 2009.

Bäumler, Quirin. *El Infierno de Caquiaviri.* 2010, silver pencil drawing on transparent foil, 317 x 765 cm.

Bäumler, Quirin. *La Muerte de Caquiaviri.* 2010, silver pencil drawing on transparent foil, 313 x 419 cm.

Beck, Martin. "Display: Eine Begriffsklärung." Forms of Exhibitions, Conference, 8–11 May 2009, Kunstverein Hamburg, Presentation.

Belting, Hans and Andrea Buddensieg, editors. *The Global Art World: Audiences, Markets, and Museums.* Hatje Cantz, 2009.

Bennett, Tony and Chris Healy, editors. Introduction. *Assembling Culture.* Routledge, 2011, pp. 3–10.

Bennett, Tony and John Frow, editors. Introduction: Vocabularies of Culture. *The SAGE Handbook of Cultural Analysis.* Sage, 2013, pp. 2–11.

Bennett, Tony and Patrick Joyce, editors. Introduction. *Material Powers: Cultural Studies, History and the Material Turn.* Routledge, 2010, pp. 1–20.

Bennett, Tony. "'Culture Studies' and the Culture Complex." *Handbook of Cultural Sociology,* edited by John R. Hall et al., Routledge, 2010, pp. 23–34.

Bennett, Tony. "Culture after Distinction." *Culture, Class, Distinction*, edited by Tony Bennett et al., Routledge, 2006, pp. 9–23.

Bennett, Tony. "Exhibition, Difference and the Logic of Culture." *Museum Frictions: Public Cultures/Global Transformations*, edited by Ivan Karp et al., Duke UP, 2006, pp. 46–69.

Bennett, Tony. "The Exhibitionary Complex." *New Formations*, no. 4, 1988, pp. 73–102.

Bennett, Tony. "The Exhibitionary Complex." *Thinking about Exhibitions*, edited by Reesa Greenberg et al., Routledge, 1996, pp. 81–112.

Bennett, Tony. "The Work of Culture." *Cultural Sociology*, vol. 1, no. 1, 2007, pp. 31–48.

Bennett, Tony. *Critical Trajectories: Culture, Society, Intellectuals*. Blackwell, 2007.

Bennett, Tony. *Culture: A Reformer's Science*. Sage, 1998.

Bennett, Tony. *Making Culture: Changing Society.* Routledge, 2013.

Benning, James. *Twenty Cigarettes.* 2011, video (colour, sound, HD; 99 min).

Berrió, Gaspar Miguel de. *Descripción del Cerro Rico e Imperial Villa de Potosí.* 1758, oil on canvas, 182 x 262 cm, Museo Colonial Charcas, Universidad San Francisco Xavier de Chuquisaca, Sucre.

Bishop, Claire and Liam Gillick, editors. "Letters and Responses: Contingent Factors. A Response to Claire Bishop's 'Antagonism and Relational Aesthetics.'" *October*, no. 115, Winter 2006, pp. 95–107.

Bishop, Claire. "Antagonism and Relational Aesthetics." *October*, no. 110, Fall 2004, pp. 51–79.

Bishop, Claire. "The Social Turn: Collaboration and Its Discontents." *Artforum*, Feb. 2006, pp. 179–185.

Bishop, Claire. *Artificial Hells: Participatory Art and the Politics of Spectatorship.* Verso. 2012.

Bismarck, Beatrice von and Irit Rogoff. "Curating/Curatorial: A Conversation between Irit Rogoff and Beatrice von Bismarck." *Cultures of the Curatorial,* edited by Beatrice von Bismarck et al., Sternberg, 2012, pp. 21–41.

Bismarck, Beatrice von et al., editors. Introduction. *Cultures of the Curatorial.* Sternberg Press, 2012, pp. 2–12.

Bismarck, Beatrice von and Benjamin Meyer-Krahmer, editors. *Cultures of the Curatorial 3. Hospitality: Hosting Relations in Exhibitions*, Sternberg Press, 2016.

Bismarck, Beatrice von. "Display/Displacement." *Re-Visionen des Displays. Ausstellungs-Szenarien, ihre Lektüre und ihr Publikum*, edited by Sigrid Schade et al., JRP Ringier, 2008, pp. 69–82.

Bismarck, Beatrice von. "Game Within the Game: Institution, Institutionalisation and Art Education." *Art and Its Institutions: Current Conflicts, Critique and Collaborations*, edited by Nina Möntmann, Black Dog Publishing, 2006, pp. 124–32.

Bismarck, Beatrice von. "In the Space of the Curatorial: Art, Training, and Negotiation." *Crosskick: European Art Academies Hosted by German Kunst-*

vereine. A Format Linking Art Education and Curatorial Practice, edited by Leonie Baumann et al., Walter König, 2009, pp. 42–45.

Bos, Saskia and Liam Gillick. "Towards a Scenario: Debate with Liam Gillick." *Modernity Today: Bijdragen tot Actuele Artistieke Theorievorming = Contributions to a Topical Artistic Discourse,* edited by Saskia Bos and Karina van Santen, de Appel, 2004, pp. 74–86.

Bourdieu, Pierre. *Distinction: A Social Critique of the Judgement of Taste.* Translated by Richard Nice. Harvard UP, 1984.

Bourdieu, Pierre. *Outline of a Theory of Practice.* Translated by Richard Nice. Cambridge UP, 1977,

Bourdieu, Pierre. *Rules of Art.* Translated by Susan Emanuel. Polity Press, 1996.

Bourdieu, Pierre. *The Field of Cultural Production: Essays on Art and Literature.* Edited by Randal Johnson, Columbia UP, 1993.

Bourdieu, Pierre. *The Logic of Practice.* Translated by Richard Nice. Polity Press, 1990.

Bourriaud, Nicolas. *Relational Aesthetics.* Les presses du réel, 2002.

Brecht, Bertold. *Schriften zum Theater: Über eine Nicht-Aristotelische Dramatik.* Edited by Werner Hecht, Suhrkamp, 1990.

Brock, Bazon. "Der Hang zum Gesamtkunstwerk." *Der Hang zum Gesamtkunstwerk: Europäische Utopien seit 1800,* edited by Harald Szeemann, Sauerländer, 1983, pp. 2–24.

Brunner, Otto et al., editors. Introduction. *Geschichtliche Grundbegriffe: Historisches Lexikon zur Politisch-Sozialen Sprache in Deutschland.* Vol.1, Klett-Cotta, 2004, pp. I–XXV.

Buchloh, Benjamin H. D. "Conceptual Art 1962–1969: From the Aesthetic of Administration to the Critique of Institutions." *October,* no. 55, Winter 1990, pp. 105–43.

Buden, Boris. "Towards the Heterosphere: Curator as Translator." *Performing the Curatorial Within and Beyond Art,* edited by Maria Lind, Sternberg Press, 2012, pp. 23–44.

Burchell, Graham et al., editors. *The Foucault Effect: Studies in Governmentality.* University of Chicago Press, 1991.

Castoriadis, Cornelius. *The Imaginary Institution of Society.* MIT Press, 1987.

Certeau, Michel de. *The Practice of Everyday Life.* Translated by Steven F. Rendall, University of California Press, 2011.

Chambres d'Amis. Curated by Jan Hoet, S.M.A.K., Gent, 21 June–21 Sep. 1986.

Charlesworth, J.J. "Not About Institutions, But Why We Are So Unsure of Them." *ICA,* www.ica.org.uk/18217/Essays/Not-about-institutions-but-why-we-are-so-unsure-of-them-by-JJ-Charlesworth.html. Accessed 14 Nov. 2012.

Christov-Bakargiev, Carolyn and Liam Gillick. "In Conversation." *The Producers: Contemporary Curators in Conversation (4),* edited by Susan Hiller and Sarah Martin, Baltic, 2002, pp. 34–45.

Chto Delat?/What is to be done? *Perestroika Timeline.* 2009/2013, materials and dimensions variable.

Collaborative Practices, Part One. Curated by Maria Lind, Katharina Schlieben and Judith Schwarzbart, Kunstverein Munich, Summer 2004.

"Columbia. Titles and Captions." *Chisenhale Gallery,* www.chisenhale.org. uk/archive/exhibitions/images/Michael_Fullerton_Columbia_Titles1_. pdf. Accessed 9 Dec. 2010.

Creischer et al., "1000 Words: Alice Creischer, Max Jorge Hinderer and Andreas Siekmann Talk about 'Principio Potosí.'" *Artforum,* Sep. 2010, pp. 300-303.

Creischer, Alice et al., editors. *The Potosí Principle. How Can We Sing the Song of the Lord in an Alien Land?* Walther König, 2010.

Creischer, Alice, Christian von Borries and Andreas Siekmann. *Dubai—Expanded Horizons: Re-enactment of a press conference, music performance.* 2009, performance and installation, Temporäre Kunsthalle, Berlin, Germany.

David, Catherine and Jean-François, editors. *Politics, Poetics: Documenta X.* Hatje Cantz, 1997.

David, Catherine and Paul Sztulman, editors. *Documenta X: Short Guide / Kurzführer.* Hatje Cantz, 1997.

Debord, Guy. *The Society of the Spectacle.* Zone Books, 1994.

Deleuze, Gilles and Felix Guattari. *A Thousand Plateaus: Capitalism and Schizophrenia.* Translated by Brian Massumi. University of Minnesota Press, 1987.

Descartes, René. *The Philosophical Writings of Descartes.* Translated by John Cottingham, Robert Stoothoff and Dugald Murdoch. 3 vols, 1984. Cambridge UP, 2006.

Diederichsen, Diederich. *On (Surplus) Value in Art.* Sternberg Press, 2008.

Documenta 5. Artistic direction by Harald Szeemann. Kassel, 30 June–8 Oct. 1972.

Documenta X. Artistic direction by Catherine David. Kassel, 21 June–28 Sep. 1997.

Documenta 11. Artistic direction by Okwui Enwezor. Kassel, 8 June–15 Sep. 2002.

Documenta 13. Artistic direction by Carolyn Christov-Bakargiev. Kassel, 9 June–16 Sep. 2012.

Doherty, Claire. "New Institutionalism and the Exhibition as Situation." *Protections: Das Ist Keine Ausstellung / Protections: This Is Not An Exhibition,* edited by Adam Budak et al. Museum Johanneum, 2006, pp. 60–79.

Doujak, Ines. *Witches.* 2010, sculptures (materials and dimensions variable).

Drabble, Barnaby and Dorothee Richter. *Curating Degree Zero.* http://www. curatingdegreezero.org. Accessed 21 Feb. 2015.

Draxler, Helmut and Christoph Gurk. "Phantasm and Politics: A Series of Events on Real Longings and the Desire for Relevance in Theatre, Art and Music." *Hebbel am Ufer,* www.english.hebbel-am-ufer.de/programme/archive/phantasm-and-politics. Accessed 30 Aug. 2014.

Duman, Alberto. "When Travesty Becomes Form." *Mute*, vol. 2 , no. 9, Fall 2008, pp. 94–101.

Dumas, Marlene. *Young Men (Man Kind)*. 2002–2007, series of drawings, dimensions variable.

Eigenheer, Marianne et al., editors. *Curating Critique*. Revolver, 2007.

Eisler, Rudolf. "Materie." *Kant-Lexikon. Nachschlagewerk zu Kants sämtlichen Schriften, Briefen und handschriftlichem Nachlass*. http://www.textlog.de/32997.html. Accessed 26. Sep. 2017.

El Dahab, Mai Abu. "On How to Fall With Grace—or Fall Flat on Your Face." *Notes for an Art School*, edited by El Dahab et al., Idea Books, 2006, pp. 4–10.

Farocki, Harun. *The Silver and the Cross*. 2010, 2 channel video installation, 17 min., colour, sound.

Farzin, Media. "An Open History of the Exhibition-as-School." *Anton Vidokle—Produce, Distribute, Discuss, Repeat*, edited by Anton Vidokle and Brian Sholis, Lukas and Sternberg, 2009, pp. 31–47.

Fazeli, Taraneh. "Class Consciousness." *Artforum*, Summer 2010, pp. 129–32.

Ferguson, Bruce W. "Exhibition Rhetorics: Material Speech and Utter Sense." *Thinking about Exhibitions*, edited by Reesa Greenberg et al., Routledge, 1996, pp. 175–90.

Filipovic, Elena et al., editors. *The Biennial Reader: An Anthology on Large-Scale Perennial Exhibitions of Contemporary Art*. Hatje Cantz, 2010.

Filipovic, Elena. "The Global White Cube." *The Manifesta Decade: Debates on Contemporary Art Exhibitions and Biennials in Post-Wall Europe*, edited by Elena Filipovic and Barbara Vanderlinden, MIT Press, 2005, pp. 63–85.

"Former West: About." *Former West*, www.formerwest.org/About. Accessed 21 Feb. 2015.

Former West: Documents, Constellations, Prospects. Haus der Kulturen der Welt, Berlin, 18–24 Mar. 2013.

"Former West—International Research, Publishing, and Exhibition Project, 2009–2012." *e-flux*, www.e-flux.com/announcements/international-research-publishing-and-exhibition-project-20098-2012/. Accessed 31 Jan. 2013.

"Former West: Team." *Former West*, www.formerwest.org/Team. Accessed 23 Feb. 2015.

Foucault, Michel. "Of Other Spaces." *The Visual Culture Reader*, edited by Nicolas Mirzeoff, Routledge, 2002, pp. 229–37.

Foucault, Michel. *Archeology of Knowledge*. Translated by A.M. Sheridan Smith. Routledge, 2002.

Foucault, Michel. *Power/Knowledge: Selected Interviews and Other Writings*. Edited by Colin Gordon, Harvester Press, 1980.

Franke, Anselm. "Magic Circles: Exhibitions under the Conditions of the Society of Control." *Manifesta Journal*, no. 7, 2009, pp. 8–11.

Freee. *Protest Drives History*. 2008, billboard poster, colour, 4 x 12 m. Institute of Contemporary Arts, London.

Fullerton, Michael. *BASF Magic Gold.* 2010, pigment, plinth, 30 x 32 x 136 cm.

Fullerton, Michael. *Gothic Version of the Ring Laser Gyroscope Used in Final Flight of the Space Shuttle Columbia STS-107.* 2010, mirror, laser, smoke machine, plinth, 150 cm x 100 cm x 30 cm.

Fullerton, Michael. *Using Polish Technology, Alan Turing Devised a more Sophisticated Machine to Crack ENIGMA.* 2010, screen print on newsprint, 220 x 295 cm.

Fullerton, Michael. *Why Your Life Sucks (Alan Turing).* 2010, oil on linen, 46 x 60 cm.

Geertz, Clifford. *The Interpretation of Cultures.* Basic Books, 1973.

Geiger, Marcus. *Untitled.* 2013, materials and dimensions variable.

Gell, Alfred. *Art and Agency: An Anthropological Theory.* Claredon Press, 1998.

Gillick, Liam. "Maybe it Would be Better if We Worked in Groups of Three? Part 1 of 2: The Discursive." *e-flux Journal,* no. 2, Jan. 2009, www.e-flux.com/journal/maybe-it-would-be-better-if-we-worked-in-groups-of-three-part-1-of-2-the-discursive. Accessed 5 May 2009.

Gillick, Liam. "Maybe it Would be Better if We Worked in Groups of Three? Part 2 of 2: The Experimental Factory." *e-flux Journal,* no. 3, Feb. 2009, www.e-flux.com/journal/maybe-it-would-be-better-if-we-worked-in-groups-of-three-part-2-of-2-the-experimental-factory. Accessed 5 May 2009.

Gillick, Liam. "The Binary Stadium: Anton Vidokle, Intermediary or Locus." *Anton Vidokle—Produce, Distribute, Discuss, Repeat,* edited by Anton Vidokle and Brian Sholis, Lukas and Sternberg, 2009, pp. 47–55.

"Global Art Museum." *ZKM,* www.globalartmuseum.de/site/home. Accessed 21 July 2014.

Gordon, Douglas. *Hysterical.* 1994/1995, two-channel projection, 29 minutes, dimensions variable.

Green, Renée, editor. Introduction. *Negotiations in the Contact Zone.* Assirio and Alvim, 2003, pp. 2–26.

Greenberg, Reesa et al., editors. *Thinking about Exhibitions.* Routledge, 1996.

Grigely, Joseph. *Exhibition Prosthetics.* Sternberg, 2010.

Gripp-Hagelstange, Helga, editor. *Niklas Luhmanns Denken: Interdisziplinäre Einflüsse und Wirkungen.* UVK, 2000.

Groys, Boris. "Politics of Installation." *Boris Groys. Going Public,* edited by Julieta Aranda et al., Sternberg Press, 2010, pp. 50–69.

Groys, Boris. Interview by Charles Esche and Maria Hlavajova. *Former West,* 18 Jan. 2009, www.formerwest.org/ResearchInterviews/BorisGroys. Accessed 7 Jan. 2013.

Habermas, Jürgen. *On The Pragmatics Of Communication.* Edited by Maeve Cook, MIT Press, 1998.

Hadley+Maxwell. "Find Us At the Kitchen Door." *Art Lies,* no. 59, Fall 2008, pp. 18–23.

Hall, Stuart. "The Centrality of Culture: Notes on the Cultural Revolutions of Our Time." *Media and Cultural Regulation*, edited by Kenneth Thompson, Sage, 1997, pp. 207–238.

Hannula, Mika, editor. *Stopping the Process?: Contemporary Views on Art and Exhibitions.* Nordic Institute for Contemporary Art, 1998.

Harding, Anna, editor. Curating: the Contemporary Art Museum and Beyond. Academy Group, 1997.

Hayes, Sharon. *In the Near Future.* 2009, multiple slide projection, 35mm colour slides, dimensions variable.

Hegel, Georg W. F. *Die Naturphilosophie.* Edited by Hermann Glockner and Karl Ludwig Michelet, Frommann, 4th ed., 1965.

Heidegger, Martin. *Basic Writings: Martin Heidegger.* Edited by David Farrell Krell, Routledge (Routledge Classics), 2011.

Hlavajova, Maria et al., editors. *Former West: Documents, Constellations, Prospects.* Basis voor actuele kunst, 2013.

Hlavajova, Maria et al., editors. *On Horizons: A Critical Reader in Contemporary Art.* Basis voor actuele kunst, 2011.

Hlavajova, Maria et al., editors. *On Knowledge Production: A Critical Reader in Contemporary Art.* Basis voor actuele kunst, 2008.

Hoegsberg, Milena. "Notes on Self-Reflexive Curatorial Strategies in the 2010 Taipei Biennial and Shanghai Biennial." *Manifesta Journal*, no. 11, 2010, pp. 95–101.

Hoffmann, Jens. "God is a Curator." *MIB-Men in Black: Handbook of Curatorial Practice*, edited by Christoph Tannert and Ute Tischler, Revolver, 2004, pp. 103–108.

Hoffmann, Jens. "Overture." *The Exhibitionist*, no. 1, pp. 2–5.

International Exhibition of New Theatre Techniques. Organized by Frederick Kiesler. Konzerthaus, Vienna, 1924.

"Introductory Notes. Charles Esche and Maria Hlavajova." *Former West*, www.formerwest.org/ResearchCongresses/1stFormerWestCongress/Text/IntroductoryNotes. Accessed 28 Nov. 2012.

IRWIN. *NSK Passport Office Berlin.* 1992/2013, materials and dimensions variable.

Kant, Immanuel. *Kritik der Urteilskraft.* Edited by Wilhelm Weischedel, 21st ed, Suhrkamp, 2014.

Kester, Grant. "Letter to the Editor: Another Turn. Grant Kester Responds to Claire Bishop." *Artforum*, May 2006, pp. 22–24.

Kester, Grant. *Conversation Pieces: Community and Communication in Modern Art.* University of California Press, 2014.

Koselleck, Reinhart. *The Practice of Conceptual History: Timing History, Spacing Concepts.* Translated by Todd Samuel Presner et al., Stanford University Press, 2002.

Kravagna, Christian. "Postkoloniale Austellungen im Kunstfeld." *Handbuch Ausstellungstheorie und -praxis*, edited by ARGE/Schnittpunkt, UTB, 2013, pp. 51–65.

Lacan, Jacques. *Schriften I.* Edited by Norbert Haas, Suhrkamp, 1975.

Laclau, Ernesto and Chantal Mouffe. *Hegemony and Socialist Strategy.* Verso, 1985.

Laclau, Ernesto. "Horizon, Ground, and Lived Experience." *On Horizons: A Critical Reader in Contemporary Art,* edited by Maria Hlavajova et al., Basis voor actuele kunst, 2011, pp. 100–112.

Latour, Bruno and Peter Weibel, editors. Introduction. *Making Things Public: Atmospheres of Democracy.* MIT Press, 2005, pp. 5–27.

Latour, Bruno and Steve Woolgar. *Laboratory Life: The Social Construction of Scientific Facts.* 1979. Reprint, Sage, 1981.

Latour, Bruno. "An Attempt at a 'Compositionist Manifesto.'" *New Literary History,* vol. 41, no. 3, 2010, pp. 471–90.

Latour, Bruno. "From Realpolitik to Dingpolitik or How to Make Things Public." *Making Things Public: Atmospheres of Democracy,* edited by Bruno Latour and Peter Weibel, MIT Press 2005, pp. 14–43.

Latour, Bruno. *Pandora's Hope.* Harvard UP, 1999.

Latour, Bruno. *Politics of Nature: How to Bring the Sciences into Democracy.* Harvard UP, 1994.

Latour, Bruno. *Reassembling the Social: An Introduction into Actor-Network-Theory.* Oxford UP, 2005.

Latour, Bruno. *We Have Never Been Modern.* Translated by Catherine Porter, Harvard UP, 1993.

"Learning Place, Boris Buden." *Former West,* www.formerwest.org/DocumentsConstellationsProspects/Texts/LearningPlace. Accessed 31 July 2013.

Li Ran. *Beyond Geography.* 2012, colour, sound; 23:09 min.

Lind, Maria et al. "UNP and The Building: Maria Lind and Dieter Roelstraete Talk to Anton Vidokle." *Frieze,* no. 128, Jan./Feb. 2009, pp. 114–116.

Lind, Maria, editor. Introduction. *Performing the Curatorial Within and Beyond Art.* Berlin: Sternberg Press, 2012, pp. 9–23.

Lind, Maria. "Dilemmas of Love, Humor, and Critique: Notes on the Work of Anton Vidokle." *Anton Vidokle—Produce, Distribute, Discuss, Repeat,* edited by Anton Vidokle and Brian Sholis, Lukas and Sternberg, 2009, pp. 21–31.

Locher, Thomas. *Reading Of.* 2013, text, MD, various dimensions.

Luhmann, Niklas. *Einführung in die Systemtheorie.* Edited by Dirk Baecker, Carl-Auer-Systeme, 2009.

Luhmann, Niklas. *Social Systems.* Translated by John Bednarz, Jr., with an introduction by Dirk Baecker, Stanford UP, 1995.

Luhmann, Niklas. *Theories of Distinction: Redescribing the Descriptions of Modernity.* Edited by William Rasch, Stanford UP, 2002.

Luhmann, Niklas. *Theory of Society: Volume 1.* Translated by Rhodes Barret, Stanford UP, 2012.

Luhmann, Niklas. *Theory of Society: Volume 2.* Translated by Rhodes Barret. Stanford UP, 2013.

Lütticken, Sven. "Unknown Knowns: On Symptoms in Contemporary Art." *On Knowledge Production: A Critical Reader in Contemporary Art,* edited by Maria Hlavajova et al., Basis voor actuele kunst, 2008, pp. 84–107.

Maestro de Caquiaviri. *Infierno.* Ca. 1739, oil on canvas, 317 x 756 cm, Church of Caquiaviri, La Paz.

Maestro de Caquiaviri. *Muerte.* Ca. 1739, oil on canvas, 313 x 419 cm, Church of Caquiaviri, La Paz.

Maharaj, Sarat. "'Xeno-Epistemics': Makeshift Kit for Visual Art as Knowledge Production." *Documenta 11—Platform 5: Exhibition,* edited by Okwui Enwezor, Hatje-Cantz, 2002, pp. 71–84.

Making Things Public: Atmospheres of Democracy. Curated by Bruno Latour and Petwer Weibel, ZKM, Karlsruhe, 20 Mar.–3 Oct. 2005.

Malik, Suhail. "Educations Sentimental and Unsentimental: Repositioning the Politics of Art and Education." *Redhook Journal: Curating and Its Institutions,* www.bard.edu/ccs/redhook/educations-sentimental-and-unsentimental-repositioning-the-politics-of-art-and-education. Accessed 10 Sep. 2012.

Marchart, Oliver. "The Curatorial Function—Organizing the Ex/Position." *Curating Critique,* edited by Marianne Eigenheer et al., Revolver, 1997, pp. 164–70.

Marchart, Oliver. *Hegemonie im Kunstfeld: die Documenta-Ausstellungen Dx, D11, D12 und die Politik der Biennalisierung.* Walther König (N. B. K. Diskurs), 2008.

Martha Rosler: If You Lived Here Still. e-flux, New York, 28 Aug.–14 Nov. 2009.

Martinon, Jean-Paul, editor. Introduction, *The Curatorial: A Philosophy of Curating.* Bloomsbury, 2013, pp. 3–22.

Michael Fullerton: Columbia. Chisenhale Gallery, London, 10 Sep.– 24. Oct. 2010.

"Michael Fullerton: Columbia." *Chisenhale Gallery,* www.chisenhale.org.uk/archive/exhibitions/index.php?id=109. Accessed 9 Dec. 2010.

Michael Fullerton: Meaning Inc. Glasgow Print Studio, 28 June–15 Aug. 2015.

"Michael Fullerton—Meaning Inc." *Glasgow Print Studio,* www.gpsart.co.uk/Home/DisplayExhibition/107?year=2014. Accessed 12 Jan. 2015.

Mik, Aernout. *Untitled.* 2013, performance.

Miller, Daniel, editor. "Agency." *Materiality.* Duke UP, 2005, pp. 28–39.

Misiano, Victor et al. editors. "Editorial: The Grammar of the Exhibition." *Manifesta Journal,* no. 7, 2009.

Molinari, Eduardo and Archivo Clemente. *The Soy Children.* 2010, installation, drawing, collages, photographs.

Mona Vatamanu and Florin Tudor: Surplus Value. Basis voor actuele kunst, Utrecht, 5 Sep.–9 Nov. 2009.

Möntmann, Nina, editor. *Art and Its Institutions: Current Conflicts, Critique and Collaborations.* Black Dog Publishing, 2006.

Möntmann, Nina. *Kunst als Sozialer Raum.* Walter König, 2002.

Moreira, Ines. "Backstage and Processuality: Unfolding the Installation Sites of Curatorial Projects." *The Curatorial: A Philosophy of Curating*, edited by Jean-Paul Martinon, Bloomsbury, 2013, pp. 231–242.

Mouffe, Chantal. *On the Political*. Routledge, 2005.

Mouffe, Chantal. *The Democratic Paradox*. Verso, 2005.

Nassehi, Armin and Gerd Nollmann, editors. *Bourdieu und Luhmann: Ein Theorievergleich*. Suhrkamp 2004.

"Night School." *New Museum*, www.museumashub.org/node/48. Accessed 9 Feb. 2015.

Nollert, Angelika et al., editors. *A.C.A.D.E.M.Y.* Revolver, 2006.

Obrist, Hans Ulrich. *Hans Ulrich Obrist: Interviews Vol. 2*. Edited by Charles Arsène-Henry, Charta, 2010.

Obrist, Hans Ulrich. *Hans Ulrich Obrist: Interviews, Vol. 1*. Edited by Thomas Boutoux, Charta, 2003.

Obrist, Hans Ulrich and Gilane Tawadros. "In Conversation." *The Producers: Contemporary Curators in Conversation* (2), edited by Susan Hiller and Sarah Martin, Baltic, 2001, pp. 14–22.

O'Doherty, Brian. *Inside the White Cube: the Ideology of the Gallery Space*. University of California Press, 1999.

O'Neill, Paul and Mick Wilson, editors. *Curating and the Educational Turn*. Open Editions, 2010.

O'Neill, Paul and Mick Wilson, editors. *Curating Research*. Open Editions, 2015.

O'Neill, Paul, editor. *Curating Subjects*. Open Editions, 2007.

O'Neill, Paul. "The Curatorial Turn: From Practice to Discourse." *The Biennial Reader: An Anthology on Large-Scale Perennial Exhibitions of Contemporary Art*, edited by Elena Filipovic et al., Hatje Cantz, 2010, pp. 240–58.

O'Neill, Paul. *The Culture of Curating and the Curating of Culture(s)*. MIT Press, 2012.

Parret, Herman. *Semiotics and Pragmatics: an Evaluative Comparison on Conceptual Frameworks*. Benjamins, 1983.

Parsons, Talcott and Edward Shils, editors. *Toward a General Theory of Action*. Cambridge UP, 1951.

Phillips, Andrea. *Public Acting: From Public Art to Art's Publicity*. Unpublished Essay, 2011.

"Public Editorial Meetings." *Former West*, www.formerwest.org/PublicEditorialMeetings. Accessed 21 Feb. 2015.

Pratt, Mary-Louise. *Imperial Eyes: Travel Writing and Transculturation*. Routledge, 1992.

Rancière, Jacques. "The Emancipated Spectator." *Artforum*, Mar. 2007, pp. 271–281.

Rancière, Jacques. *The Emancipated Spectator*. Verso, 2009.

Rancière, Jacques. *The Ignorant Schoolmaster*. Stanford UP, 1991.

Rancière, Jacques. *The Politics of Aesthetics*. Continuum, 2004.

Rand, Steve and Heather Kouris, editors. *Cautionary Tales: Critical Curating.* Apexart, 2007.

Raunig, Gerald. "Instituent Practices: Fleeing, Instituting, Transforming." *Art and Contemporary Critical Practice,* edited by Gerald Raunig and Gene Ray, Mayfly Books, 2009.

Ricoeur, Paul. *Freud and Philosophy: an Essay on Interpretation.* Translated by Dennis Savage, Yale UP, 1970.

"Rirkrit Tiravanija: Untitled (Free/Still). 1992/1995/1997/2011-." *Moma Multimedia Vodcast,* www.moma.org/collection/object.php?object_id=147206. Accessed 15 Feb. 2012.

Rogoff, Irit. "Academy as Potentiality." *A.C.A.D.E.M.Y.,* edited by Angelika Nollert et al., Revolver, 2006, pp. 13–20.

Rogoff, Irit. "Turning." *e-flux Journal,* no. 59, Nov. 2014. www.e-flux.com/journal/turning/. Accessed 11 Dec. 2014.

Rose, Gillian. *Visual Methodologies: An Introduction to the Interpretation of Visual Materials.* Sage, 2001.

Rosenfeld, Elske. *Our Brief Autumn of Utopia.* 2010, text and video material, dimensions variable.

Rosler, Martha and Anton Vidokle. "Exhibition as School as Work of Art." *Art Lies,* no. 59, Fall 2008, pp. 70–77.

Rosler, Martha. *Semiotics of the Kitchen.* 1975, video (black and white, sound; 6:09 min), Museum of Modern Art, New York.

Rugg, Judith and Michèle Sedgwick, editors. *Issues in Curating Contemporary Art and Performance.* Intellect, 2007.

"Russian Avant-Garde Revisited." *Former West,* www.formerwest.org/ResearchSeminars/RussianAvantgardeRevisited/Program. Accessed 12 Dec. 2014.

Sarotte, Mary Elise. *1989: The Struggle to Create Post-Cold War Europe.* Princeton UP, 2009.

Schade, Sigrid et al., editors. *Re-Visionen des Displays. Ausstellungs-Szenarien, ihre Lektüre und ihr Publikum.* JRP Ringier, 2008.

Schlieben, Katharina. "The Crux of Polyphonic Language, or the Thing as Gathering." *Manifesta Journal,* no, 8, 2010, pp. 16–20.

Schlingensief, Christoph. *Ausländer Raus.* 2013, installation by Nina Wetzel in cooperation with Matthias Lilienthal and with films by Paul Poet.

Schmitt, Carl. *The Concept of the Political.* Translated by George Schwab, 1996. Chicago UP, 2007.

Schützeichel, Rainer. *Soziologische Kommunikationstheorien.* UVK, 2004.

"Seminar 4: Tirdad Zolghadr: That's Why You Always Find Me in the Kitchen at Parties." *Unitednationsplaza Archive,* www.unitednationsplaza.org/event/5. Accessed 9 Feb. 2015.

"Seminar 5: Liam Gillick: Five Short Texts on the Possibility of Creating an Economy of Equivalence." *Unitednationaplaza Archive,* www.unitednationsplaza.org/event/6. Accessed 9 Feb. 2015.

Sharon Hayes: In The Near Future. Contemporary Art Gallery, Vancouver, 8 Apr.–5 June 2011.

"Sharon Hayes: In the Near Future." *CAG*, http://www.contemporaryart-gallery.ca/exhibitions/sharon-hayes-in-the-near-future-2/. Accessed 22 Feb. 2015.

Sheikh, Simon. "Constitutive Effects: The Techniques of the Curator." *Curating Subjects*, edited by Paul O'Neill, Open Editions, 2007, pp. 147–85.

Sheikh, Simon. "Objects of Study or Commodification of Knowledge? Remarks on Artistic Research." *Art and Research*, vol. 2 , no. 2. www.artandresearch.org.uk/v2n2/sheikh.html. Accessed 8 Aug. 2009.

Sheikh, Simon. "Talk Value: Cultural Industry and the Knowledge Economy." *On Knowledge Production: A Critical Reader in Contemporary Art,* edited by Maria Hlavajova et al., Basis voor actuele kunst 2008, pp. 182–97.

Sheikh, Simon. "Vectors of the Possible: Art Between Spaces of Experience and Horizons of Expectation." *On Horizons: A Critical Reader in Contemporary Art,* edited by Maria Hlavajova et al., Basis voor actuele kunst, 2011, pp. 152–68.

Sheikh, Simon. *Exhibition Making and the Political Imaginary: On Modalities and Potentialities of Curatorial Practice.* Dissertation, Lund University, 2012. Available at: https://lup.lub.lu.se/luur/download?func=downloadFileandrecordOId=2520477andfileOId=2520478. Accessed 5 May 2013.

Sheikh, Simon. *In the Place of the Public Sphere.* b_books, 2005.

Shepard Steiner and Trevor Joyce, editors. *Cork Caucus: On Art, Possibility and Democracy.* National Sculpture Factory, 2006.

Sherman, Daniel and Irit Rogoff, editors. *Museum Culture: Histories, Discourses, Spectacles.* Routledge, 1994.

Sholis, Brian, editor. Preface. *Anton Vidokle—Produce, Distribute, Discuss, Repeat.* Lukas and Sternberg, 2009, pp. 7–11.

Smith, Terry et al., editors. *Antinomies of Art and Culture: Modernity, Postmodernity, Contemporaneity.* Duke UP, 2008.

Smith, Terry. *Thinking Contemporary Curating.* Independent Curators International (ICI Perspectives on Curating), 2012.

Sonsbeek '93. Curated by Valerie Smith, Sonsbeek Park, Arnhem, 5 June–26 Sep. 1993.

Spivak, Gayatri Chakravorty. *Outside in the Teaching Machine.* Psychology Press, 1993.

Staniszewski, Mary Anne. *The Power of Display: A History of Exhibition Installations at the Museum of Modern Art.* MIT Press, 1998.

Sternfeld, Nora. "Being Able to Do Something." *The Curatorial: A Philosophy of Curating,* edited by Jean-Paul Martinon, Bloomsbury, 2013, pp. 151–56.

Sternfeld, Nora. "Kuratorische Ansätze." *Handbuch Ausstellungstheorie- und Praxis,* edited by ARGE schittpunkt, Böhlau UTB, 2013, pp. 73–81.

Steyerl, Hito. "Documentarism as Politics of Truth." *eipcp*, Mar. 2003, www.eipcp.net/transversal/1003/steyerl2/en. Accessed 15 Mar. 2013.

Steyerl, Hito. *Universal Embassy.* 2004, mini-DV, sound, 4 min.

Szewczyk, Monika. "Anton Vidokle and the Anaesthics of Administration." *Anton Vidokle — Produce, Distribute, Discuss, Repeat,* edited by Anton Vidokle and Brian Sholis, Lukas and Sternberg, 2009, pp. 55–69.

Taipeh Biennial 2010. Curated by Hongjohn Lin and Tirdad Zolghadr, 7 Sep.–14 Nov. 2010.

"Talcott Parsons." *Metzler Philosophen Lexikon: Von den Vorsokratikern bis zu den Neuen Philosophen.* 3rd ed., 2003.

Tannert, Chritoph and Ute Tischler, editors. *MIB–Men in Black: Handbook of Curatorial Practice.* Revolver, 2004.

The Global Contemporary: Art Worlds after 1989. Curated by Andrea Buddensieg and Peter Weibel. ZKM, Karlsruhe, 17 Sep. 2011–5 Feb. 2012.

The Interventionist: Art in the Social Sphere. Curated by Nato Thompson and Greg Sholette, MASS MoCA, North Adams, 28 May 2004–20 Mar. 2005.

The Karl Marx School of English Language, David Riff and Dmitry Gutov. *Rosy Dawn of Capital.* 2010, paintings, sound, materials and dimensions variable.

The Potosí Principle: How Can We Sing the Song of the Lord in an Alien Land? Curated by Alice Creischer, Andreas Siekmann and Max-Jorge Hinderer. Haus der Kulturen der Welt, Berlin, 8 Oct 2010–2 Jan 2011.

"The Potosí Principle: How Can We Sing the Song of the Lord in an Alien Land?" Leaflet. Haus der Kulturen der Welt. Berlin, 10 Oct. 2010. Print.

This is What Democracy Looks Like. Curated by Keith Miller, New York University, Gallatin Gallery, 28 Oct.–18 Nov. 2011.

Thompson, Nato Michelle White. "Curator as Producer." *Art Lies,* no. 59, Autumn 2008, pp. 60–66.

Tiravanija, Rirkrit. *Untitled 1992/1995 (free/still).* 1992, refrigerator, table, chairs, wood, drywall, food and other materials, dimensions variable, Museum of Modern Art, New York.

Uchill, Rebecca. "Hanging Out, Crowding Out or Talking Things Out: Curating the Limits of Discursive Space." *Journal of Curatorial Studies,* vol. 1, no. 1, 2012, pp. 27–43.

"Unitednationsplaza." *Studio MC,* www.minc.ws/index.php?category=2andcategory_1=0andcategory_2=81andcategory_3=0. Accessed 9 Sep. 2017.

Utopia Station. Curated by Hans-Ulrich Obrist, Molly Nesbit and Rirkrit Tiravanija, Arsenale, 50th Venice Biennial, Venice, 15 June–2 Nov. 2003.

Valdés, Lucas. *Retrato Milagroso de San Francisco de Paula.* Ca. 1710, oil on canvas, 90 x 117.5 cm, Museo de Bellas Artes, Seville.

Vanderlinden, Barbara, and Elena Filipovic, editors. *The Manifesta Decade: Debates on Contemporary Art Exhibitions and Biennials in Post-Wall Europe.* MIT Press, 2005.

Vectors of the Possible. Curated by Simon Sheikh, Basis voor actuele kunst, Utrecht, 11 Sep.–28 Nov. 2010.

"Vectors of the Possible." Leaflet. Basis voor actuele kunst. Utrecht, 10 Nov. 2010. Print

Velazquéz, Diego. *Las Meninas, or The Family of Felipe IV.* Ca. 1656, oil on canvas, 318 x 276 cm, Museo Nacional del Prado, Madrid.

Verwoert, Jan. "Gathering People Like Thoughts." *Anton Vidokle —Produce, Distribute, Discuss, Repeat,* edited by Anton Vidokle and Brian Sholis, Lukas and Sternberg, 2009, pp. 11–21.

Verwoert, Jan. "This is Not an Exhibition. On the Practical Ties and Symbolic Differences between the Agency of the Art Institution and the Work of Those on its Outside." *Art and Its Institutions: Current Conflicts, Critique and Collaborations,* edited by Nina Möntmann. Black Dog Publishing, 2006, pp. 132–42.

Vidokle, Anton and Brian Kuan Wood. "Breaking the Contract." *e-flux Journal,* no. 37, Sep. 2012, www.e-flux.com/journal/breaking-the-contract/. Accessed 16 Nov. 2012.

Vidokle, Anton and Julieta Aranda. *Time/Bank.* 2009/2013, multimedia installation, materials and dimensions variable.

Vidokle, Anton and Tirdad Zolghadr, editors. *Printed Project (6): I Can't Work Like This.* Visual Arts Ireland, 2006.

Vidokle, Anton. "Art without Artists?" *e-flux Journal,* no. 16, May 2010, www.e-flux.com/journal/art-without-artists. Accessed 19 Sep. 2017.

Vidokle, Anton. "Exhibition as School in a Divided City." *Notes for an Art School,* edited by Mai Abu El Dahab et al., Idea Books, 2006, pp. 11–17.

Vidokle, Anton. "From Exhibition to School: Notes from Unitednationsplaza." *Art School (Propositions for the 21st Century),* edited by Steve Madoff, MIT Press, 2009.

Vidokle, Anton. "Opening Remarks: Night School." *New Museum,* www.newmuseum.org/Anton_Vidokle_Night_School_Opening_Remarks.pdf. Accessed 11 Dec. 2008.

Vidokle, Anton. *New York Conversations.* 2011, DVD, 64:40 min., 4:3, b/w, stereo. New York: Lukas and Sternberg.

Vielstimmigkeit: Collaborative Practices, Part Two. Curated by Katharina Schlieben and Sønke Gau, Shedhalle, Zurich. 24 Apr.– 15 May 2005.

Wall, Jeff. *Man With A Rifle.* 2000, transparent positive in light box, 289 x 226 cm, Museum Moderner Kunst Stiftung Ludwig (MUMOK), Vienna.

Wall, Jeff. *Milk.* 1984, silver dye bleach transparency, aluminium light box, 204.5 x 245.1 x 22.2 cm, Museum of Modern Art, New York.

Wappler, Friederike, editor. *Neue Bezugsfelder in Kunst und Gesellschaft / New Relations in Art and Society.* JRP Ringier, 2011.

"Where the West Ends?" *Former West,* www.formerwest.org/ResearchSeminars/WhereTheWestEnds/Program. Accessed 12 Dec. 2014.

Williams, Raymond. *Keywords: A Vocabulary of Culture and Society.* Oxford UP, 1976.

Williams, Raymond. "The Analysis of Culture." *Culture, Ideology and Social Process: A Reader,* edited by Tony Bennett et al., The Open University, 1981, pp. 43–52.

Wilson, Mick. "Curatorial Moments and Discursive Turns." *Curating Subjects*, edited by Paul O'Neill, Open Editions, 2007. pp. 201–216.

Zolghadr, Tirdad. "Notes from the Editor." *Redhook Journal*, Fall 2011, www.bard.edu/ccs/redhook/notes-from-the-editor. Accessed 11 Aug. 2012.